21世纪英语专业系列教材　　　　　　　总主编　胡壮麟

英语泛读教程

（第二版）

第2册

主　编：潘守文　胡文征　姜亚军

副主编：张生庭

编　者：孙明丽　沈红梅　侯冰洁　唐颖　周晓凤

北京大学出版社
PEKING UNIVERSITY PRESS

图书在版编目（CIP）数据

英语泛读教程. 第2册/潘守文，胡文征，姜亚军主编. —2版. —北京：北京大学出版社，2013.1
（21世纪英语专业系列教材）
ISBN 978-7-301-20812-0

Ⅰ. 英… Ⅱ. ①潘…②胡…③姜… Ⅲ. 英语–阅读教学–高等学校–教材 Ⅳ. H319.4

中国版本图书馆CIP数据核字（2012）第127674号

书　　　名：	英语泛读教程（第二版）第2册
著作责任者：	潘守文　胡文征　姜亚军　主编
责 任 编 辑：	郝妮娜
标 准 书 号：	ISBN 978-7-301-20812-0/H·3080
出 版 发 行：	北京大学出版社
地　　　址：	北京市海淀区成府路205号　100871
网　　　址：	http://www.pup.cn　新浪官方微博：@北京大学出版社
电 子 信 箱：	zbing@pup.pku.edu.cn
电　　　话：	邮购部 62752015　发行部 62750672　编辑部 62759634　出版部 62754962
印 刷 者：	三河市博文印刷有限公司
经 销 者：	新华书店
	787毫米×1092毫米　16开本　16印张　490千字
	2008年9月第1版
	2013年1月第2版　2019年9月第3次印刷
定　　价：	39.00元

未经许可，不得以任何方式复制或抄袭本书之部分或全部内容。
版权所有，侵权必究
举报电话：010-62752024　电子信箱：fd@pup.pku.edu.cn

《21世纪英语专业系列教材》
编写委员会

（以姓氏笔画排序）

王立非	王守仁	王克非
王俊菊	文秋芳	石　坚
申　丹	朱　刚	仲伟合
刘世生	刘意青	殷企平
孙有中	李　力	李正栓
张旭春	张庆宗	张绍杰
杨俊峰	陈法春	金　莉
封一函	胡壮麟	查明建
袁洪庚	桂诗春	黄国文
梅德明	董洪川	蒋洪新
程幼强	程朝翔	虞建华

总　序

　　北京大学出版社自2005年以来已出版《语言与应用语言学知识系列读本》多种，为了配合第十一个五年计划，现又策划陆续出版《21世纪英语专业系列教材》。这个重大举措势必受到英语专业广大教师和学生的欢迎。

　　作为英语教师，最让人揪心的莫过于听人说英语不是一个专业，只是一个工具。说这些话的领导和教师的用心是好的，为英语专业的毕业生将来找工作着想，因此要为英语专业的学生多多开设诸如新闻、法律、国际商务、经济、旅游等其他专业的课程。但事与愿违，英语专业的教师们很快发现，学生投入英语学习的时间少了，掌握英语专业课程知识甚微，即使对四个技能的掌握也并不比大学英语学生高明多少，而那个所谓的第二专业在有关专家的眼中只是学到些皮毛而已。

　　英语专业的路在何方？有没有其他路可走？这是需要我们英语专业教师思索的问题。中央领导关于创新是一个民族的灵魂和要培养创新人才等的指示精神，让我们在层层迷雾中找到了航向。显然，培养学生具有自主学习能力和能进行创造性思维是我们更为重要的战略目标，使英语专业的人才更能适应21世纪的需要，迎接21世纪的挑战。

　　如今，北京大学出版社外语部的领导和编辑同志们也从教材出版的视角探索英语专业的教材问题，从而为贯彻英语专业教学大纲做些有益的工作，为教师们开设大纲中所规定的必修、选修课程提供各种教材。《21世纪英语专业系列教材》是普通高等教育"十一五"国家级规划教材和国家"十一五"重点出版规划项目《面向新世纪的立体化网络化英语学科建设丛书》的重要组成部分。这套系列教材要体现新世纪英语教学的自主化、协作化、模块化和超文本化，结合外语教材的具体情况，既要解决教学内容、教学方法和教育技术的时代化，也要坚持弘扬以爱国主义为核心的民族精神。因此，今天北京大学出版社在大力提倡专业英语教学改革的基础上，编辑出版各种英语专业技能、英语专业知识和相关专业知识课程的教材，以培养具有创新性思维和具有实际工作能力的学生，充分体现了时代精神。

　　北京大学出版社的远见卓识，也反映了英语专业广大师生盼望已久的心愿。由北京大学等全国几十所院校具体组织力量，积极编写相关教材。这就是说,这套教材是由一些高等院校有水平有经验的第一线教师们制定编写大纲,反复讨论,特别是考虑到在不同层次、不同背景学校之间取得平衡,避免了先前的教材或偏难或偏易的弊病。与此同时,一批知名专家教授参与策划和教材审定工作,保证了教材质量。

  当然,这套系列教材出版只是初步实现了出版社和编者们的预期目标。为了获得更大效果,希望使用本系列教材的教师和同学不吝指教,及时将意见反馈给我们,使教材更加完善。

  航道已经开通,我们有决心乘风破浪,奋勇前进!

胡壮麟

北京大学蓝旗营

第二版前言

国家级规划教材《英语泛读教程》自2008年问世以来，受到了全国英语专业老师和学生的一致好评。过去五年的教材使用与教学实践证明，本教材选材方向正确，既兼顾语言表达与人文知识的相得益彰，又注重西方文化传统与现代文化的融会贯通，既注重经典传承，也关注时代变迁。

《英语泛读教程》第二版基本保持了第一版的编写思想。修订内容之一是更换了部分课文，以求选材的时代性、内容的丰富性、文本的趣味性和文体的多样性。在筛选文章的过程中，我们既考虑提升学生的英语水平与人文知识基础，也注重整套教材内容的前后衔接。

第二版对课文后面的练习也做了调整。具体的考量有三：第一，注重从具体课文到所涉及领域之间的递进关系，通过具体的课文使学生对相关领域的知识有所了解。第二，注重学生对篇章结构的理解。第三，注重课内阅读与课外阅读之间的配合。具体修订内容如下：

一、为了提高学生的学习兴趣，本次修订替换了约30%的课文，新的课文内容多启发人文思考，更能体现通过文化思考来带动语言习得，同时注重学生思辨能力的提升。

二、移除各单元练习中的翻译部分，加入了词汇题，有助于学生进一步掌握和复习课文中的重点词汇。

三、新增命题拓展。通过此题的延伸，可以引导学生有意识地进行批评性阅读，从而使其更深刻地领会和理解西方文化的内涵与实质。

四、新设一个引导性的课外拓展题，让学生自己学会如何围绕课本提供的主题进行拓展学习，从大学基础学习阶段就培养良好的自主深入学习的习惯，更有利于学生知识面的扩展。

五、每个单元后面新增二十分钟的阅读材料，材料选自历年英语专业四级阅读真题，以提高学生的限时阅读水平，提升学生阅读的有效性。

我们相信，通过此次修订，这套泛读教材将更好地服务于英语人才的培养。借此机会，感谢为本套教材改版而默默奉献的老师们，也感谢北京大学出版社的领导、各位编辑和工作人员为本套教材的成长所提供的关爱与支持。

  英语专业教学任重道远，教材建设永无止境。本套教材旨在适应新形势下的英语专业教学，探索教学新路，缺点与不足之处在所难免，衷心希望得到专家学者的批评指正，听到广大师生的改进意见。

编者

2013 年 1 月

第一版前言

英语专业的本分是什么？英语语言能力的重要性毋庸置疑，却不是英语专业的本分。与高校许多文科专业相类似，英语专业的本分是人文素质的培养，是洞察人文现象的能力的培养，是思考力、鉴别力、判断力的培养，依此洞悉、鉴别、吸收英语国家的文化成就，并与中华文化精华融会贯通，促进人的全面发展和社会进步。

然而实际情况却不能尽如人意。很多人误以为英语专业的本分就是英语语言能力的提高，客观上将英语语言能力培养与人文素质培养割裂开来，使之相互脱节，导致英语教学效率低下，加上应试教育推波助澜，英语专业学生对英语国家文化只停留在现象的表面，而无意追问现象背后的文化内涵和精髓，不去深入思考，不追求理论高度，不能构建系统的专业知识，不能洞察、鉴别、吸收英语国家优秀文化，更谈不上与中华文化融会贯通，不能履行英语专业的本分，因此在高校处境尴尬。常有人说英语专业不是一个专业，这让英语专业师生痛心疾首。不是一个专业意味着不是一门学问，不是一门学问意味着没学问、没知识、没头脑、没思想，只能当匠人，不能成大器，不能成为民族的栋梁。

成为民族的栋梁，是英语专业师生的梦想。时代在发展，旧的人才标准已经不能适应时代发展的要求，只具有英语语言技能的人才已经算不上真正的人才。时代的发展要求英语专业必须充分利用所属高校的人文资源，逐步打通文、史、哲的界限，构建以学术研究为核心的英语人才培养体系，以学术研究促进英语实践能力、独立思考能力和人文素质的提高，培养英语基本功扎实、独立思考能力强、通晓英语国家文化和中华文化、人文素质优秀的新型英语人才。实践证明，将学生当学者，将课文当文献，英语语言能力、独立思考能力、自主学习能力、人文素质同时培养，不仅符合《高等学校英语专业英语教学大纲》的要求，而且切实可行，理应成为英语教材编写的指导原则。本册书在上述英语教学理念指导下完成，与以往以应试为目的的英语泛读教材有所不同，现就本书特点说明如下：

1. 本书供高校英语专业一年级第二学期使用，起点高，要求学生具有较好的英语基础和人文修养,旨在帮助学生从语言技能与人文修养两个方面提高自己。本书所选的24篇课文不仅语言规范而且具有相当的思想内涵,大部分作者为英语国家的文化精英。课文不仅涉及英语国家的文化现象,更包含英语学者对这些文化现象的深入思考,不是单纯的语言技能训练资料,而是英语专业学生洞察英语国家文化不可或缺的参考文献。

2. 课文开门见山,直接进入课文题目和内容,引导学生迅速进入阅读状态,集中精力捕捉关键信息。

3. 生词释义简洁明了,完全采用英文释义,完全回避汉译,旨在引导学生完全进入英语状态并运用英语进行判断思维。本书为一些生词提供了多个释义,旨在培养学生鉴别语言细微差别的能力。

4. 文化注释言简意赅,意在为学生提供便捷的文化参考,具有百科全书的功能。

5. 本书意在为学生的独立思考提供广阔的空间,无意将本书编者对课文的理解强加于学生,因此取消了以往常见的多项选择题,淡化唯一答案和绝对答案,努力将以学生为中心的英语教学理念落到实处,设计了具有探讨性、启发性、辐射性的练习题,引导学生穿越语言现象和文化现象的表面进入英语国家文化的深层,独立探索,独立判断。

6. 练习I、II围绕课文内容进行提问,旨在锻炼学生的判断力、逻辑推理能力、文献综述能力和快速组织语言进行表达辩论的能力。练习III、IV仍然围绕课文内容展开训练,旨在训练学生灵活使用英语的能力和英译汉的能力。练习V、VI为扩展练习,既为了督促学生有目的地扩大阅读范围,也为了引导学生举一反三,将刚学到的内容与以往学到的内容融会贯通,形成完整而良好的知识结构。

本册教材由吉林大学外国语学院英语系负责编写,由潘守文、胡文征担任主编,负责整体设计与审稿,并与孙明丽、沈红梅、侯冰洁、唐颖、周晓凤老师一起承担选材及编写工作,其间得到了本套教材其他分册主编的帮助,北京大学出版社张冰主任、刘强编辑也为本册书编写付出了心血,编者在此一并表示感谢。本册教材疏漏之处,诚请广大读者批评指正,提出宝贵意见和建议。

编 者
2008年8月

Contents

Unit One 1
- **Text A** What to Listen for in Music 1
- **Text B** The Eloquent Sounds of Silence 12
- **Twenty Minutes' Reading** 18

Unit Two 22
- **Text A** Your Speech Is Changing 22
- **Text B** How to Talk about the World 30
- **Twenty Minutes' Reading** 36

Unit Three 40
- **Text A** A Love Affair with Books 40
- **Text B** The Lost Art of Reading 48
- **Twenty Minutes' Reading** 58

Unit Four 62
- **Text A** Thinking as a Hobby 62
- **Text B** The Art of Living Simply 74
- **Twenty Minutes' Reading** 83

Unit Five 87
- **Text A** Once More to the Lake 87
- **Text B** The Almost Perfect State 94
- **Twenty Minutes' Reading** 105

Unit Six 108
- **Text A** Middle Age, Old Age 108
- **Text B** Men Are Very Delicate 116
- **Twenty Minutes' Reading** 123

Unit Seven 127
- **Text A** Beauty 127
- **Text B** Cinderella's Stepsisters 134
- Twenty Minutes' Reading 140

Unit Eight 143
- **Text A** In Praise of Idleness 143
- **Text B** To Err Is Human 151
- Twenty Minutes' Reading 158

Unit Nine 163
- **Text A** On National Prejudice 163
- **Text B** Politics and the English Language 170
- Twenty Minutes' Reading 181

Unit Ten 184
- **Text A** Daydreams of What You'd Rather Be 184
- **Text B** Culture and Food Habits 193
- Twenty Minutes' Reading 200

Unit Eleven 204
- **Text A** Photographs of My Parents 204
- **Text B** Two Ways to Belong in America 212
- Twenty Minutes' Reading 220

Unit Twelve 224
- **Text A** Three Types of Resistance to Oppression 224
- **Text B** Loneliness... An American Malady 232
- Twenty Minutes' Reading 238

Unit One

What to Listen for in Music
Aaron Copland*

We all listen to music according to our separate capabilities. But, for the sake of analysis, the whole listening process may become clearer if we break it up into its component parts, so to speak. In a certain sense we all listen to music on three separate planes. For lack of a better terminology, one might name these: (1) the sensuous plane, (2) the expressive plane, (3) the sheerly musical plane. The only advantage to be gained from mechanically splitting up the listening process into these hypothetical planes is the clearer view to be had of the way in which we listen.

The simplest way of listening to music is to listen for the sheer pleasure of the musical sound itself. That is the sensuous plane. It is the plane on which we hear music without thinking, without considering it in any way. One turns on the radio while doing something else and absentmindedly bathes in the sound. A kind of brainless but attractive state of mind is engendered by the mere sound appeal of the music.

You may be sitting in a room, reading this (essay). Imagine one note struck on the piano. Immediately that one note is enough to change the room proving that the sound element in music is a powerful and mysterious agent, which it would be foolish to deride or belittle.

The surprising thing is that many people who consider themselves qualified music lovers abuse that plane of listening. They go to concerts in order to loose themselves. They use music as a consolation or an escape. They enter an ideal world where one doesn't have to think of the realities of everyday life. Of course they

terminology /ˌtɜːmɪˈnɒlədʒɪ/ *n.* a system of words used to name things in a particular discipline
sensuous /ˈsenʃʊəs/ *a.* giving pleasure to the mind or body through the senses
sheerly /ʃɪəlɪ/ *adv.* entirely, completely, utterly
engender /ɪnˈdʒendə/ *v.* **a.** call forth; produce; create **b.** make children
appeal /əˈpiːl/ *n.* attractiveness that interests or pleases or stimulates sb.
agent /ˈeɪdʒənt/ *n.* **a.** an active and efficient cause; capable of producing a certain effect **b.** a substance that exerts some force or effect
deride /dɪˈraɪd/ *v.* treat or speak of with contempt
belittle /bɪˈlɪtəl/ *v.* **a.** express a negative opinion of **b.** lessen the authority, dignity, or reputation of
abuse /əˈbjuːz, əˈbjuːs/ *v.* **a.** change the inherent purpose or function of something **b.** use wrongly or improperly or excessively
loose /luːs/ *v.* **a.** grant freedom to; free from confinement **b.** turn loose or free from restraint
consolation /ˌkɒnsəˈleɪʃən/ *n.* **a.** the comfort you feel when consoled in times of disappointment **b.** the act of consoling; giving relief in affliction

aren't thinking about the music either. Music allows them to leave it, and they go off to a place to dream, dreaming because of and apropos of the music yet never quite listening to it.

Yes, the sound appeal of music is a potent and primitive force, but you must not allow it to use up a disproportionate share of your interest. The sensuous plane is an important one in music, a very important one, but it does not constitute the whole story.

There is no need to digress further on the sensuous plane. Its appeal to every normal human being is self-evident. There is, however, such a thing as becoming more sensitive to the different kinds of sound stuff as used by various composers. For all composers do not use that sound stuff in the same way. Don't get the idea that the value of music is commensurate with its sensuous appeal or that the loveliest sounding music is made by the greatest composer. If that were so, Ravel* would be a greater composer than Beethoven*. The point is that the sound element varies with each composer, that his usage of sound forms an integral part of his style and must be taken into account when listening. The reader can see, therefore, that a more conscious approach is valuable even on this primary plane of music listening.

The second plane on which music exists is what I have called the expressive one. Here, immediately, we tread on controversial ground. Composers have a way of shying away from any discussion of music's expressive side. Did not Stravinsky* himself proclaim that his music was an "object", a "thing" with a life of its own and with no other meaning than its own purely musical existence? This intransigent attitude of Stravinsky's may be due to the fact that so many people have tried to read different meanings into so many pieces. Heaven knows it is difficult enough to say precisely what it is that a piece of music means, to say it definitely, to say it finally so that everyone is satisfied with your explanation. But that should not lead one to the other extreme of denying to music the right to be "expressive". My own

apropos of /ˌæprəˈpəʊ/ of an appropriate or pertinent nature; concerning
disproportionate /ˌdɪsprəˈpɔːʃənɪt/ *adj.* out of proportion, not proportionate
digress /daɪˈgres/ *v.* **a.** especially from the main subject of attention or course of argument in writing, thinking, or speaking **b.** wander from a direct or straight course
self-evident /ˈself ˈevɪdənt/ *adj.* so obvious that there is no need for proof or explanation
commensurate /kəˈmenʃərɪt/ *a.* corresponding in size or degree or extent
integral /ˈɪntɪgrəl/ *a.* **a.** existing as an essential constituent or characteristic **b.** constituting the undiminished entirety; lacking nothing essential especially not damaged
tread /tred/ *v.* put down or press the foot, place the foot
controversial /ˌkɒntrəˈvɜːʃəl/ *adj.* causing a lot of disagreement, because many people have strong opinions about the subject being discussed
shy away *v. p.* to avoid doing sth because you are not confident enough or you are worried or nervous about it
proclaim /prəˈkleɪm/ *v.* **a.** declare formally; declare someone to be something; **b.** state or announce
intransigent /ɪnˈtrænsɪdʒənt/ *adj.* unwilling to change your ideas or behaviour in a way that seems unreasonable

belief is that all music has an expressive power, some more and some less, but that all music has a certain meaning behind the notes and that meaning behind the notes constitutes, after all, what the piece is saying, what the piece is about. This whole problem can be stated quite simply by asking, "is there a meaning to music?" My answer to that would be, "yes". And "can you state in so many words what the meaning is?" My answer to that would be, "no". Therein lies the difficulty.

Simple-minded souls will never be satisfied with the answer to the second of these questions. They always want to have a meaning, and the more concrete it is the better they like it. The more the music reminds them of a train, a storm, a funeral or any other familiar conception the more expressive it appears to be to them. This popular idea of music's meaning — stimulated and abetted by the usual run of musical commentator —should be discouraged wherever and whenever it is met. One timid lady once confessed to me that she suspected something seriously lacking in her appreciation of music because of her inability to connect it with anything definite. This is getting the whole thing backward, of course.

Still, the question remains, how close should the intelligent music lover wish to come to pinning a definite meaning to any particular work? No closer than a general concept, I should say. Music expresses, at different moments, serenity or exuberance, regret or triumph, fury or delight. It expresses each of these moods, and many others, in a numberless variety of subtle shadings and differences. It may even express a state of meaning for which there exists no adequate word in any language. In that case, musicians often like to say it has only a purely musical meaning. What they really mean to say is that no appropriate word can be found to express the music's meaning and that, even if it could, they do not feel the need finding it.

But whatever the professional musician may hold, most musical novices still search for specific words with which to pin down their musical reactions. That is why they always find Tschaikovsky* easier to "understand" than Beethoven. In the first place, it is easier to pin a meaning-word on a Tschaikovsky piece than on a Beethoven one. Much easier. Moreover, with the Russian composer, every time you come back to a piece of his it almost always says

therein /ˌðeərˈɪn/ *adv.* in that place, or in that piece of writing
stimulate /ˈstɪmjuːleɪt/ *v.* to encourage someone by making them excited about and interested in sth.; stir feelings in
abet /əˈbet/ *v.* to help somebody do something wrong or illegal; assist or encourage, usually in some wrong-doing
pin /pɪn/ *v.* to understand something clearly or be able to describe it exactly
serenity /sɪˈrenəti/ *n.* peace or calmness
exuberance /ɪgˈzjuːbərəns/ *n.* happiness and joyful enthusiasm
novice /ˈnɒvɪs/ *n.* someone new to a field or activity

the same thing to you, whereas with Beethoven it is often quite difficult to put your finger right on what he is saying. And any musician will tell you that is why Beethoven is the greater composer. Because music which always says the same thing to you will necessarily soon become dull music, but music whose meaning is slightly different with each hearing has a greater chance of remaining alive.

fugue /fju:g/ *n.* a piece of music that begins with a simple tune which is then repeated by other voices or instrumental parts with small variations
Clavichord /ˈklævɪkɔːd/ *n.* an early stringed instrument like a piano but with more delicate sound
resignedly /rɪˈzaɪnɪdlɪ/ *adv.* **a.** with resignation and acceptance; in a resigned manner **b.** in a hopeless resigned manner
pessimistically /pesɪˈmɪstɪklɪ/ *adv.* with pessimism; in a pessimistic manner
vigor /ˈvɪgə/ *n.* **a.** active strength of body or mind **b.** an imaginative lively style (especially that of writing)

Listen, if you can, to the forty-eight fugue themes of Bach's* *Well Tempered Clavichord*. Listen to each theme, right after another. You will soon realize that each theme mirrors a different world of feeling. You will soon realize that the more beautiful a theme seems to you the harder it is to find any word that will describe it to your complete satisfaction. Yes, you certainly know whether it is a gay theme or a sad one. You will be able, in other words, in your own mind to draw a frame of emotional feeling around your theme. Now study the sad one a little closer. Try to pin down the exact quality of its sadness. Is it pessimistically sad or resignedly sad; is it fatefully sad or smilingly sad?

Let us suppose that you are fortunate and can describe to your own satisfaction in so many words the exact meaning of your chosen theme. There is still no guarantee that anyone else will be satisfied. Nor need they be. The important thing is that each one feel for [themselves] the specific expressive quality of a theme or, similarly, an entire piece of music. And if it is a great work of art, don't expect it to mean exactly the same thing to you each time you return to it.

Themes or pieces need not only express one emotion, of course.

Take such a theme as the first main one of Beethoven's *Ninth Symphony*, for example. It is clearly made up of different elements. It does not say only one thing. Yet anyone hearing it immediately gets a feeling of strength, a feeling of power. It isn't a power that comes simply because the theme is played loudly. It is a power inherent in the theme itself. The extraordinary strength and vigor of the theme results in the listener's receiving an impression that a forceful statement has been made.

But one should never try and boil it down to the fateful hammer of life, etc., that is where the trouble begins. The musician, in his exasperation says it means nothing but the notes themselves, whereas the nonprofessional is only too anxious to hang on to any explanation that gives [them] the illusion of getting closer to the music's meaning.

> **boil down to a.** be the essential element of **b.** be cooked until very little liquid is left
> **exasperation** /ɪɡˌzæspəˈreɪʃən/ *n.* **a.** an exasperated feeling of annoyance **b.** actions that cause great irritation (or even anger)
> **hang on to** *v.* continue doing something in spite of difficulties
> **manipulation** /məˌnɪpjʊˈleɪʃən/ *n.* exerting shrewd or devious influence especially for one's own advantage
> **engrossed** /ɪnˈɡrəʊst/ giving or marked by complete attention to
> **arpeggio** /ɑːˈpedʒɪəʊ/ a chord whose notes are played in rapid succession rather than simultaneously
> **staccato** /stəˈkɑːtəʊ/ *n.* (music) marked by or composed of disconnected parts or sounds
> **layman** /ˈleɪmən/ *n.* a person who is not trained, qualified, or experienced in a particular subject or activity

Now, perhaps the reader will know better what I mean when I say that music does have an expressive meaning but that we cannot say in so many words what the meaning is.

The third plane of which music exists is the sheerly musical plane.

Besides the pleasurable sound of music and the expressive feeling that it gives off, music does exist in terms of the notes themselves and of their manipulation. Most listeners are not sufficiently conscious of this third plane.

Professional musicians, on the other hand, are, if anything, too conscious of the mere notes themselves. They often fall into the error of becoming so engrossed with their arpeggios and staccatos that they forget the deeper aspects of the music they are performing. But from the layman's standpoint, it is not so much a matter of getting over bad habits on the sheerly musical plane as of increasing one's awareness of what is going on, as far as the notes are concerned.

When the person in the street listens to the "notes themselves" with any degree of concentration, he is most likely to make some mention of the melody. Either they hears a pretty melody or they do not, and they generally let it go at that. Rhythm is likely to gain their attention next, particularly if it seems exciting. But harmony and tone color are generally taken for granted, if they are thought of consciously at all. As for music's having a definite form of some kind, that idea seems never to have occurred to them.

It is very important for all of us to become more alive to the music on its sheerly musical plane. After all, an actual musical material is being used.

correlate /ˈkɒrɪˌleɪt/ bring into a mutual, complementary, or reciprocal relation
instinctively /ɪnˈstɪŋktɪvlɪ/ *adv.* as a matter of instinct
simultaneously /sɪməlˈteɪnɪəslɪ/ *adv.* at the same time
carried away so excited, angry or interested as to be out of control

The intelligent listener must be prepared to increase their awareness of the musical material and what happens to it. They must hear the melodies, the rhythms, the harmonies, the tone color in a more conscious fashion. But above all they must, in order to follow the line of the composer's thought, know something of the principals of musical form. Listening to all of these elements is listening on the sheerly musical plane.

Let me repeat that I have split up mechanically the three separate planes on which we listen merely for the sake of greater clarity. Actually we never listen to one or the other of these planes. What we do is to correlate them — listening in all three ways at the same time. It takes no mental effort, for we do it instinctively.

Perhaps an analogy with what happens to us when we visit the theater will make this instinctive correlation clearer. In the theater, you are aware of the actors and actresses, costumes, sets, sounds and movements. All of these give one the sense that the theater is a pleasant place to be in. They constitute the sensuous plane in our theatrical reactions.

The expressive plane in the theater would be derived from the feeling that you get from what is happening on the stage. You are moved to pity, excitement, or gaiety. It is this general feeling, generated aside from the particular words being spoken, a certain emotional something which exists on the stage, that is analogous to the expressive quality in music.

It is easy enough to see that the theatergoer never is conscious of any of these elements separately. They are aware of them all at the same time. The same is true of music listening. We simultaneously and without thinking listen on all three planes.

In a sense, the ideal listener is both inside and outside the music at the same moment, judging it and enjoying it, wishing it would go one way and watching it go another — almost like the composer at the moment they compose it; because in order to write their music, the composer must also be inside and outside their music, carried away by it and yet coldly critical of it. A subjective attitude is implied in both creating and listening to music.

Cultural Notes

1. **Aaron Copland** (1900—1990) was a celebrated American composer, composition teacher, writer, and later in his career a conductor of his own and other American music. As Copland was instrumental in forging a distinctly American style of composition, he is often referred to as "the Dean of American Composers"; he is best known for the works he wrote in the 1930s and 1940s in a deliberately accessible style often referred to as Populist and which the composer labeled his "vernacular" style. These works with his own style include the ballets *Appalachian Spring, Billy the Kid* and *Rodeo*, his *Fanfare for the Common Man* and *Third Symphony*. The open, slowly changing harmonies of many of his works are archetypical of what many people consider to be the sound of American music, evoking the vast American landscape and pioneer spirit. In addition to his ballets and orchestral works, he produced music in many other genres including chamber music, vocal works, opera and film scores.

2. **Maurice Ravel** (1875—1937) a French composer known especially for his melodies, orchestral and instrumental textures and effects, was among the most significant and influential composers of the early twentieth century. Much of his piano music, chamber music, vocal music and orchestral music has entered the standard concert repertoire. Ravel's piano compositions, such as *Jeux d'eau, Miroirs, Le tombeau de Couperin* and *Gaspard de la nuit*, demand considerable virtuosity from the performer, and his orchestral music, including *Daphnis et Chloé* uses a variety of sound and instrumentation. Ravel is perhaps known best for his orchestral work *Boléro* (1928).

3. **Ludwig van Beethoven** (1770—1827) was a German composer and pianist. A crucial figure in the transition between the Classical and Romantic eras in Western art music, he remains one of the most famous and influential of all composers. His best known compositions include 9 symphonies, 5 concertos for piano, 32 piano sonatas, and 16 string quartets. He also composed other chamber music, choral works (including the celebrated *Missa Solemnis*). Beethoven was a great musical innovator, widening the scope of sonata, symphony, concerto and quartet, and combining vocals and instruments in a new way. His personal life was marked by a struggle against deafness, and some of his most important works were composed during the last 10 years of his life, when he was quite unable to hear.

4. **Igor Fyodorovich Stravinsky** (1882—1971) was a Russian pianist, composer and conductor, born on June 17, 1882 in Oranienbaum, Russia. As one of the most influential composers in the twentieth century and the touchstone of modern western music, he adopted all the important musical style trends of his time, ranging from the classics to modern forms. His most famous works included the ballets *The Firebird, Petrushka* and *The Rite of Spring*. Stravinsky died on April 6, 1971.

5. **Pyotr Ilyich Tschaikovsky** (1840—1893) anglicised as Peter Ilyich Tschaikovsky, was a Russian composer whose works included symphonies, concertos, operas, ballets, chamber music, and a choral setting of *The Russian Orthodox Divine Liturgy*. Some of these are among the most popular concert and theatrical music in the classical repertoire. He was the first Russian composer whose music made a lasting impression internationally, which he bolstered with appearances as a guest conductor later in his career in Europe and the United States. One of these appearances was at the inaugural concert of Carnegie Hall in New York City in 1891. Tchaikovsky was honored in 1884 by Emperor Alexander III, and awarded a lifetime pension in the late 1880s.

6. **Johann Sebastian Bach** (1685—1750) was a German composer, organist, harpsichordist, violist, and violinist of the Baroque Period. He enriched many established German styles through his skill in counterpoint, harmonic and motivic organisation, and the adaptation of rhythms, forms, and textures from abroad, particularly from Italy and France. Many of Bach's works are still known today, such as *the Brandenburg Concertos, the Mass in B minor, the Well-Tempered Clavier*, his cantatas, chorales, partitas, passions, and organ works. His music is revered for its intellectual depth, technical command, and artistic beauty.

Comprehension Exercises

I. Answer the following questions based on the text.

1. What are we listening for in a piece of music?
2. How many planes could a piece of music be broken into according to the author? What are they respectively?
3. How do you understand the fact that many people who consider themselves qualified music lovers abuse the sensuous plane of listening?

4. What are the major functions of music?
5. What is the author's attitude towards these different planes of music at the end of the text?

II. Decide whether each of the following statements is true or false according to the text.

1. According to Aaron Copland, the listening process will be easy to analyze if it is divided into different planes.
2. The value of music is always commensurate with its sensuous appeal and the loveliest music is always made by the greatest composer.
3. There is a meaning to any piece of music and it is an easy thing for the listeners to state the meaning of the music in his own words.
4. According to the text, most inexperienced listeners will be all too ready to search for concrete words to define their reactions to music.
5. When we listen to music, we always hang on to only one plane instead of all the three planes of it at the same time.

III. Select the most suitable word or phrases and fill in the following blanks in their proper form.

self-evidence	integral	commensurate	digress	controversial
instinctive	shy away	layman	engross	manipulation
pessimism	therein	boil down to	resign	novice
stimulate	intransigent	proclaim		

1. To understand why I wrote that report, let me _____ to give you some information about my background.
2. At first sight it seems _____ that falling incomes, rising prices and a squeeze on welfare will mean larger numbers find themselves below the breadline.
3. Likewise, China is rich in cultural resources, but has had difficulty harnessing these resources to build soft power _____ with its hard power.
4. Science has demonstrated that we, as a species, are a(n) _____ part of biodiversity.
5. Their intervention is set to spark another round of debate over the government's _____ plans.
6. They tried to criticize the leadership and _____ from direct challenge.
7. Knox herself is expected to address the court in a final appeal to _____ her innocence.

8. Of late, he's been seen by even his most staunch supporters as too ready to retreat from critical ground when confronted by _____ Republicans.

9. The treaty was imposed by force, and _____ lay the cause of its ineffectiveness.

10. Ministers have recently talked of the need to _____ private investment to maintain growth.

11. I'm a _____ at these things, Lieutenant. You're the professional.

12. _____, I telegraphed back and told him that it was all right with me if he insisted on adopting the second plan.

13. What these farmers want to obtain _____ just one thing. It is land.

14. They hardly seem to notice one another because they are so _____ in their own activity.

15. I'm a _____. What I'm going to say may expose myself to ridicule, yet I still want to say a few words.

IV. Try to paraphrase the following sentences, paying special attention to the underlined parts.

1. The only advantage to be gained from mechanically splitting up the listening process into these hypothetical planes is the clearer view to be had of the way in which we listen.

    _____
    _____

2. The surprising thing is that many people who consider themselves qualified music lovers abuse that plane of listening. They go to concerts in order to loose themselves.

    _____

3. This popular idea of music's meaning — stimulated and abetted by the usual run of musical commentator — should be discouraged wherever and whenever it is met.

    _____

4. But whatever the professional musician may hold, most musical novices still search for specific words with which to pin down their musical reactions.

    _____

5. The musician, in his exasperation says it means nothing but the notes themselves, whereas the nonprofessional is only too anxious to hang on to any explanation that gives them the illusion of getting closer to the music's

meaning.

_____
_____

V. Discuss with your partner about each of the three statements and write an essay in no less than 250 words about your understanding of one of them.

1. We all listen to music according to our separate capabilities. But, for the sake of analysis, the whole listening process may become clearer if we break it up into its component parts, so to speak.
_____
_____

2. Don't get the idea that the value of music is commensurate with its sensuous appeal or that the loveliest sounding music is made by the greatest composer.
_____
_____

3. In a sense, the ideal listener is both inside and outside the music at the same moment, judging it and enjoying it, wishing it would go one way and watching it go another — almost like the composer at the moment they compose it.
_____
_____

VI. List four websites where we can learn more about Aaron Copland and his understanding of music and provide a brief introduction to each of them.

1. _____
_____
_____ .

2. _____
_____
_____ .

3. _____
_____
_____ .

4. _____
_____
_____ .

Text B

The Eloquent Sounds of Silence
Pico Iyer*

Every one of us knows the sensation of going up, on retreat, to a high place and feeling ourselves so lifted up that we can hardly imagine the circumstances of our usual lives, or all the things that make us fret. In such a place, in such a state, we start to recite the standard litany: that silence is sunshine where company is clouds; that silence is rapture, where company is doubt; that silence is golden, where company is brass.

But silence is not so easily won. And before we race off to go prospecting in those hills, we might usefully recall that fool's gold is much more common and that gold has to be panned for, dug out from other substances. "All profound things and emotions of things are preceded and attended by Silence," wrote Herman Melville*, one of the loftiest and most eloquent of souls. Working himself up to an ever more thunderous cry of affirmation, he went on, "Silence is the general consecration of the universe. Silence is the invisible laying on of the Divine Pontiff's hands upon the world. Silence is the only Voice of our God." For Melville, though, silence finally meant darkness and hopelessness and self-annihilation. Devastated by the silence that greeted his heartfelt novels, he retired into a public silence from which he did not emerge for more than 30 years. Then, just before his death, he came forth with his final utterance—the luminous tale of *Billy Budd**—and showed that silence is only as worthy as what we can bring back from it.

We have to earn silence, then, to work for it: to make it not an absence but a presence; not emptiness but repletion. Silence is something more than just a pause; it is that enchanted place where space is cleared and time is stayed and the horizon itself expands. In silence, we often say, we

retreat /rɪˈtriːt/ *n.* a quiet, secluded place that one goes to in order to rest
fret /fret/ *v.* **a.** to be agitated or irritated **b.** to make resentful or angry
litany /ˈlɪtəni/ *n.* a prayer consisting of a series of invocations by the priest with responses from the congregation
company /ˈkʌmpəni/ *n.* **a.** companionship; fellowship **b.** a group of people together for some purpose
rapture /ˈræptʃə/ *n.* **a.** a state of being carried away by overwhelming emotion **b.** a state of elated bliss
prospect /ˈprɒspekt/ *v.* to explore for useful or valuable things or substances, such as minerals
fool's gold a common mineral that has a pale yellow color, sometimes mistaken for gold
pan /pæn/ *v.* to wash dirt in a pan to separate out the precious minerals
lofty /ˈlɒfti/ *adj.* of unusually high quality of thinking, feeling, desires, etc.
consecration /ˌkɒnsɪˈkreɪʃən/ *n.* a solemn commitment of your life or your time to some cherished purpose
laying on the act of contacting sth. with your hand
pontiff /ˈpɒntɪf/ *n.* (usu. cap.) the Pope
annihilation /əˌnaɪəˈleɪʃən/ *n.* total destruction
devastate /ˈdevəsteɪt/ *v.* to destroy completely
come forth a. to come out of **b.** to happen or occur as a result of sth.
luminous /ˈluːmɪnəs/ *adj.* softly bright or radiant
repletion /rɪˈpliːʃən/ *n.* the state of being replete; superabundant fullness

can hear ourselves think; but what is truer to say is that in silence we can hear ourselves not think, and so sink below ourselves into a place far deeper than mere thought allows. In silence, we might better say, we can hear someone else think.

Or simply breathe. For silence is responsiveness, and in silence we can listen to something behind the clamor of the world. "A man who loves God, necessarily loves silence," wrote Thomas Merton*, who was, as a Trappist, a connoisseur, a caretaker of silences. It is no coincidence that places of worship are places of silence: if idleness is the devil's playground, silence may be the angels'. It is no surprise that silence is an anagram of license. And it is only right that Quakers* all but worship silence, for it is the place where everyone finds his God, however he may express it. Silence is an ecumenical state, beyond the doctrines and divisions created by the mind. If everyone has a spiritual story to tell of his life, everyone has a spiritual silence to preserve.

So it is that we might almost say silence is the tribute we pay to holiness; we slip off words when we enter a sacred space, just as we slip off shoes. A "moment of silence" is the highest honor we can pay someone; it is the point at which the mind stops and something else takes over (words run out when feelings rush in). A "vow of silence" is for holy men the highest devotional act. We hold our breath, we hold our words; we suspend our chattering selves and let ourselves "fall silent" and fall into the highest place of all.

It often seems that the world is getting noisier these days: in Japan, which may be a model of our future, cars and buses have voices, doors and elevators speak. The answering machine talks to us, and for us, somewhere above the din of the TV; the Walkman preserves a public silence but ensures that we need never—in the bathtub, on a mountaintop, even at our

clamor /ˈklæmə/ *n.* a loud continuous usu. confused noise or shouting
Trappist /ˈtræpɪst/ *n.* member of an order of monks noted for austerity and a vow of silence
connoisseur /ˌkɒnəˈsɜː/ *n.* an expert able to appreciate a field, esp. in the fine arts
anagram /ˈænəgræm/ *n.* a word or phrase spelled by rearranging the letters of another word or phrase
license /ˈlaɪsəns/ *n.* **a.** excessive freedom; lack of due restraint **b.** a legal document giving official permission
ecumenical /ˌiːkjʊˈmenɪkəl/ *adj.* universal, general
tribute /ˈtrɪbjuːt/ *n.* sth. given or done as an expression of esteem
slip off words to be silence
devotional /dɪˈvəʊʃənəl/ *adj.* relating to worship
din /dɪn/ *n.* **a.** a loud harsh noise **b.** the act of making a noisy disturbance

clangor /ˈklæŋə/ *n.* a sharp, harsh, ringing sound
blast /blɑːst/ *n.* **a.** a sudden very loud noise. **b.** an explosion (as of dynamite) **c.** a strong current of air
agitate /ˈædʒɪteɪt/ *v.* to cause to be excited
deity /ˈdeɪːɪtɪ/ *n.* a god or goddess; a heathen god
exultation /ˌeɡzʌlˈteɪʃən/ *n.* the utterance of sounds expressing great joy
signature tune a melody used to identify a performer or a dance band or radio/TV program
charge /tʃɑːdʒ/ *v.* to fill
province /ˈprɒvɪns/ *n.* the proper sphere or extent of your activities
assert /əˈsɜːt/ *v.* **a.** to insist on having one's opinions and rights recognized **b.** to affirm solemnly and formally as true
treacherous /ˈtretʃərəs/ *adj.* **a.** tending to betray **b.** dangerously unstable and unpredictable
paper over to cover up; to conceal
imperative /ɪmˈperətɪv/ *n.* some duty that is essential and urgent
babble /ˈbæbəl/ *v.* **a.** to talk foolishly **b.** to utter meaningless sounds like a baby, or utter in an incoherent way
unmake /ˌʌnˈmeɪk/ *v.* to deprive of certain characteristics
awe /ɔː/ *n.* **a.** an overwhelming feeling of wonder or admiration **b.** a profound fear inspired by a deity

desks—be without the clangor of the world. White noise becomes the aural equivalent of the clash of images, the nonstop blast of fragments that increasingly agitates our minds. As Ben Okri*, the young Nigerian novelist, puts it, "When chaos is the god of an era, clamorous music is the deity's chief instrument."

There is, of course, a place for noise, as there is for daily lives. There is a place for roaring, for the shouting exultation of a baseball game, for hymns and spoken prayers, for orchestras and cries of pleasure. Silence, like all the best things, is best appreciated in its absence: if noise is the signature tune of the world, silence is the music of the other world, the closest thing we know to the harmony of the spheres. But the greatest charm of noise is when it ceases. In silence, suddenly, it seems as if all the windows of the world are thrown open and everything is as clear as on a morning after rain. Silence, ideally, hums. It charges the air. In Tibet, where the silence has a tragic cause, it is still quickened by the fluttering of prayer flags, the tolling of temple bells, the roar of wind across the plains, the memory of chant.

Silence, then, could be said to be the ultimate province of trust: it is the place where we trust ourselves to be alone; where we trust others to understand the things we do not say; where we trust a higher harmony to assert itself. We all know how treacherous are words, and how often we use them to paper over embarrassment, or emptiness, or fear of the larger spaces that silence brings, "Words, words, words" commit us to positions we do not really hold, the imperatives of chatter, words are what we use for lies, false promises and gossip. We babble with strangers; with intimates we can be silent. We "make conversation" when we are at a loss; we unmake it when we are alone, or with those so close to us that we can afford to be alone with them.

In love, we are speechless; in awe, we say, words fail us.

Cultural Notes

1. **Pico Iyer** (1957—) is one of the most revered and respected travel writers alive today. He was born in England, raised in California, and educated at Eton, Oxford, and Harvard. His essays, reviews, and other writings have appeared in *Time, Conde Nast Traveler, Harper's, the New Yorker, Sports Illustrated,* and *Salon.com.* His books include *Video Night in Kathmandu, The Lady and the Monk, Cuba and the Night, Falling off the Map, Tropical Classical,* and *The Global Soul.* They have been translated into several languages and published in Europe, Asia, South America, and North America.

2. **Herman Melville** (1819—1891) was an American author, best-known for his masterpiece *Moby Dick* (1851), a whaling adventure recognized as a masterpiece 30 years after Melville's death. The fictionalized travel narrative of *Typee* (1846) is Melville's most popular book during his lifetime. ***Billy Budd*** is the novel he wrote in the last five years of his life and published posthumously in 1924.

3. **Thomas Merton** (1915—1968) was arguably the most influential American Catholic author of the twentieth century. His autobiography, *The Seven Storey Mountain,* has sold over one million copies and has been translated into over fifteen languages. He wrote over sixty other books and hundreds of poems and articles on topics ranging from monastic spirituality to civil rights, nonviolence, and the nuclear arms race.

4. **Quakers** are members of the Religious Society of Friends, a faith that emerged as a new Christian denomination in England during a period of religious turmoil in the mid-1600's, and is practiced today, in a variety of forms, around the world. To members of this religion, the words "Quaker" and "Friend" mean the same thing.

Comprehension Exercises

I. Answer the following questions based on the text.

1. What might be the most essential statement that the author tries to convey?
2. Why is silence not so easily won?
3. Why do Quakers almost worship silence?
4. When is silence best appreciated?
5. Why does the author think silence could be said to be the ultimate province of trust?

II. Decide whether each of the following statements is true or false according to the text.

1. Everybody loves the sensation of going up to a high place.
2. Herman Melville was finally destroyed by silence.
3. Silence is just a pause, an absence and emptiness.
4. The author does not like sports and music at all.
5. The greatest charm of noise is when it is absent.

III. Select the most suitable word or phrases and fill in the following blanks with their proper form.

agitate	assert	awe	babble	blast	charge
clamor	company	devastate	exultation	fret	imperative
luminous	prospect	province	rapture	retreat	treacherous
tribute					

1. Hot Springs has become a destination for weary hikers and tourists seeking a relaxing _____.
2. He was working all hours and constantly _____ about everyone else's problems.
3. Don't worry. You would definitely be happy in the _____ of fellow travellers around the evening fire.
4. Lang wears so much product in his hair that when he sways in _____ to his playing his head looks like a porcupine in a typhoon.
5. Unfortunately, we still feel that there is little _____ of seeing these big questions answered.
6. But scientists warn that climate change could also result in larger and more frequent storm surges which will _____ these countries.
7. There, spread out as far as I could see, were literally thousands of tiny, _____ objects that glowed in the black sky like fireflies.
8. Even Myanmar's military regime has realized that the public _____ for effective leadership cannot be silenced.
9. Still, not a few protests emerged against his tyrannical rule and _____ for a more representative political system.
10. People from all walks of life in the world paid _____ to Steve Jobs, together with eager Apple fans.
11. The police were reported to have _____ their way into the house using explosives when there was an obstruction for them to save the hostage.
12. Carl and Martin were _____ by the idea that they might inherit their

grandmother's possessions when she died.

13. Consciousness has long been the _____ of philosophers and psychologists, and most doctors steer clear of their abstract speculations.

14. After the war, the army made an attempt to _____ its authority in the south of the country.

15. Plane crashes in Alaska are somewhat common because of the _____ weather and mountainous terrain.

IV. Try to paraphrase the following sentences, paying special attention to the underlined parts.

1. White noise becomes the aural equivalent of the clash of images, the non-stop blast of fragments that increasingly agitates our minds.

2. In love, we are speechless; in awe, we say, words fail us.

3. Silence, then, could be said to be the ultimate province of trust.

4. Silence is responsiveness, and in silence we can listen to something behind the clamor of the world.

5. If idleness is the devil's playground, silence may be the angels'.

V. Discuss with your partner about each of the three statements and write an essay in no less than 250 words about your understanding of one of them.

1. Silence, like all the best things, is best appreciated in its absence.

2. Silence is the tribute we pay to holiness.

3. Silence is something more than just a pause.

VI. List four websites where we can learn more about Pico Iyer and provide a brief introduction to each of them.

1. _____
   _____
   _____.
2. _____
   _____
   _____.
3. _____
   _____
   _____.
4. _____
   _____
   _____.

Twenty Minutes' Reading

You are required to read the following two sections within 20 minutes.

SECTION A

Saying "thank you" is probably the first thing most of us learn to do in a foreign language. After all, we're brought up to be polite, and it is important to make a good impression upon other people — especially across national divides.

So, what exactly are you supposed to say when "thank you" is only the 20th most popular way to express gratitude? According to a recent survey, 19 other ways of expressing appreciation finished ahead of "thank you" in a poll of 3,000 people.

Pollsters found almost half of those asked preferred the more informal "cheers", while others liked to use such expressions as "ta", "great" and "nice one".

So, just what is the appropriate form of words to express your thanks?

Fortunately, the clue is in the language itself. "Cheers", despite its popularity, is considered an informal way to say thank you — and this is a definite clue as to when you can best use it.

For instance, when going for a drink with friends, a smile and a "cheers" by way of thanks is not only appropriate to the situation, it is also culturally accurate.

"Ta", originated from the Danish word "tak", was the second-most popular expression of thanks, and is also commonly used in informal situations, along with phrases such as "nice one", and "brilliant". Interestingly, one word that didn't make it into the top 20 was "thanks", Thank you's shorter, more informal cousin.

"Thanks" can be useful, as it is able to bridge the divide between the formality of "thank you" and the downright relaxed "cheers".

Certain words can double as an expression of thanks as well as delight. Again, the words themselves offer the clue as to when best to use them.

For example, words like "awesome", "brilliant" and "you star" featured highly in the new poll and they can hint at both your pleasure at someone's action, as well as serving to express your thanks. If you are on the receiving end of a "new" thank you, you can respond with a simple "no problem", or "sure".

Of course, in certain circumstances, a simple wave, nod or smile may be appropriate. For instance, if a car driver slows down to let you cross the road, simply raising your hand in acknowledgement is enough to show that you appreciate the driver's consideration.

Sometimes, formality is necessary, and "thank you" is still the best choice in such situations. But students should not worry about when exactly to use certain expressions.

Many people in Western countries are worried that good manners are in decline. People are tired of seeing their acts of kindness and service pass without comment. So don't think your "thank you" was clumsy or awkwardly formal. The chances are, if you said "thank you", you made someone's day. You star.

1. We can tell from the results of the poll that_____.
    A. people are unconcerned about politeness nowadays
    B. "thank you" remains the best expression of gratitude
    C. there is a variety of expressions of appreciation
    D. there are more formal expressions than informal ones
2. Which word/phrase does NOT appear in the top 20?
    A. Thanks.   B. Cheers.   C. Brilliant.   D. You star.
3. According to the passage, which is an appropriate response to "awesome" or "brilliant"?
    A. Thanks.   B. Cheers.   C. Nice one.   D. Sure.
4. According to the passage, the way in which we express our gratitude depends on all the following EXCEPT_____.
    A. culture   B. gender   C. formality   D. circumstance
5. In the last paragraph the author encourages people to_____.
    A. show their gratitude to others   B. behave themselves well
    C. continue their acts of kindness   D. stop worrying about bad manners

SECTION B

From 2007 to 2010, American households lost $11 trillion in real estate, savings, and stocks. More than half of all U.S. workers either lost their jobs or were forced to take cuts in hours or pay during the recession. The worst may be behind them now, but the shocking losses of the past few years have reshaped nearly every facet of their lives — how they live, work, and spend — even the way they think about the future.

For Cindy, the recession began when her husband was relocated to Rhinelander, Wisconsin, by his company, forcing the family to move in a hurry. The couple bought a new house but were unable to sell their two-bedroom home in Big Lake, Minnesota. With two mortgages(抵押借款) and two young children to care for, Cindy couldn't imagine how to stretch her husband's paycheck to keep her family fed.

Then she stumbled upon an online community called Blotanical, a forum for gardeners, many with an interest in sustainability. "The more I read and discussed these practices, the more I realized this would help not only our budget but also our health," she says.

Cindy admits that before the recession, she was a city girl with no interest in growing her own dinner. "I grew flowers mostly — I didn't think about plants that weren't visually interesting." But to stretch her budget, she began putting in vegetables and fruit — everything from strawberry beds to apple trees — and as her first seedlings grew, her spirits lifted. She no longer thinks of gardening and making her own jams as just a money saver; they're a genuine pleasure. "It's brought us closer together as a family, too," she says. Her kids voluntarily pitch in with(主动帮助)the garden work, and the family cooks together instead of eating out. The food tastes better — it's fresher and organic — and the garden handily fulfills its original purpose: cost cutting. Now she spends about $200 to $300 a month on groceries, less than half of the $650 a month that she used to lay out.

After discovering how resourceful she can be in tough times, Cindy is no longer easily discouraged. "It makes me feel proud to be able to say I made it myself," she says. "I feel accomplished, and I'm more confident about attempting things I've never done before." Now she avoids convenience stores and has begun learning to knit, quilt, and make her own soap. "I don't think I would have ever begun this journey if it weren't for the recession," she says. "I have a feeling that from now on, it will affect my family's health and happiness for the better."

6. We learn from the first paragraph that the recession_____.
   A. affected Americans in certain occupations
   B. is over with some of the losses recovered
   C. had only brought huge losses in savings and stocks
   D. had great impact on Americans' work and life
7. What made the family's financial situation even worse was that they_____.
   A. didn't know anyone in Rhinelander
   B. couldn't sell their home in Big Lake
   C. had two children to raise
   D. moved to Rhinelander in a hurry
8. Which of the following statements is correct?
   A. Cindy had already had a keen interest in sustainability.
   B. Cindy had developed a hobby of gardening before the recession.
   C. Cindy had seen the benefits of gardening in a different way.
   D. Cindy had already planned to meet the gardeners.
9. In addition, Cindy views gardening as a genuine pleasure because gardening_____.
   A. built up family ties and kids' enthusiasm
   B. enabled her to make her own jams
   C. helped her cut living costs almost by half
   D. enabled her to know more about plants
10. What does Cindy think of the different times she has gone through?
    A. It gave the couple and their kids a tough lesson.
    B. It left a lasting psychological impact on the family.
    C. It would come again and affect the family.
    D. It gave her confidence and optimism.

Unit Two

Text A

Your Speech Is Changing
Bergen Evans*

If a contemporary Rip van Winkle* had slept for forty years and awakened today, he would have to go back to school before he could understand a daily newspaper or a magazine. He would never have heard of atomic bombs, babysitters, coffee breaks, flying saucers, or contact lenses—nor of eggheads, mambo, microfilm, nylons, neptunium, parking meters, or smog.

Many new words have been added to the English language in the past forty years; and since Shakespeare*'s time the number of words in the language has increased more than five times, from 140,000 to somewhere between 700,000 and 8000,000. Most of these new words have not come from borrowing, but from the natural growth of language—adaptation of elements already in the language.

The language has always changed, but the rate of change has been uneven; minor changes have slowly accumulated in every generation, but there have been periods of rapid change as well. The most important of these periods occurred during the two hundred and fifty years after 1066, the year the Normans conquered England*. Before the conquest, the inhabitants of England spoke Anglo-Saxon*, a complex Germanic language. The Normans were Norsemen who, after generations of raiding, had settled in northern France in the tenth century and by

babysitter /ˈbeɪbɪˌsɪtə/ *n.* **a.** a person to take charge of a child while the parents are temporarily away **b.** warship used for convoy, guard and anti-submarine purposes
coffee break a brief rest, as from work
flying saucer UFO
egghead /ˈeghed/ *n.* a person who is very highly educated but not very good at practical things
mambo /ˈmæmbəʊ/ *n.* a fast ballroom dance of Carib-bean origin, rhythmically similar to the rumba and cha-cha but having a more complex pattern of steps
microfilm /ˈmaɪkrəʊfɪlm/ *n.* a film for photographing a printed page reduced to a very small size
neptunium /nepˈtjuːnɪəm/ *n.* a radioactive metallic element that is chemically similar to uranium and is obtained in nuclear reactors esp as a by-product in the production of plutonium
somewhere /ˈsʌmweə/ *adv.* used when you are giving a number that is not exact
accumulate /əˈkjuːmjʊleɪt/ *v.* to make or become greater in quantity or size

1066 were speaking a form of French. After their conquest of England they instituted Norman French as the dominant language—the language of the upper classes, of law, of government, and of such commerce as there was.

For more than two centuries nobody who was anybody spoke Anglo-Saxon. It is doubtful that Richard the Lion-hearted*, for example, spoke one word of English in his entire life—*Angle-ish* was strictly for the churls. As Wamba the Jester pointed out to Curth the Swineherd in Scott's *Ivanhoe**, while animals were living and had to be cared for, they were Saxon—*cow, calf, sheep,* and *pig*—but when they were dressed for the table, when the rewards of labor were to be enjoyed, they were Norman French—*beef, veal, mutton,* and *pork*.

institute /ˈɪnstɪtjuːt/ *v.* to introduce or start sth.
dominant /ˈdɒmɪnənt/ *adj.* most important, prevailing
commerce /ˈkɒmɜːs/ **a.** an interchange of goods on a large scale between different countries or different parts of the same country; trade; business **b.** social communication
anybody /ˈenɪˌbɒdɪ/ *pron.* a person of some importance
churl /tʃɜːl/ *n.* ill-bred person
dress /dres/ *v.* to prepare meat or fish for cooking or eating by removing the parts that are not usually eaten
alteration /ˌɔːltəˈreɪʃən/ *n.* a change in sth.
comic /ˈkɒmɪk/ funny or humorous
villain /ˈvɪlən/ *n.* the main bad character in an old play, film, or story
draw apart to move slowly away from each other
riot /ˈraɪət/ *v.* **a.** to behave violently in a public place **b.** to indulge without restraint
defiant /dɪˈfaɪənt/ *adj.* showing lack of respect or a refusal to obey someone
exuberance /ɪɡˈzjuːbərəns/ *n.* luxuriance, state of being full of life and vigor
overlord /ˈəʊvəlɔːd/ *n.* ruler

Nevertheless, the masses went right on speaking Anglo-Saxon. It was used every day for generations, by millions of common people who merely said things as effectively as they could and then got on with the business of living; never did a language become more "corrupted" by alterations, foreign words, and errors. By about three hundred years after the Norman conquest, Anglo-Saxon had re-established itself as the language of the upper classes, as *English,* and had become a flexible, exact, splendid, and moving instrument of expression. Norman French, meanwhile, had become something comic, spoken by the villains in the old mystery plays just for a laugh.

The seventeenth and eighteenth centuries, during which printing became established, saw the stabilization of spelling and, more important, the establishment of colonies in America. Immediately the language of the New World and that of the Old World began to draw apart; American speech developed its own rhythms and vigor, found or adapted special words for its own needs, and, in western areas, rioted with a sort of defiant exuberance. It became a language of the people, somewhat as Anglo-Saxon had been during the rule of the Norman overlords.

In writing, too, a change has taken place. The use of the colloquial in American writing is increasing rather than diminishing, although its opponents sometimes label it as "pandering to the masses" and a "debasement" of the language. The increasing use of the colloquial in our writing is an interesting change that is bound to have far-reaching consequences. Our common, informal speech has always been colloquial; that is what the word *colloquial* means. The sensible man speaks colloquially most of the time. When he tries to be formal or unusually impressive, he speaks the way he thinks he writes—and usually makes a fool of himself; worse, he often fails to convey his meaning. Yet whenever he stops to think, the common man feels guilty about his speech and feels that he ought to be more formal, that he ought not to use in writing (about which he retains a semiliterate awe) the expressions that just come naturally to his mind. Thus, when he sees a language form marked "colloq." in the dictionary, he thinks he ought not to use it at all, although actually the colloquial meaning of most words is the "real" meaning to him.

Opposed to the increased use of the colloquial is a minor but increasingly vocal group that insists on rules and correctness, basing that stand on a liking for absolutes; they may be motivated in part by a sense of insecurity produced by the rapidly changing social status of millions. At best, the demands of this group, if acceded to, will sacrifice vigor to propriety; at worst, they are producing a new kind of bad grammar — the uncertainty and pretentiousness that lead to the substitution of *myself* for *me* ("he gave it to John and myself"), to sticking ly on the ends of adverbs that don't need it ("our missile program is moving fastly"), to such vulgar elegances as "Whom shall I say is calling?"

The enormous enlargement of our vocabulary, the increasing use in our writing of the spoken idiom, and changes in our pronunciation are not the only changes that are taking place, however. There have also been significant grammatical alterations in our language. Such changes take place only by generations or decades, at the fastest, so they pass unnoticed by all but grammarians; yet even the layman can perceive them when

pander to to provide sth. that satisfies unreasonable wishes
debasement /dɪˈbeɪsmənt/ *n.* reduction of the quality or value of something
far-reaching *adj.* having a wide influence
impressive /ɪmˈpresɪv/ *adj.* causing admiration
convey /kənˈveɪ/ *v.* to express; make your feelings, ideas or thoughts know to other people
guilty /ˈɡɪlti/ *adj.* **a.** having broken a law or disobeyed a moral or social rule **b.** having or showing a feeling of guilt **c.** uncomfortable
semiliterate /ˌsemiˈlɪtərɪt/ *adj.* hardly able to read and write
vocal /ˈvəʊkəl/ *adj.* expressing yourself freely and noisily
motivate /ˈməʊtɪveɪt/ *v.* to provide someone with a reason for doing sth.
accede to to agree to do or accept sth.
propriety /prəˈpraɪəti/ *n.* correctness of social or moral behavior
pretentiousness /prɪˈtenʃəsnɪs/ *n.* the act of trying to be more important or clever than is really the case
vulgar /ˈvʌlɡə/ *adj.* showing a lack of fine feeling or good judgment in the choice of what is beautiful
elegance /ˈelɪɡəns/ *n.* pleasing and stylish appearance

he is told that something that seems "quite all right" to him was regarded as erroneous only a few years ago.

Take, for example, the extraordinary increase in the use of the infinitive, one of the characteristics of modern American speech and writing. Ask any educated American to point out what is wrong with "The government has a duty to protect the worker" or "We have a plan to keep the present tariff" and chances are he couldn't see anything wrong in either sentence. Yet in 1925 Fowler*, a noted grammarian, listed both of these sentences as ungrammatical, arguing that they should read "of protecting" and "of keeping".

A further example of change in our grammar is the great increase in the use of what are called "empty" verbs. Where people used to say "Let's drink" or "Let's swim", there is now a strong tendency to say "Let's have a drink" or "Let's take a swim". Where people formerly said "It snowed heavily", we are inclined to say "There was a heavy snowfall". Our fathers "decided"; we, on the other hand, more often "reach a decision".

Nobody knows why all these changes are being made; perhaps we are in the process of reducing our verbs to a few basic words, like those handy household tools where one handle serves as a blade, screwdriver, hammer, corkscrew, and a dozen other things. If this is so, it may mark a change as significant as that which took place after the Norman conquest.

Whatever the reasons for the changes that are taking place, the vocabulary will probably continue to expand, because the expansion of our knowledge and experience requires the invention of new words or the adaptation of old ones. Meaning will depend more and more upon word order and context, and spelling will become simpler, with fewer common variants. Pronunciation, because of the great mobility of our population and the spread of radio and television, will tend to become more uniform.

One thing by now seems certain—that the speech of the men who lost to the Norman invaders will not die; that language, preserved by the sturdy, surly, freedom-loving commoners who did not attempt to ingratiate themselves with their conquerors by learning their speech, will adapt and endure.

layman /'leɪmən/ n. a person who is not trained in a particular profession or subject
erroneous /ɪˈrəʊniəs/ adj. mistaken or incorrect
sturdy /'stɜːdɪ/ adj. strong and unlikely to break or be hurt
surly /'sɜːlɪ/ adj. rude and unpleasant
ingratiate /ɪnˈɡreɪʃɪeɪt/ v. to gain favor with someone by making yourself pleasant to them and saying things that will please them

Cultural Notes

1. **Bergen Evans** (1904—1978) was a well-known American expert on the English language. He taught English literature at Northwestern University for over forty years, hosted the CBS television show *The Last Word* (1957—1959), and wrote various books and short works.
2. **Rip van Winkle** is a character in the short story *Rip van Winkle* by American writer Washington Irving (1783—1859). Rip slept overnight before the War of Independence, woke up and found that twenty years had passed, during which big social changes had occurred.
3. **William Shakespeare** (1564—1616) was an English poet, dramatist and actor, often called the English national poet and considered by many to be the greatest dramatist of all time.
4. **The Norman Conquest** refers to the conquest by the French-speaking Normans under Duke William in 1066. After defeating the English at Hastings, William was crowned as King of England.
5. **Anglo-Saxon,** the original Germanic element in the English language, is plain, simple, blunt, monosyllabic, and often rude or vulgar.
6. Nicknamed **Richard the Lion-hearted,** Richard I (1157—1199) was king of England during the years 1189—1199.
7. **Ivanhoe** (1820) is a historical novel written by British writer Sir Walter Scott (1771—1832). The novel is set in the late 12th century, when the English people, or Anglo-Saxons, led a hard life under the rule of their Norman conquerors.
8. **Henry Watson Fowler** (1858—1933) was an English lexicographer. Together with his brother, he worked on *The King's English* (1906), a trenchant and witty book of modern English usage and misusage, and on *The Concise Oxford Dictionary of Current English* (1911) and *The Pocket Oxford Dictionary* (1924). After the death of his brother in 1918, H. W. Fowler completed *A Dictionary of Modern English Usage* (1926) alone. These works became invaluable reference books for writers, editors, and all those interested in the usage of modern English.

Comprehension Exercises

I. Answer the following questions based on the text.

1. Why does the author mention Rip van Winkle at the beginning of the text?
2. What language did the Normans speak before 1066?
3. What language was established as the most important language in England after the Norman Conquest?
4. What changes had happened to English and Norman French by about three hundred years after the Norman Conquest?
5. What changes happened to the English Language, with the establishment of colonies in America?
6. What is the author's opinion of colloquial language?

II. Decide whether each of the following statements is true or false according to the text.

1. Words such as egghead, mambo, microfilm, nylon, etc. appeared in the twentieth century.
2. Languages have been changing at the same speed.
3. The first truly significant period of change in the English language began in the eleventh century.
4. For more than two hundred years after the Norman Conquest, people in England spoke Norman French.
5. If rigid rules are imposed on a language, it will lose its vigor.
6. There have been no great grammatical changes in English.

III. Select the most suitable word or phrases and fill in the following blanks in their proper form.

accede	accumulate	alteration	babysitter	churl
comic	convey	debase	defiant	dress
erroneous	exuberance	far-reaching	ingratiate	institute
motivate	overlord	pander	riot	villain

1. How are you going to grow a successful business and _____ wealth using that method?
2. The newly organized government will _____ a number of measures to better safeguard the public.
3. He must have had some ups and downs in life to make him such a _____. Do you know anything of his history?

4. The poor child never cried or protested when I was _____ her wounds, which deeply impressed me.

5. It is no doubt that making some simple _____ to your diet will make you feel fitter.

6. The defeated leader appeared to remain _____ as ever, even while he was encircled by men brandishing guns.

7. Three weeks later, another political _____ erupted, this time in the neighborhood of this tumultuous region.

8. The new company continued to benefit from Brazil's _____ domestic economy, with stable growth and a swelling middle class.

9. As a newly recruited party member, he has offended the party's traditional base by _____ to the rich and the middle classes.

10. The economy is in danger of collapse unless _____ reforms are implemented in this country.

11. Gold has become a hedge against the stock market where it once was a hedge against currency _____, or against commodity price inflation.

12. When I returned to my factory from abroad, I tried to _____ the wonder of this machine to my boss.

13. For a long time, we had been wondering why he didn't just _____ to our demands at the outset.

14. Some people just need something fun to _____ them to get up and get moving positively and creatively.

15. I would say that a more likely explanation of your pal's actions against you is that he is trying to _____ himself with his girlfriend.

IV. Try to paraphrase the following sentences, paying special attention to the underlined parts.

1. After their conquest of England they instituted Norman French as the dominant language — the language of the upper classes, of low, of government, and of such commerce as there was.

   _____

   _____

2. For more than two centuries nobody who was anybody spoke Anglo-Saxon.

   _____

   _____

3. ...but when they were dressed for the table, when the rewards of labor were to be enjoyed, they were Norman French ...

   _____

   _____

4. American speech <u>developed its own rhythms and vigor</u>, found or adapted special words for its own needs, and, in western areas, <u>rioted with</u> a sort of <u>defiant exuberance</u>.
   _____
   _____

5. At best, the demands of this group, <u>if acceded to</u>, will <u>sacrifice vigor to propriety</u>.
   _____
   _____

V. Discuss with your partner about each of the three statements and write an essay in no less than 250 words about your understanding of one of them.

1. Something that was regarded as erroneous only a few years ago seems quite all right now.
   _____
   _____

2. Nobody knows why all the language changes are being made.
   _____
   _____

3. Meaning will depend more and more upon word order and context, and spelling will become simpler, with fewer common variants.
   _____
   _____

VI. List four websites where we can learn more about Bergen Evans or the change of language and provide a brief introduction to each of them.

1. _____
   _____
   _____.

2. _____
   _____
   _____.

3. _____
   _____
   _____.

4. _____
   _____
   _____.

Text B

How to Talk about the World
*Peter Farb**

Most people assume that a text in one language can be accurately translated into another language, so long as the translator uses a good bilingual dictionary. But that is not so, because words that are familiar in one language may have no equivalent usage in another. The word *home*, for example, has special meaning for English speakers, particularly those who live in the British Isles. To an Englishman, a *home* is more than the physical structure in which he resides; it is his castle, no matter how humble, the place of his origins, fondly remembered, as well as his present environment of happy family relationships. *This is my home* says the Englishman, and he thereby points not only to a structure but also to a way of life. The same feeling, though, cannot be expressed even in a language whose history is as closely intertwined with English as is French. The closest a Frenchman can come is *Voilá ma maison* or *Voilá mon logis*—words equivalent to the English *house* but certainly not to the English *home*.

Mark Twain* humorously demonstrated the problems of translation when he published the results of his experiment with French. He printed the original version of his well-known story "The Celebrated Jumping Frog of Calaveras County", followed by a Frenchman's translation of it, and then a literal translation from the French back into English. Here are a few sentences from each version:

Twain's Original Version: "Well, there was a feller here once by the name of Jim Smiley, in the winter of '49—or maybe it was the spring of '50—I don't recollect exactly, somehow though what makes me think it was one or the other is because I remember the big flume wasn't finished when he first come to the camp."

bilingual /baɪˈlɪŋgwəl/ *adj.* spoken or written in two languages
reside /rɪˈzaɪd/ *v.* to live
intertwine /ˌɪntəˈtwaɪn/ *v.* to twine together
literal translation an exact, word-for-word translation
recollect /ˌrekəˈlekt/ *v.* to remember
flume /fluːm/ *n.* (in a gold-mining camp) an artificial channel or open pipe through which water passes

French Version: (omitted)

Literal Retranslation into English: "It there was one time here an individual known under the name of Jim Smiley; it was in the winter of '49, possibly well at the spring of '50, I no me recollect exactly. That which makes me to believe that it was one or the other, it is that I shall remember that the grand flume was no achieved when he arrives at the camp for the first time."

bizarre /bɪˈzɑː/ *adj.* very strange
ineptness /ɪˈneptnɪs/ *n.* foolishness or a poor performance
disastrous /dɪˈzɑːstrəs/ *adj.* terrible
ultimatum /ˌʌltɪˈmeɪtəm/ *n.* statement of final condition not open for discussion
laden /ˈleɪdn/ *adj.* loaded with; carrying
anecdote /ˈænɪkdəʊt/ *n.* a short interesting story about a particular person or event
obligatory categories of grammar required grammatical classes of words
aspect /ˈæspekt/ *n.* a verb form, esp. related to sense of time, as in the English perfect with go in I have gone

Twain, of course, exaggerated his example of bizarre translation—but sometimes such ineptness can have disastrous consequences. At the end of July 1945, Germany and Italy had surrendered and the Allies* issued an ultimatum to Japan to surrender also. Japan's premier called a press conference at which he stated that his country would *mokusatsu* the Allied ultimatum. The word *mokusatsu* was an extremely unfortunate choice. The premier apparently intended it to mean that the cabinet would "consider" the ultimatum. But the word has another meaning, "take no notice of," and that was the one the English-language translators at Domei, Japan's overseas broadcasting agency, used. The world heard that Japan had rejected the ultimatum—instead of that Japan was still considering it. Domei's mistranslation led the United States to send B-29s, laden with atomic bombs, over Hiroshima* and Nagasaki*. Apparently, if *mokusatsu* had been correctly translated, the atomic bomb need never have been dropped.

Such anecdotes about failures in translation do not get at the heart of the problem, because they concern only isolated words and not the resistance of an entire language system to translation. For example, all languages have obligatory categories of grammar that may be lacking in other languages. Russian—like many languages but not like English—has an obligatory category for gender which demands that a noun, and often a pronoun, specify whether it is masculine, feminine, or neuter. Another obligatory category, similarly lacking in English, makes a verb state whether or not an action has been completed. Therefore, a Russian finds it impossible to translate accurately the English sentence *I hired a worker* without having much more information. He would have to know whether the *I* who was speaking was a man or a woman, whether the action of *hired* had a completive or noncompletive aspect ("already hired" as opposed to "was in the process of hiring"), and whether the *worker* was a man or a woman.

unwieldy /ʌnˈwiːldi/ *adj.* large, heavy, and awkward to move
render /ˈrendə/ *v.* to translate
rip /rɪp/ to tear
intersection /ˌɪntəˈsekʃən/ *n.* a place where roads or lines cross
thoroughfare /ˈθʌrəfeə/ *n.* main road or street (usu. busy)
eccentricity /ˌeksenˈtrɪsɪtɪ/ *n.* peculiarity; strangeness

Or imagine the difficulty of translating into English a Chinese story in which a character identified as a *biaomei* appears. The obligatory categories to which this word belongs require that it tell whether it refers to a male or a female, whether the character is older or younger than the speaker, and whether the character belongs to the family of the speaker's father or mother. *biaomei* therefore can be translated into English only by the unwieldy statement "a female cousin on my mother's side and younger than myself". Of course, the translator might simply establish these facts about the character the first time she appears and thereafter render the words as "cousin", but that would ignore the significance in Chinese culture of the repetition of these obligatory categories.

The Russian and Chinese examples illustrate the basic problem in any translation. No matter how skilled the translator is, he cannot rip language out of the speech community that uses it. Translation obviously is not a simple two-way street between two languages. Rather, it is a busy intersection at least five thoroughfares meet—the two languages with all their eccentricities, the cultures of the two speech communities, and the speech situation in which the statement was uttered.

Cultural Notes

1. **Peter Farb** (1925—1980) was a naturalist, linguist, anthropologist, and a free-lance writer on many topics, spanning from human culture to the geological formation of North America. His *Face of America: The Natural History of a Continent* (1964) became so popular that President Kennedy presented it to the heads of one hundred foreign governments.

2. **Mark Twain** (1835—1910) was an American writer, journalist, and humorist. The short story "The Celebrated Jumping Frog of Calaveras County" (1865) marked the beginning of his literary career. He won a worldwide audience for his novels *Tom Sawyer* and *Huckleberry Finn*. Sensitive to the sound of language, Twain introduced colloquial speech into American fiction. According to Ernest Hemingway, "All modern American literature comes from one book by Mark Twain called *Huckleberry Finn*...."

3. **The Allies** of World War II were mainly the United Kingdom, the United States, the Soviet Union, and France. Other allied nations included Australia, Canada, China, Denmark, New Zealand, Poland, Yugoslavia and so on. The involvement of many of the Allies in World War II was natural and inevitable, because they were either invaded or under the direct threat of invasion by the Axis.
4. **Hiroshima** and **Nagasaki** are two seaport cities of Japan. In early August 1945, two atomic bombs made by the allied powers (USA and UK) were dropped on Hiroshima and Nagasaki respectively. These brought the long Second World War to a sudden end.

Comprehension Exercises

I. Answer the following questions based on the text.

1. How is the English word "home" different from the French equivalent in connotations or associations?
2. What does the experiment Mark Twain made demonstrate?
3. What example does Farb use to show that inaccurate translation may have very serious consequences?
4. Why does Farb say that the anecdotes such as Domei mistranslation "do not get at the heart of the problem"?
5. What would the translator have to know in order to translate "I hired a worker" into Russian?
6. Why is the English translation of Chinese "*biaomei*" unsatisfactory?
7. What does Farb mean to say by "five thoroughfares"?
8. What conclusion does Farb intend to draw?

II. Decide whether each of the following statements is true or false according to the text.

1. A text in one language can be accurately translated into another language.
2. Words familiar in one language always have equivalent usage in another language.
3. Poor translation can cause very serious consequences.
4. Momei's mistranslation was solely responsible for the atomic bombings in Hiroshima and Nagasaki.
5. Russian nouns have a gender category while English nouns don't.

III. Select the most suitable word or phrases and fill in the following blanks in their proper form if necessary.

anecdote	aspect	bilingual	bizarre	disastrous
eccentricity	exaggerate	ineptness	intersection	laden
liberal	recollect	render	reside	rip
specify	thoroughfare	ultimatum	unwieldy	

1. In future, the programme will be _____, using Chinese alongside English so that it could be accessible to different groups of people.
2. Happiness does not _____ in strength or money; instead it is a mental state of satisfaction.
3. Over the years I have seen referees become more _____ on their interpretation of the laws of the game.
4. Ramona spoke with warmth when she _____ the amiable and generous doctor who used to be working at the community hospital.
5. The book, most impartial readers would surely agree, is rambling, contradictory and often simply _____.
6. As a general rule, the defining feature of modern videogame storytelling is its _____ — its near-total lack of imagination, ambition, technical proficiency, and, well, brains.
7. Johnson said the debate has been disappointing because opponents have substituted _____ for fact.
8. We feel miserable to hear the _____ news that the vegetable harvest of this region is behind schedule.
9. They issued an _____ to the police to rid the area of racist attackers, or they will take the law into their own hands.
10. The old scullery maid is coming from the market, her basket _____ with vegetables, wading through the slush and drenched with the rain.
11. He observed in the magazine that a crucial _____ of political change should involve the education of the masses.
12. His relatives from the countryside came panting up to his door with their _____ baggage.
13. We must now consider the implications of his actions, seek the truth and _____ a judgment.
14. Looking at the _____ in her new dress, she flew into a rage, reluctant to say any words with the culprit.
15. Later police arrested dozens of protesters for apparently blocking a(n) _____ leading to the base.

Unit Two

IV. Try to paraphrase the following sentences, paying special attention to the underlined parts.

1. Twain, of course, <u>exaggerated his example of bizarre translation</u> — but sometimes such <u>ineptness</u> can have disastrous consequences.

2. Such anecdotes about failures in translation do not <u>get at the heart of the problem</u>, because they concern only <u>isolated words</u> and not the <u>resistance</u> of an entire language system to translation.

3. Russian — like many languages but not like English — has <u>an obligatory category</u> for gender which <u>demands</u> that a noun, and often a pronoun, <u>specify</u> whether it is masculine, feminine or neuter.

4. No matter how skilled the translator is, he cannot <u>rip language out of the speech community</u> that uses it.

5. Rather, it is <u>a busy intersection at least five thoroughfares meet</u> — the two languages with <u>all their eccentricities</u>, the cultures of the two <u>speech communities</u>, and the speech situation in which the statement was uttered.

V. Discuss with your partner about each of the three statements and write an essay in no less than 250 words about your understanding of one of them.

1. A text in one language can be accurately translated into anther language.

2. Words that are familiar in one language may have no equivalent usage in another.

3. Translation obviously is not a simple two-way street between two languages.

VI. List four websites where we can learn more about Peter Farb and provide a brief introduction to each of them.

1. _____
   _____
   _____.

2. _____
   _____
   _____.

3. _____
   _____
   _____.

4. _____
   _____
   _____.

Twenty Minutes' Reading

You are required to read the following two sections within 20 minutes.

 **SECTION A**

"I'm a little worried about my future," said Dustin Hoffman in *The Graduate*. He should be so lucky. All he had to worry about was whether to have an affair with Mrs Robinson. In the sixties, that was the sum total of post-graduation anxiety syndrome.

Hoffman's modern counterparts are not so fortunate. The Mrs Robinsons aren't sitting around at home any more, seducing graduates. They are out in the workplace, doing the high-powered jobs the graduates want, but cannot get. For those fresh out of university, desperate for work but unable to get it, there is a big imbalance between supply and demand. And there is no narrowing of the gap in sight.

The latest unemployment figures show that 746,000 of 18—24 year-olds are unemployed — a record rate of 18 per cent. Many of those will have graduated this summer. They are not panicking yet, but as the job rejections mount up, they are beginning to feel alarmed.

Of course, it is easy to blame the Government and, in particular, the target that Labour has long trumpeted — 50 per cent of school-leavers in higher education. That was not too smart. The Government has not only failed to meet its target — the actual figure is still closer to 40 per cent — but it has raised expectations to unrealistic levels.

Parents feel as badly let down as the young people themselves. Middle-class families see their graduate offspring on the dole (救济金) queue and wonder why they bothered paying school fees. Working-class families feel an even keener sense of disappointment. For many such families, getting a child into university was the fulfillment of a lifelong dream. It represented upward social and financial mobility. It was proof that they were living in a dynamic, economically successful country. That dream does not seem so rosy now.

Graduate unemployment is not, ultimately, a political problem ready to be solved. Job-creation schemes for graduates are very low down in ministerial in-trays. If David Cameron's Conservatives had a brilliant idea for guaranteeing every graduate a well-paid job, they would have unveiled it by now. It is a social problem, though a more deep-seated social problem than people perhaps realize.

1. The author begins with an episode from The Graduate in order to_____.
    A. support the fact that more women are working now
    B. emphasize the sharp contrast between now and then
    C. demonstrate that there were much fewer graduates than now
    D. show that few graduates started working right after graduation
2. With regard to job opportunities for young graduates, the author sounds_____.
    A. pessimistic   B. hopeful   C. indifferent   D. furious
3. The author is _____ the Labour Government's target: 50% of school leavers in higher education.
    A. in favour of   B. doubtful about
    C. strongly critical of   D. mildly critical of
4. Which of the following statements about parents' feelings is CORRECT?
    A. Working-class parents feel just as disappointed.
    B. Parents and their children feel equally disappointed.
    C. Middle-class parents feel more disappointed.
    D. Parents feel more disappointed than their children.
5. Towards the end of the passage, the author implies that_____.
    A. there will be job-creation schemes for graduates
    B. graduate unemployment is more of a political issue
    C. the Conservatives are doing far from enough to solve the issue
    D. graduate unemployment is both a political and a social issue

SECTION B

No matter how many times you have seen images of the golden mask of boy king Tutankhamen, come face to face with it in Egypt's Cairo Museum, and you will suck in your breath.

It was on Nov 4, 1923, that British archaeologist Howard Carter stumbled on a stone at the base of the tomb of another pharaoh(法老)in Luxor that eventually led to a sealed doorway.

Then, on Nov 23, Carter found a second door and when he stuck his head through it, what he saw was to stun the world. Inside lay the great stone coffin, enclosing three chests of gilded wood.

A few months later, when a crane lifted its granite cover and one coffin after another was removed, Carter found a solid block of gold weighing 110 kg. In it was the mummy(木乃伊)of the 19-year-old Tutankhamen, covered in gold with that splendid funeral mask. And all this lay buried for more than 3,000 years.

Months after my trip to Egypt, I can relive the rush of emotion I felt and sense the hush that descended on the crammed Cairo Museum's Tutankhamen gallery.

Cairo, a dusty city of 20 million people, is a place where time seems to both stand still and rush into utter chaos. It is a place where the ancient and contemporary happily go along on parallel tracks.

Take the Great Pyramids of Giza, sitting on the western edge of the city. Even as the setting sun silhouettes these gigantic structures against the great desert expanse, a call for prayer floats over semi-finished apartment blocks filled with the activity of city life.

While careful planning for the afterlife may lie buried underground in Cairo, it is noise and confusion on the streets. Donkey carts battle for space with pedestrians and the only operative road rule is "might is right". But it is a city that is full of life — from the small roadside restaurants to the coffee shops where men and women smoke the shisha(水烟壶).

Donkey carts piled high with flat-breads magically find their way in and out the maddening traffic; young women in long skirts and headscarves hold hands with young men in open collar shirts, while conversations dwell on Kuwait's chances at the soccer World Cup.

6. According to the context, "suck in your breath" means "feel a sense of _____".
   A. awe   B. horror   C. doubt   D. delight
7. Which of the following statements about the discovery of the mummy is incorrect?
   A. The masked mummy was covered in gold.
   B. The discovery of the mummy came as a surprise.
   C. The mummy was first discovered by a British archaeologist.
   D. The mummy was found lying right inside the stone coffin.
8. Which word CANNOT be used to describe the city of Cairo?
   A. Crowdedness.   B. Quiet.   C. Noise.   D. Confusion.
9. Which pair words/phrases indicates contrast?
   A. gigantic structure; great desert expanse
   B. a call for prayer; men and women with the shisha
   C. chaos; maddening
   D. coffee shops; pyramids
10. What is the author's attitude towards Cairo?
    A. Positive.   B. Negative.   C. Objective.   D. Not clear.

Unit Three

A Love Affair with Books
Bernadete Piassa*

When I was young, I thought that reading was like a drug which I was allowed to take only a teaspoon at a time, but which, nevertheless, had the effect of carrying me away to an enchanted world where I experienced strange and forbidden emotions. As time went by and I took that drug again and again, I became addicted to it. I could no longer live without reading. Books became an intrinsic part of my life. They became my friends, my guides, my lovers—my most faithful lovers.

I didn't know I would fall in love with books when I was young and started to read. I don't even recall when I started to read and how. I just remember that my mother didn't like me to read. In spite of this, every time I had an opportunity I would sneak somewhere with a book and read one page, two pages, three, if I was lucky enough, always feeling my heart beating fast, always hoping that my mother wouldn't find me, wouldn't shout as always: "Bernadete, don't you have anything to do?" For her, books were nothing. For me, they were everything.

In my childhood I didn't have a big choice of books. I lived in a small town in Brazil, surrounded by swamp and farms. It was impossible to get out of town by car; there weren't roads. By train it took eight hours to reach the next village. There were airplanes, small airplanes, only twice a week. Books couldn't get to my town very easily. There wasn't a library there, either. However, I was lucky: my uncle was a pilot.

enchanted /ɪnˈtʃɑːntɪd/ *adj.* bewitched, captivated, delighted
addicted /əˈdɪktɪd/ *adj.* compulsively or physiologically dependent on sth. habit-forming
intrinsic /ɪnˈtrɪnsɪk/ *adj.* inherent; belonging to a thing by its very nature
sneak /sniːk/ *v.* to go stealthily or furtively

My uncle, who owned a big farm and also worked flying people from place to place in his small airplane, had learned to fly, in addition, with his imagination. At home, he loved to sit in his hammock on his patio and travel away in his fantasy with all kinds of books. If he happened to read a best-seller or a romance, when he was done he would give it to my mother, who also liked to read although she didn't like me to. But I would get to read the precious book anyway, even if I needed to do this in a hiding place, little by little.

hammock /ˈhæmək/ n. a hanging bed of canvas or rope netting (usu. suspended between two trees)
patio /ˈpætɪəʊ/ n. paved outdoor area adjoining a residence
fantasy /ˈfæntəsɪ/ n. a. imagination unrestricted by reality b. fiction with a large amount of fantasy in it
devour /dɪˈvaʊə/ v. a. to enjoy avidly, as of a book b. to eat greedily
appalled /əˈpɔːld/ adj. struck with fear or dread
tuck /tʌk/ v. a. to fold under b. to press into a narrower compass
intriguing /ɪnˈtriːɡɪŋ/ adj. capable of arousing interest or curiosity

I remember very well one series of small books. Each had a green cover with a drawing of a couple kissing on it. I think the series had been given to my mother when she was a teenager because all the pages were already yellow and almost worn out. But although the books were old, for me they seemed alive, and for a long time I devoured them, one by one, pretending that I was the heroine and my lover would soon come to rescue me. He didn't come, of course. And I was the one who left my town to study and live in Rio de Janeiro*, taking only my clothes with me. But inside myself I was taking my passion for books that would never abandon me.

I had been sent to study in a boarding school, and I was soon appalled to discover that the expensive all-girls school had even fewer books than my house. In my class there was a bookshelf with maybe fifty books, and almost all of them were about the lives of saints and the miracles of Christ. I had almost given up the hope of finding something to read when I spotted, tucked away at the very end of the shelf, a small book already covered by dust. It didn't seem to be about religion because it had a more intriguing title, *The Old Man and the Sea*. It was written by an author that I had never heard of before: Ernest Hemingway*. Curious, I started to read the book and a few minutes later was already fascinated by Santiago, the fisherman.

I loved that book so much that when I went to my aunt's house to spend the weekend, I asked her if she had any books by the man who had written it. She lent me *For Whom the Bell Tolls,* and I read it every Sunday I could get out of school, only a little bit at a time, only one teaspoon at a time. I started to wait anxiously for those Sundays. At the age of thirteen I was deeply in love with Ernest Hemingway.

When I finished all of his books that I could find, I discovered Herman Hesse*, Graham Greene*, Aldous Huxley*, Edgar Allan Poe*. I could read them only on Sundays, so during the week I would dream or think about the world I had discovered in their books.

At that time I thought that my relationship with books was kind of odd, something that set me apart from the world. Only when I read the short story "Illicit Happiness" by Clarice Lispector*, a Brazilian author, did I discover that other people could enjoy books as much as I did. The story is about an ugly, fat girl who still manages to torture one of the beautiful girls in her town only because the unattractive girl's father is the owner of a bookstore, and she can have all the books she wants. With sadistic refinement, day after day she promises to give to the beautiful girl the book the girl dearly wants, but never fulfills her promise. When her mother finds out what is going on, she gives the book to the beautiful girl, who then runs through the streets hugging it and, at home, pretends to have lost it only to find it again, showing an ardor for books that made me exult. For the first time I wasn't alone. I knew that someone else also loved books as much as I did.

My passion for books continued through my life, but I had to surmount another big challenge when, at the age of thirty-one, I moved to New York. Because I had almost no money, I was forced to leave all my books in Brazil. Besides, I didn't know enough English to read in this language. For some years I was condemned again to the darkness; condemned to live without books, my friends, my guides, my lovers.

But my love for books was so strong that I overcame even this obstacle. I learned to read in English and was finally able to enjoy my favorite authors again.

Although books have always been part of my life, they still hold a mystery for me, and every time I open a new one, I ask myself which pleasures I am about to discover, which routes I am about to travel, which emotions I am about to sink in. Will this new book touch me as a woman, as a foreigner, as a romantic soul, as a curious person? Which horizon is it about to unfold to me, which string of my soul is it bound to touch, which secret is it about to unveil for me?

sadistic /səˈdɪstɪk/ *adj.* deriving pleasure from inflicting pain on another
refinement /rɪˈfaɪnmənt/ *n.* the quality of excellence in thought and manners and taste
dearly /ˈdɪəlɪ/ *adv.* **a.** at a high price or terrible cost **b.** very much
ardor /ˈɑːdə/ *n.* intense feeling of love
exult /ɪɡˈzʌlt/ *v.* **a.** to express great joy **b.** to feel extreme happiness
surmount /səˈmaʊnt/ *v.* to deal with successfully
condemn /kənˈdem/ *v.* **a.** to express strong disapproval of **b.** to force someone into an unhappy state of affairs
unveil /ʌnˈveɪl/ *v.* to reveal by removing a veil from (a person or sth. new)

Sometimes, the book seduces me not only for the story it tells, but also because of the words the author uses in it. Reading Gabriel Garcia Marquez*'s short story "The Hand somest Drowned Man in the World", I feel dazzled when he writes that it took "the fraction of centuries for the body to fall into the abyss". The fraction of centuries! I read those words again and again, infatuated by them, by their precision, by their hidden meaning. I try to keep them in my mind, even knowing that they are already part of my soul.

seduce /sɪˈdjuːs/ *v.* to lure or entice away from duty, principles, or proper conduct
dazzled /ˈdæzəl/ *adj.* stupefied or dizzied by sth. overpowering
fraction /ˈfrækʃn/ *n.* a small part or item forming a piece of a whole
abyss /əˈbɪs/ *n.* a bottomless gulf, or pit; hell
infatuate /ɪnˈfætjʊeɪt/ *v.* to arouse unreasoning love or passion in and cause to behave in an irrational way
point /pɔɪnt/ *n.* idea contained in sth. said or done
tiresome /ˈtaɪəsəm/ *adj.* **a.** annoying **b.** tiring or uninteresting
subversive /səbˈvɜːsɪv/ *adj.* in opposition to a civil authority or government
lackluster /ˈlækˌlʌstə/ *adj.* lacking brilliance or vitality

After reading so many books that touch me deeply, each one in its special way, I understand now that my mother had a point when she tried to keep me away from books in my childhood. She wanted me to stay in my little town, to marry a rich and tiresome man, to keep up with the traditions. But the books carried me away; they gave me wings to fly, to discover new places. They made me dare to live another kind of life. They made me wish for more, and when I couldn't have all I wished for, they were still there to comfort me, to show me new options.

Yes, my mother was right. Books are dangerous; books are subversive. Because of them I left a predictable future for an unforeseeable one. However, if I had to choose again, I would always choose the books instead of the lackluster life I could have had. After all, what joy would I find in my heart without my books, my most faithful lovers?

Cultural Notes

1. **Bernadete Piassa**, a senior project director of the marketing research team of Mattson Jack Group, Inc. based in Philadelphia, grew up in rural Brazil. In this prize-winning essay from a national writing contest, she describes how she was eager to read but was discouraged from reading the few that she could find.
2. **Rio de Janeiro** is the former capital and 2nd largest city of Brazil, famous as a tourist attraction.
3. **Ernest Hemingway** (1899—1961) was a famous American novelist and short-story writer and is regarded as one of the great American writers of the

20th century. During World War I he served as an ambulance driver in the Italian infantry and was wounded. Later, while working in Paris as a correspondent for *the Toronto Star*, he became involved with the expatriate literary and artistic circle surrounding Gertrude Stein. During the Spanish Civil War, Hemingway served as a correspondent on the loyalist side. From this experience came his novel, *For Whom the Bell Tolls* (1940). He fought in World War II and then settled in Cuba in 1945. His novel *The Old Man and the Sea* (1952) celebrates the indomitable courage of an aged Cuban fisherman—Santiago. In 1954, Hemingway was awarded the Nobel Prize for Literature. Increasingly plagued by ill health and mental problems, he committed suicide by shooting himself in 1961.

4. **Herman Hesse** (1877—1962), a German-Swiss writer, received the Goethe Prize of Frankfurt in 1946 and the Peace Prize of the German Booksellers in 1955.

5. **Graham Greene** (1904—1991) was an English playwright, novelist, short story writer, travel writer and critic whose works explore the ambivalent moral and political issues of the modern world. Greene combined serious literary acclaim with wide popularity. Although Greene objected strongly to being described as a "Catholic novelist" rather than as a "novelist who happened to be Catholic", Catholic religious themes are at the root of many of his novels. Works such as *The Quiet American* also show an avid interest in international politics.

6. **Aldous Huxley** (1894—1963) was an English writer and one of the most prominent members of the famous Huxley family, best known for his dystopian novel *Brave New World* (1931). Besides novels, he published travel books, histories, poems, plays, and essays on philosophy, arts, sociology, religion and morals.

7. **Edgar Allan Poe** (1809—1849) was an American poet, short story writer, editor, critic and one of the leaders of the American Romantic Movement. Best known for his tales of the macabre, Poe was one of the early American practitioners of the short story and a progenitor of detective fiction and crime fiction. He is also credited with contributing to the emergent science fiction genre.

8. **Clarice Lispector** (1920—1977) was a Brazilian writer universally recognized as the most original and influential Brazilian woman writer of her time. In feminist circles, she is revered as an intensely feminine writer who articulates the needs and concerns of every woman in pursuit of self-awareness.

9. **Gabriel García Márquez** (1928—   ) is a Colombian-born author and journalist, winner of the 1982 Nobel Prize for Literature and a pioneer of the Latin American "Boom". His masterpiece, *One Hundred Years of Solitude,* tells the story of the rise and fall, birth and death of a mythical town of Macondo through the history of the Buendi'a family.

Comprehension Exercises

I. Answer the following questions based on the text.
1. What's the main idea of the text?
2. In what ways were books "like a drug" to Piassa?
3. Why did Piassa's mother discourage her from reading?
4. How did books affect her life?
5. What might you get to know about the Brazilian culture?

II. Decide whether each of the following statements is true or false according to the text.
1. Piassa's mother did not enjoy reading.
2. As a child, Piassa had to struggle to find access to books.
3. The books Piassa read were largely romance.
4. Piassa was not interested in books with religious contents.
5. Piassa implies that girls interested in reading books are usually beautiful.
6. Piassa finally understands her mother's reasons for keeping books from her.

III. Select the most suitable word or phrases and fill in the following blanks in their proper form.

abyss	addicted	appalled	ardor	condemn
dazzled	devour	enchanted	exult	fantasy
fraction	infatuate	intriguing	intrinsic	seduce
sneak	subversive	surmount	tuck	unveil

1. Nowadays many people are particularly _____ by the Internet's ability to seamlessly blend community, knowledge and consumption.
2. When you are _____ to something, whether it's a substance, an activity or a person, it seems as if nothing can replace it.
3. Although these children haven't been taught anything about music, they apparently have this sort of _____ reaction to music.

4. Not a few of us begin to be worried about the fact that health-care spending will essentially _____ all our future wage increases and economic growth.

5. Helen was _____ by the news she got on the Internet that three children were drowned in that very stream.

6. Hackers use anonymous electronic greeting cards to _____ their malicious software onto unprotected computers.

7. The food arrives quickly and I _____ into my excellent lamb while Fukuyama eats slowly as he thinks about his answers.

8. The rainforest around our house sometimes brings forth such _____ creatures that all my children enjoyed observing them.

9. All the participants were greatly affected and deeply touched by his great revolutionary _____ .

10. What distinguishes these developing country women is their ability to _____ obstacles traditionally faced by small enterprises.

11. For that matter, even wanting to parade our own brilliance and _____ in other people's errors is not very nice, although it is certainly very human.

12. Markets had risen after European officials promised to _____ a far-reaching rescue plan by that date.

13. At the very first sight of her, John became _____ with the blonde French teacher fresh from the city of Lyon.

14. As Miss White, the math teacher, went into the classroom, she was _____ by the resplendent trappings of crimson and gold right away.

15. The play was promptly banned as it was believed to contain some _____ and even treasonous element.

IV. Try to paraphrase the following sentences, paying special attention to the underlined parts.

1. At home, he loved to sit in his hammock <u>on his patio</u> and <u>travel away in his fantasy with all kinds of books</u>.

   _____

   _____

2. I had almost given up the hope of finding something to read when I <u>spotted, tucked away</u> at the very end of the shelf, a small book already covered by dust.

   _____

3. At that time I thought that my relationship with books was <u>kind of odd</u>, some-

thing that set me apart from the world.

4. When her mother finds out what is going on, she gives the book to the beautiful girl, who then runs through the streets hugging it and, at home, pretends to have lost it only to find it again, showing an ardor for books that made me exult.

5. I read those words again and again, infatuated by them, by their precision, by their hidden meaning. I try to keep them in my mind, even knowing that they are already part of my soul.

V. Discuss with your partner about each of the three statements and write an essay in no less than 250 words about your understanding of one of them.

1. Books are dangerous.

2. Books are subversive.

3. Books give people wings to fly.

VI. List four websites where we can learn more about Bernadete Piassa and provide a brief introduction to each of them.

1.

2.

3.

4. _____
   _____
   _____ .

The Lost Art of Reading
David L. Ulin

One evening not long ago, my fifteen-year-old son, Noah, told me that literature was dead. We were at the dinner table, discussing *The Great Gatsby,* * which he was reading for a ninth-grade humanities class. Part of the class structure involved annotation, which Noah detested; it kept pulling him out of the story to stop every few lines and make a note, mark a citation, to demonstrate that he'd been paying attention to what he read. "It would be so much easier if they'd let me read it," he lamented, and listening to him, I couldn't help but recall my own classroom experiences, the endless scansion of poetry, the sentence diagramming, the excavation of metaphor and form. I remembered reading, in junior high school, *Lord of the Flies** — a novel Noah had read (and loved) at summer camp, writing to me in a Facebook message that it was "seriously messed up" — and thinking, as my teacher detailed the symbolic structure, finding hidden nuance in literally every sentence, that what she was saying was impossible. How, I wondered, could William Golding have seeded his narrative so consciously and still have managed to write? How could he have kept track of it all? Even then, I knew I wanted to be a writer, had begun to read with an eye toward how a book or story was built, and if this was what it took, this overriding sense of consciousness, then I would never be smart enough.

Now, I recognize this as one of the fallacies of teaching literature in the classroom, the need to seek a reckoning with everything, to imagine

annotation /ænəˈteɪʃ(ə)n/ *n.* the activity of adding notes to a text or diagram, often in order to explain it
citation /saɪˈteɪʃ(ə)n/ *n.* a passage or phrase quoted from a book or other piece of writing
demonstrate /ˈdemənstreɪt/ *v.* **a.** establish the validity of something, as by an example, explanation or experiment **b.** provide evidence for; stand as proof of
scansion /ˈskænʃ(ə)n/ *n.* the analysis of the metrical structure of verse
diagram /ˈdaɪəɡræm/ *n.* a drawing intended to explain how something works; a drawing showing the relation between the parts
excavation /ˌekskəˈveɪʃ(ə)n/ *n.* the act of digging; the act of extracting ores or coal etc. from the earth
nuance /ˈnjuːɑːns, njuːˈɑːns/ *n.* a subtle difference in meaning or opinion or attitude
overriding /ˌəʊvəˈraɪdɪŋ/ *adj.* having superior power and influence; the most important
fallacy /ˈfæləsi/ *n.* a misconception resulting from incorrect reasoning; an idea which many people believe to be true, but which is in fact false because it is based on incorrect information or reasoning
reckoning /ˈrekənɪŋ/ *n.* a calculation made about something, especially a calculation that is not very exact

a framework, a rubric, in which each little piece makes sense. Literature — at least the literature to which I respond — doesn't work that way; it is conscious, yes, but with room for serendipity, a delicate balance between craft and art. This is why it's often difficult for writers to talk about their process, because the connections, the flow of storytelling, remain mysterious even to them. "I have to say that, for me, it evolved spontaneously. I didn't have any plan," Philip Roth* once said of a scene in his 2006 novel *Everyman*, and if such a revelation can be frustrating to those who want to see the trick, the magic behind the magic, it is the only answer for a writer, who works for reasons that are, at their essence, the opposite of schematic: emotional, murky, not wholly identifiable — at least, if the writing's any good. That kind of writing, though, is difficult to teach, leaving us with scansion, annotation, all that sound and fury, a buzz of explication that obscures the elusive heartbeat of a book.

For Noah, I should say, this was not the issue — not on those terms, anyway. He merely wanted to finish the assignment so he could move on to something he preferred. As he is the first to admit, he is not a reader, which is to say that, unlike me, he does not frame the world through books. He reads when it moves him, but this is hardly constant; like many of his friends, his inner life is entwined within the circuits of his laptop, its electronic speed and hum. He was unmoved by my argument that *The Great Gatsby* was a terrific book; *yeah, yeah, yeah,* his hooded eyes seemed to tell me, *that's what you always say*. He was unmoved by my vague noises about Fitzgerald and modernity, by the notion that among the peculiar tensions of reading the novel now, as opposed to when it first came out, is an inevitable double vision, which suggests both how much and how little the society has changed. He was unmoved by my observation that, whatever else it might be, *The Great Gatsby* had been, and remains, a piece of popular fiction, defining its era in a way a novel would be hard-pressed to do today.

This is the conundrum, the gorilla in the midst of any conversation about literature in contemporary culture, the question of

rubric /ˈruːbrɪk/ *n.* **a.** a title or heading under which something operates or is studied; **b.** set of rules or instructions
serendipity /ˌserənˈdɪpɪti/ *n.* the luck some people have in finding or creating interesting or valuable things by chance
schematic /skɪˈmætɪk/ *a.* represented in simplified or symbolic form
buzz /bʌz/ *n.* a long continuous sound, like the noise a bee makes when it is flying
elusive /ɪˈluːsɪv/ *a.* difficult to find, describe, remember, or achieve
entwine /ɪnˈtwaɪn/ *v.* **a.** tie or link together; **b.** spin or twist together so as to form a cord
circuit /ˈsɜːkɪt/ *n.* the complete circle that an electric current travels
laptop /ˈlæptɒp/ *n.* a portable computer small enough to use in your lap
hum /hʌm/ *n.* a low continuous sound
hard-pressed *a.* having a lot of problems and not enough money or time
conundrum /kəˈnʌndrəm/ *n.* a problem or puzzle which is difficult or impossible to solve

dilution and refraction, of whether and how books matter, of the impact they can have. We talk about the need to read, about reading at risk, about reluctant readers (mostly preadolescent and adolescent boys such as Noah), but we seem unwilling to confront the fallout of one simple observation: literature doesn't, *can't*, have the influence it once did. For Kurt Vonnegut,* the writer who made me want to be a writer, the culprit was television. "When I started out," he recalled in 1997, "it was possible to make a living as a freelance writer of fiction, and live out of your mailbox, because it was still the golden age of magazines, and it looked as though that could go on forever. Then television, with no malice whatsoever — just a better buy for advertisers — knocked the magazines out of business." For new media reactionaries such as Lee Siegel and Andrew Keen, the problem is technology, the endless distractions of the Internet, the breakdown of authority in an age of blogs and Twitter, the collapse of narrative in a hyperlinked, multi-networked world. What this argument overlooks, of course, is that literary culture as we know, it was the product of a technological revolution, one that began with Johannes Gutenberg's invention of movable type. We take books and mass literacy for granted, but in reality, they are a recent iteration, going back not even a millennium. Less than four hundred years ago — barely a century and a half after Gutenberg — John Milton could still pride himself without exaggeration on having read every book then available, the entire history of written thought accessible to a single mind. When I was in college, a friend and I worked on a short film, never finished, in which Milton somehow found himself brought forward in time to lower Manhattan's Strand bookstore, where the sheer volume of titles ("18 Miles of Books" is the store's slogan) provoked a kind of mental overload, causing him to run screaming from the store out into Broadway, only to be struck down by a New York City bus.

Milton (the real one, anyway) was part of a lineage, a conversation, in which books — indeed, print itself — made a difference in the world. The same might be said of Thomas Paine,* who in January 1776 published *Common Sense* as an anonymous pamphlet and in so doing lighted the fuse of the American Revolution. Colonial America

dilution /daɪˈluːʃən/ *n.* **a.** a liquid that has been diluted with water or another liquid, so that it becomes weaker; **b.** weakening (reducing the concentration) by the addition of water or a thinner
refraction /rɪˈfrækʃən/ *n.* **a.** the change in direction of a propagating wave (light or sound) when passing from one medium to another; **b.** the amount by which a propagating wave is bent
fallout /ˈfɔːlaʊt/ *n.* **a.** the radioactive particles that settle to the ground after a nuclear explosion; **b.** any adverse and unwanted secondary effect
culprit /ˈkʌlprɪt/ *n.* the person who is guilty of a crime, or responsible for damage, a problem, etc.
freelance /ˈfriːlɑːns/ *a.* working independently for several different companies or organizations rather than being directly employed by one
malice /ˈmælɪs/ *n.* behaviour intended to harm people or their reputations, or cause them embarrassment and upset
hyperlinked /ˈhaɪpəˌlɪŋkt/ *a.* linked to another HTML document or another part of this kind of HTML document
iteration /ɪtəˈreɪʃ(ə)n/ *n.* doing or saying again; a repeated performance
overload /əʊvəˈləʊd/ *n.* an excessive burden

insurrectionism /ˌɪnsəˈrekʃən/ *n.* the principle of revolt against constituted authority

blogosphere /ˈblɒgsfɪə/ *n.* all the weblogs on the Internet, considered collectively

refutation /ˌrefjʊˈteɪʃən/ *n.* **a.** the speech act of answering an attack on your assertions **b.** any evidence that helps to establish the falsity of sth.

rack up **a.** gain points in a game **b.** defeat thoroughly

disseminate /dɪˈsemɪˌneɪt/ *v.* spread information or knowledge so that it reaches many people or organizations

template /ˈtemplɪt/ *n.* a model or standard for making comparisons

saturation /ˌsætʃəˈreɪʃən/ *n.* the process or state that occurs when a place or thing is filled completely with people or things, so that no more can be added

vantage point *n.* a place or position from which you can see a lot of things

obsessive /əbˈsesɪv/ *a.* having an irrationally strong and continuous interest in sth. exclusively

lead–up *n.* preparations

polemic /pɒˈlemɪk/ *n.* a controversy (especially over a belief or dogma)

afterthought /ˈɑːftəˌθɔːt/ *n.* **a.** thinking again about a choice previously made; **b.** an addition that was not included in the original plan

was a hotbed of print insurrectionism, with an active pamphlet culture that I imagine as the blogosphere of its day. Here we have another refutation to the antitechnology reactionaries, since one reason for print's primacy was that it was on the technological cutting edge. Like the blogs they resemble, most pamphlets came and went, selling a few hundred copies, speaking to a self-selected audience. *Common Sense*, on the other hand, became a colonial bestseller, racking up sales of 150,000; it was also widely disseminated and read aloud, which exposed it to hundreds of thousands more. The work was so influential that Thomas Jefferson used it as a template when he sat down a few months later to write *the Declaration of Independence,* distilling many of Paine's ideas (the natural dignity of humanity, the right to self-determination) in both content and form.

Given this level of saturation, it's not hard to make a case for *Common Sense* as the most important book ever published in America, but from the vantage point of the present, it raises questions that are less easily resolved. Could a book, any book, have this kind of impact in contemporary society? What about a movie or a website? Yes, the Daily Kos and FiveThirtyEight.com attracted devoted and obsessive traffic in the lead-up to the 2008 presidential election, but the percentages (and the effect) were nowhere near what Paine achieved. Even Michael Moore's film *Fahrenheit 9/11,* *released barely six months before the 2004 election to packed theaters and impassioned public debate, came and went in the figurative blink of an eye. Partly, that's because Moore is a propagandist and Paine a philosopher; the key to *Common Sense* is the elegance of its argument, the way it balances polemic and persuasion, addressing those on both sides of the independence issue, always careful to seek common ground. Yet equally important is the speed and fragmentation of our public conversation, which quickly moved along to Swift Boats and other issues, leaving Moore behind. By November, *Fahrenheit 9/11* was little more than an afterthought, and six years later, if we remember it at all, it's as a dated artifact, a project whose shelf life did not even last as long as the election it sought to change.

This, in an elliptical way, is what Noah was getting at. How do things stick to us in a culture where information and ideas flare up so quickly that we have no time to assess one before another takes its place? How does reading maintain its hold on our imagination, or is that question even worth asking anymore? Noah may not be a reader, but he is hardly immune to the charms of a lovely sentence; a few weeks after our conversation at the dinner table, he told me he had finished *The Great Gatsby* and that the last few chapters had featured the most beautiful writing he'd ever read. "Yes, of course," I told him, pleased at the observation, but I couldn't help thinking back to our earlier talk about the novel, which had ended with Noah standing up and saying, in a tone as blunt as a lance thrust: "This is why no one reads anymore."

"What?" I said. He was back to talking about the annotation, but there was something else, a subtext to his words.

"This is why reading is over. None of my friends like it. Nobody wants to do it anymore."

He held my gaze for a long moment, as if challenging me to make a counterargument. Briefly, I thought about responding, but there was nothing to say. On the one hand, this was the primal conflict, my son declaring his independence, telling me that reading didn't matter in a room full of books, my books, thousands of them on the shelves. I almost asked for a towel to clean up the blood.

And yet, for all that I could recognize the dynamic, I found myself unsettled in another way. Yes, Noah was reacting; yes, he was putting me in my place. What I hadn't expected, though, was that as he left the room, I would be struck by a

dated /ˈdeɪtɪd/ *a.* old-fashioned; bearing a date
elliptical /ɪˈlɪptɪkəl/ *a.* having the shape of an ellipse; referring to something indirectly
flare up a. ignite quickly and suddenly, especially after having died down; **b.** erupt or intensify suddenly
immune /ɪˈmjuːn/ *a.* **a.** relating to or conferring immunity (to disease or infection); **b.** not affected by a given influence
feature /ˈfiːtʃə/ *v.* **a.** to show a particular person or thing in a film, magazine, show, etc. **b.** to be included in sth. and be an important part of it
blunt /blʌnt/ *a.* characterized by directness in manner or speech; without subtlety or evasion
subtext /ˈsʌbˌtekst/ *n.* the implied message or subject of sth. that is said or written
counterargument /ˈkaʊntəˌrɑːgjəmənt/ *n.* an argument offered in opposition to another argument
primal /ˈpraɪməl/ *a.* having existed from the beginning; in an earliest or original stage or state
dynamic /daɪˈnæmɪk/ *a.* full of energy and new ideas, and determined to succeed
unsettled /ʌnˈsetəld/ *a.* **a.** still in doubt; **b.** not settled or established

revelation /ˌrevəˈleɪʃən/ *n.* a surprising or interesting fact made known to people

disturbing realization, one that spoke to the essence of who I was. Literature is dead, Noah had told me, this is why reading is over. And indeed, I saw now with the force of <u>revelation</u>, I could not say that he was wrong.

Cultural Notes

1. **David L. Ulin** is a book critic, and a former book editor of *the Los Angeles Times*. He is the author of *The Myth of Solid Ground: Earthquakes, Prediction, and the Fault Line Between Reason and Faith,* and the editor of *Another City: Writing from Los Angeles* and *Writing Los Angeles: A Literary Anthology,* which won him a 2002 California Book Award. He has written for *The Atlantic Monthly, The Nation,* and *The New York Times Book Review.* He was awarded a 2010 Southern California Independent Booksellers Association/Glenn Goldman Book Award for his work on *Los Angeles: Portrait of a City.* This text is adapted from his *The Lost Art of Reading: Why Books Matter in a Distracted Time.*

2. **The Great Gatsby** is a novel by American author F. Scott Fitzgerald. With the Roaring Twenties as the backdrops, this novel is described as an ironic tale of life on Long Island at the time. Since its publication in 1925, it has received favorable critical acclaims and has been widely regarded as a "Great American Novel" and a literary classic, capturing the essence of an era and the post-war "carefree madness" of American life. The Modern Library named it the second best English language novel of the 20th Century.

3. **Lord of the Flies**, published in 1954, was the first and the most famous novel by Nobel Prize-winning British writer William Golding. This novel is concerned about a group of British boys deserted on an uninhabited island who try to govern themselves, with disastrous results. In 2005 the novel was chosen by TIME magazine as one of the 100 best English-language novels from 1923 to 2005.

4. **Philip Roth** (1933—   ) is one of the greatest contemporary American novelists and also one of the most representative Jewish American writers. As an evergreen writer, his name was established with his 1959 book *Goodbye, Columbus,* a novella. As a prolific novelist, he has produced more than 30 books such as *American Pastoral* (1997), *The Human Stain* (2000), and *Everyman* (2006) mentioned in this text.

5. **Kurt Vonnegut, Jr.** (1922—2007) was one of the most prominent

20th-century American writers and stylists famous for his postmodern writings. His representative novels such as *Cat's Cradle* (1963), *Slaughterhouse-Five* (1969), and *Breakfast of Champions* (1973) blend satire, gallows humor, and science fiction. As a citizen he was a lifelong supporter of the American Civil Liberties Union and was honorary president of the American Humanist Association.

6. **Thomas Paine** (1737—1809) was an outstanding English-American political activist, author, political theorist, Enlightenment thinker and revolutionary. He produced several highly influential political pamphlets at the start of the American Revolution, inspiring the American patriots and patriotism in 1776 to declare independence from Britain. *Common Sense* is one of them, first published anonymously on January 10, 1776, signed "Written by an Englishman", and it became an immediate success, greatly encouraging the colonial people to fight for their independence; historian Gordon S. Wood described *Common Sense* as "the most incendiary and popular pamphlet of the entire revolutionary era".

7. **Lee Siegel** (1957—   ) is a New York writer and cultural critic who has written for *Harper's, The Nation, The New Republic, The New Yorker, The New York Review of Books, The New York Times, Slate,* and many other publications.

8. **Andrew Keen** (1960—   ) is a British-American entrepreneur and author. He is particularly known for his view that the current Internet culture may be debasing culture. Keen is especially concerned about the way that the current Internet culture undermines the authority of learned experts and the work of professionals.

Comprehension Exercises

I. Answer the following questions based on the text.

1. Why does the writer use "the lost art of reading" as the title? What is he trying to criticize in this text?
2. How old is the writer's son? Which grade is the boy in?
3. What is the problem with the boy? Why did the boy say "literature was dead"?
4. For what purpose does the writer mention John Milton? Why did the writer bring forward Milton to the modern world?
5. What is the writer's tone in this piece of writing?

II. Decide whether each of the following statements is true or false according to the text.

1. The writer is fond of reading literary works, especially American novels.
2. The writer's sixteen-year-old son Noah detested reading any kind of novels.
3. The teacher in the humanities class would ask students to read novels in the way they like.
4. The writers themselves know all the connections hidden in their stories and, therefore, only they can talk about their writing process very easily.
5. The writer began to have an impulse to turn to the field of writing under the influence of Philip Roth.
6. The writer imagined that John Milton would be excited to see so many books for him to read if he were brought forth to a Manhattan's Strand bookstore.
7. The writer was puzzled by the dilemma of literary reading in modern world.

III. Select the most suitable word or phrases and fill in the following blanks in their proper form.

detest	demonstrate	excavation	nuance	overriding
fallacies	serendipity	elusive	schematic	entwine
dilution	iteration	refutation	unsettled	disseminate
saturation	obsessive	immune		

1. We all have to do things we _____, at one time or another, because we are not free to consult our own wishes only.
2. Some 30,000 angry farmers arrived in the capital of this country yesterday to _____ against possible cuts in their economic subsidies.
3. To document an archeological _____ effectively, it is essential to record sites, features and finds accurately and comprehensively.
4. With eyes and facial expressions, human beings could communicate virtually every subtle _____ of their emotion there is.
5. All the parties had spent the election campaign talking about the _____ importance of health.
6. _____ and luck are by their very nature unpredictable, and therefore not part of any good plan.
7. Happiness itself can be defined in many different ways: it may have all kinds of components, it may be a life's work, or even no work at all, but we are, most of us, in pursuit of this _____ goal
8. In mapping out the constitution for his utopian society or state, Plato starts out with a _____ description of the human soul.

9. I have to say that everything you say and write is filled with holes and logical _____.

10. The media also _____ information that is crucial for the life and development of communities.

11. Different peoples are increasingly in contact with one another, cultures _____, and identities intermingle.

12. The films manufactured by Hollywood are _____ in the cinemas all over the world, available to viewers all over the world.

13. The developments leave the airline with several problems, including an _____ labor situation.

14. About 93 percent of U.S. residents are _____ to measles either because they were vaccinated or they had the disease as a child.

15. What ever the accuser said, Tom Williams the accused could give corresponding _____.

IV. Try to paraphrase the following sentences, paying special attention to the underlined parts.

1. Part of the class structure <u>involved annotation</u>, which Noah <u>detested</u>; it kept <u>pulling him out of the story</u> to stop every few lines and make a note, <u>mark a citation</u>, to demonstrate that he'd been paying attention to what he read.

   _____

   _____

2. Listening to him, I couldn't help but recall my own classroom experiences, <u>the endless scansion</u> of poetry, the sentence <u>diagramming</u>, the <u>excavation of metaphor</u> and form.

   _____

   _____

3. Now, I recognize this as one of the <u>fallacies</u> of teaching literature in the classroom, the need to <u>seek a reckoning</u> with everything, to imagine a framework, a <u>rubric</u>, in which each little piece makes sense.

   _____

   _____

4. Literature — at least the literature to which I respond — doesn't work that way; it is conscious, yes, but <u>with room for serendipity, a delicate balance between craft and art.</u>

   _____

   _____

5. That kind of writing, though, is difficult to teach, leaving us with scansion,

annotation, all that sound and fury, a buzz of explication that obscures the elusive heartbeat of a book.

6. Then television, with no malice whatsoever — just a better buy for advertisers — knocked the magazines out of business.

7. Colonial America was a hotbed of print insurrectionism, with an active pamphlet culture that I imagine as the blogosphere of its day.

8. Given this level of saturation, it's not hard to make a case for Common Sense as the most important book ever published in America, but from the vantage point of the present, it raises questions that are less easily resolved.

V. Discuss with your partner about each of the three statements and write an essay in no less than 250 words about your understanding of one of them.

1. This is why it's often difficult for writers to talk about their process, because the connections, the flow of storytelling, remain mysterious even to them (the writers themselves).

2. Literature doesn't, *can't*, have the influence it once did.

3. In the process of the literary creation, the writer has no plan beforehand; the works evolve spontaneously.

VI. List four websites where we can learn more about David L. Ulin and his major literary works and provide a brief introduction to each of them.

1. _____

2. _____
   _____
   _____.
3. _____
   _____
   _____.
4. _____
   _____
   _____.

Twenty Minutes' Reading

You are required to read the following two sections within 20 minutes.

SECTION A

We have a crisis on our hands. You mean global warming? The world economy? No, the decline of reading. People are just not doing it anymore, especially the young. Who's responsible? Actually, it's more like. What is responsible? The Internet, of course, and everything that comes with it — Facebook, Twitter (微博). You can write your own list.

There's been a warning about the imminent death of literate civilization for a long time. In the 20th century, first it was the movies, then radio, then television that seemed to spell doom for the written world. None did. Reading survived; in fact it not only survived, it has flourished. The world is more literate than ever before — there are more and more readers, and more and more books.

The fact that we often get our reading material online today is not something we should worry over. The electronic and digital revolution of the last two decades has arguably shown the way forward for reading and for writing. Take the arrival of e-book readers as an example. Devices like Kindle make reading more convenient and are a lot more environmentally friendly than the traditional paper book.

As technology makes new ways of writing possible, new ways of reading are possible. Interconnectivity allows for the possibility of a reading experience that was barely imaginable before. Where traditional books had to make do with photographs and illustrations, an e-book can provide readers with an unlimited number of links: to texts, pictures, and videos. In the future, the way people write novels, history, and philosophy will resemble nothing seen in the past.

On the other hand, there is the danger of trivialization. One Twitter group is offering its followers single-sentence-long "digests" of the great novels. War and Peace in a sentence? You must be joking. We should fear the fragmentation of reading. There is the danger that the high-speed connectivity of the Internet will reduce our attention span — that we will be incapable of reading anything of length or which requires deep concentration.

In such a fast-changing world, in which reality seems to be remade each day, we need the ability to focus and understand what is happening to us. This has always been the function of literature and we should be careful not to let it disappear. Our society needs to be able to imagine the possibility of someone utterly in tune with modern technology but able to make sense of a dynamic, confusing world.

In the 15th century, Johannes Guttenberg's invention of the printing press in Europe had a huge impact on civilization. Once upon a time the physical book was a challenging thing. We should remember this before we assume that technology is out to destroy traditional culture.

1. Which of the following paragraphs briefly reviews the historical challenges for reading?
   A. Paragraph One.　　　　　　B. Paragraph Two.
   C. Paragraph Three.　　　　　D. Paragraph Four.
2. The following are all cited as advantages of e-books EXCEPT _____.
   A. multimodal content　　　　B. environmental friendliness
   C. convenience for readers　　D. imaginative design
3. Which of the following can best describe how the author feels toward single-sentence-long novels?
   A. Ironic.　　B. Worried.　　C. Sarcastic.　　D. Doubtful.
4. According to the passage, people need knowledge of modern technology and _____ to survive in the fast-changing society.
   A. good judgment　　　　　　B. high sensitivity
   C. good imagination　　　　　D. the ability to focus
5. What is the main idea of the passage?
   A. Technology pushes the way forward for reading and writing.
   B. Interconnectivity is a feature of new reading experience.
   C. Technology is an opportunity and a challenge for traditional reading.
   D. Technology offers a greater variety of reading practice.

SECTION B

I know when the snow melts and the first robins (知更鸟) come to call, when the laughter of children returns to the parks and playgrounds, something wonderful is about to happen.

Spring cleaning.

I'll admit spring cleaning is a difficult notion for modern families to grasp. Today's busy families hardly have time to load the dishwasher, much less clean the doormat. Asking the family to spend the weekend collecting winter dog piles from the melting snow in the backyard is like announcing there will be no more Wi-Fi. It interrupts the natural order.

"Honey, what say we spend the weekend beating the rugs, sorting through the boxes in the basement and painting our bedroom a nice lemony yellow?" I say.

"Can we at least wait until the NBA matches are over?" my husband answers.

But I tell my family, spring cleaning can't wait. The temperature has risen just enough to melt snow but not enough for Little League practice to start. Some flowers are peeking out of the thawing ground, but there is no lawn to seed, nor garden to tend. Newly wakened from our winter's hibernation (冬眠), yet still needing extra blankets at night, we open our windows to the first fresh air floating on the breeze and all of the natural world demanding "Awake and be clean!"

Biologists offer a theory about this primal impulse to clean out every drawer and closet in the house at spring's first light, which has to do with melatonin, the sleepy time hormone (激素) our bodies produce when it's dark. When spring's light comes, the melatonin diminishes, and suddenly we are awakened to the dusty, virus-filled house we've been hibernating in for four months.

I tell my family about the science and psychology of a good healthy cleaning at spring's arrival. I speak to them about life's greatest rewards waiting in the removal of soap scum from the bathtub, which hasn't been properly cleaned since the first snowfall.

"I'll do it," says the eldest child, a 21-year-old college student who lives at home.

"You will? Wow!" I exclaim.

Maybe after all these years, he's finally grasped the concept. Maybe he's expressing his rightful position as eldest child and role model. Or maybe he's going to Florida for a break in a couple of weeks and he's being nice to me who is the financial-aid officer.

No matter. Seeing my adult son willingly cleaning that dirty bathtub gives me hope for the future of his 12-year-old brother who, instead of working, is found to be sleeping in the seat of the window he is supposed to be cleaning.

"Awake and be clean!" I say.

6. According to the passage, "...spring cleaning is a difficult notion for modern families to grasp" means that spring cleaning _____.
   A. is no longer an easy practice to understand
   B. is no longer part of modern family life
   C. requires more family members to be involved
   D. calls for more complicated skills and knowledge

7. Which of the following is LEAST likely to be included in family spring cleaning?
   A. Beating the rugs.   B. Cleaning the window.
   C. Restoring Wi-Fi services. D. Cleaning the backyard.

8. Why does the author say "spring cleaning can't wait"?
   A. Because there will be more activities when it gets warmer.
   B. Because the air is fresher and the breeze is lighter.
   C. Because the whole family is full of energy at spring time.
   D. Because the snow is melting and the ground is thawing.

9. Which of the following interpretations of the biologists' theory about melatonin is INCORRECT?
   A. The production of melatonin in our bodies varies at different times.
   B. Melatonin is more likely to cause sleepiness in our bodies.
   C. The reduction of melatonin will cause wakefulness in our bodies.
   D. The amount of melatonin remains constant in our bodies.

10. Which of the following can best sum up the author's overall reaction to her adult son's positive response to spring cleaning?
    A. Surprised and skeptical.   B. Elated and hesitant.
    C. Relieved and optimistic.   D. Optimistic and hesitant.

Unit Four

Thinking as a Hobby
William Golding

While I was still a boy, I came to the conclusion that there were three grades of thinking; and since I was later to claim thinking as my hobby, I came to an even stranger conclusion — namely, that I myself could not think at all.

I must have been an unsatisfactory child for grownups to deal with. I remember how incomprehensible they appeared to me at first, but not, of course, how I appeared to them. It was the headmaster of my grammar school who first brought the subject of thinking before me — though neither in the way, nor with the result he intended. He had some statuettes in his study. They stood on a high cupboard behind his desk. One was a lady wearing nothing but a bath towel. She seemed frozen in an eternal panic lest the bath towel slip down any farther; and since she had no arms, she was in an unfortunate position to pull the towel up again. Next to her, crouched the statuette of a leopard, ready to spring down at the top drawer of filing cabinet labeled A-AH. My innocence interpreted this as the victim's last, despairing cry. Beyond the leopard was a naked, muscular gentleman, who sat, looking down, with his chin on his fist and his elbow on his knee. He seemed utterly miserable.

Some time later, I learned about these statuettes. The headmaster had placed them where they would face delinquent children, because they symbolized to him the whole of life. The naked lady was the Venus of Milo.* She was Love. She was not worried about the towel. She was just busy being beautiful. The leopard was Nature, and he was being natural. The naked, muscular gentleman was not miserable. He was Rodin's Thinker, an image of pure thought. It is easy to buy small plaster models of what you think life is like.

I had better explain that I was a frequent visitor to the headmaster's study, because of

statuette /ˌstætjʊˈet/ *n.* a very small sculpture of a person or an animal which is often displayed on a shelf or stand

crouch /kraʊtʃ/ *v.* bend forward, lower oneself toward the ground

filing cabinet *n.* a piece of office furniture, usually made of metal, which has drawers in which files are kept

delinquent /dɪˈlɪŋkwənt/ *a.* repeatedly committing minor crimes; persistently bad

the latest thing I had done or left undone. As we now say, I was not integrated. I was, if anything, disintegrated; and I was puzzled. Grownups never made sense. Whenever I found myself in a <u>penal</u> position before the headmaster's desk, with the statuettes glimmering whitely above him, I would sink my head, clasp my hands behind my back and <u>writhe</u> one shoe over the other.

penal /ˈpiːnəl/ *a.* relating to the punishment of criminals
writhe /raɪð/ *v.* twists and turns violently backward and forward
opaque /əʊˈpeɪk/ *a.* difficult to see through or understand
hindquarters /ˈhaɪndkwɔːtəz/ *n.* **a.** the fleshy part of the human body that you sit on **b.** the part of a quadruped that corresponds to the human buttocks
anguish /ˈæŋgwɪʃ/ *n.* great mental suffering or physical pain
plonk /plɒŋk/ *v.* to drop or be dropped, esp. heavily or suddenly

The headmaster would look <u>opaquely</u> at me through flashing spectacles.

"What are we going to do with you?"

Well, what were they going to do with me? I would writhe my shoe some more and stare down at the worn rug.

"Look up, boy! Can't you look up?"

Then I would look up at the cupboard, where the naked lady was frozen in her panic and the muscular gentleman contemplated the <u>hindquarters</u> of the leopard in endless gloom. I had nothing to say to the headmaster. His spectacles caught the light so that you could see nothing human behind them. There was no possibility of communication.

"Don't you ever think at all?"

No, I didn't think, wasn't thinking, couldn't think — I was simply waiting in <u>anguish</u> for the interview to stop.

"Then you'd better learn — hadn't you?"

On one occasion the headmaster leaped to his feet, reached up and <u>plonked</u> Rodin's masterpiece on the desk before me.

"That's what a man looks like when he's really thinking."

I surveyed the gentleman without interest or comprehension.

"Go back to your class."

Clearly there was something missing in me. Nature had endowed the rest of the human race with a sixth sense and left me out. This must be so, I mused, on my way back to the class, since whether I had broken a window, or failed to remember Boyle's Law, or been late for school, my teachers produced me one, adult answer: "Why can't you think?"

As I saw the case, I had broken the window because I had tried to hit Jack Arney with a cricket ball and missed him; I could not remember Boyle's Law because I had never bothered to learn it; and I was late for school because I preferred looking over the bridge into the river. In fact, I was wicked. Were my teachers, perhaps, so good that they could not understand the depths of my depravity? Were they clear, untormented people who could direct their every action by this mysterious business of thinking? The whole thing was incomprehensible. In my earlier years, I found even the statuette of the Thinker confusing. I did not believe any of my teachers were naked, ever. Like someone born deaf, but bitterly determined to find out about sound, I watched my teachers to find out about thought.

There was Mr. Houghton. He was always telling me to think. With a modest satisfaction, he would tell me that he had thought a bit himself. Then why did he spend so much time drinking? Or was there more sense in drinking than there appeared to be? But if not, and if drinking were in fact ruinous to health — and Mr. Houghton was ruined, there was no doubt about that — why was he always talking about the clean life and the virtues of fresh air? He would spread his arms wide with the action of a man who habitually spent his time striding along mountain ridges.

"Open air does me good, boys — I know it!"

Sometimes, exalted by his own oratory, he would leap from his desk and hustle us outside into a hideous wind.

"Now, boys! Deep breaths! Feel it right down inside you — huge draughts of God's good air!"

He would stand before us, rejoicing in his perfect health, an open-air man. He would put his hands on his waist and take a

depravity /dɪˈprævɪtɪ/ n. very dishonest or immoral behaviour
exalt /ɪgˈzɔːlt/ v. glorify, honor or praise very highly
oratory /ˈɒrətərɪ/ n. the art of making formal speeches
hustle /ˈhʌsəl/ v. move or cause to move furtively and hurriedly

tremendous breath. You could hear the wind, trapped in the cavern of his chest and struggling with all the unnatural impediments. His body would reel with shock and his ruined face go white at the unaccustomed visitation. He would stagger back to his desk and collapse there, useless for the rest of the morning.

impediment /ɪmˈpedɪmənt/ *n.* a person or thing that makes difficult the movement, development or progress
reel /riːl/ *v.* move about in an unsteady way
high-minded /ˈhaɪˈmaɪndɪd/ *a.* of high moral or intellectual value; elevated in nature or style
nape /neɪp/ *n.* the back side of the neck
bulge /bʌldʒ/ *v.* stick out; swell or protrude outwards
detestation /ˌdiːtesˈteɪʃən/ *n.* intense hatred; abhorrence
clairvoyance /kleəˈvɔɪəns/ *n.* the alleged power of perceiving things beyond the natural range of the senses
disinterested /dɪsˈɪntrɪstɪd/ *a.* unaffected by self-interest
remorselessly /rɪˈmɔːslɪslɪ/ *adv.* without pity; in a merciless manner

Mr. Houghton was given to high-minded monologues about the good life, sexless and full of duty. Yet in the middle of one of these monologues, if a girl passed the window, tapping along on her neat little feet, he would interrupt his discourse, his neck would turn of itself and he would watch her out of sight. In this instance, he seemed to me ruled not by thought but by an invisible and irresistible spring in his nape. His neck was an object of great interest to me. Normally it bulged a bit over his collar. But Mr. Houghton had fought in the First World War alongside both Americans and French, and had come — by who knows what illogic? — to a settled detestation of both countries. If either happened to be prominent in current affairs, no argument could make Mr. Houghton think well of it. He would bang the desk, his neck would bulge still further and go red. "You can say what you like," he would cry, "but I've thought about this — and I know what I think!"

Mr. Houghton thought with his neck.

There was Miss Parsons. She assured us that her dearest wish was our welfare, but I knew even then, with the mysterious clairvoyance of childhood, that what she wanted most was the husband she never got. There was Mr. Hands — and so on.

I have dealt at length with my teachers because this was my introduction to the nature of what is commonly called thought. Through them I discovered that thought is often full of unconscious prejudice, ignorance and hypocrisy. It will lecture on disinterested purity while its neck is being remorselessly twisted toward a skirt. Technically, it is about as proficient as most businessmen's golf, as honest as most politicians' intentions, or — to come near my own preoccupation — as coherent as most books that get written. It is what I came to call grade-three thinking, though more properly, it is feeling, rather than thought.

True, often there is a kind of innocence in prejudices, but in those days I viewed grade-three thinking with an intolerant contempt and an incautious mockery. I delighted to confront a pious lady who hated the Germans with the proposition that we should love our enemies. She taught me a great truth in dealing with grade-three thinkers; because of her, I no longer dismiss lightly a mental process which for nine-tenths of the population is the nearest they will ever get to thought. They have immense solidarity. We had better respect them, for we are outnumbered and surrounded. A crowd of grade-three thinkers, all shouting the same thing, all warming their hands at the fire of their own prejudices, will not thank you for pointing out the contradictions in their beliefs. Man is a gregarious animal, and enjoys agreement as cows will graze all the same way on the side of a hill.

mockery /ˈmɒkərɪ/ *n.* showing your contempt by derision; humorous or satirical imitation
gregarious /grɪˈgeərɪəs/ *a.* enjoying being together with other people or animals
stampede /stæmˈpiːd/ *v.* act or run, usually en masse, hurriedly or on an impulse
heady /ˈhedɪ/ *a.* **a.** extremely exciting as if by alcohol or a narcotic; **b.** marked by defiant disregard for danger or consequences
skittle /ˈskɪtl/ *n.* a bowling pin of the type used in playing ninepins

Grade-two thinking is the detection of contradictions. I reached grade two when I trapped the poor, pious lady. Grade-two thinkers do not stampede easily, though often they fall into the other fault and lag behind. Grade-two thinking is a withdrawal, with eyes and ears open. It became my hobby and brought satisfaction and loneliness in either hand. For grade-two thinking destroys without having the power to create. It set me watching the crowds cheering His Majesty the King and asking myself what all the fuss was about, without giving me anything positive to put in the place of that heady patriotism. But there were compensations. To hear people justify their habit of hunting foxes and tearing them to pieces by claiming that the foxes liked it. To hear our Prime Minister talk about the great benefit we conferred on India by jailing people like Pandit Nehru* and Gandhi.* To hear American politicians talk about peace in one sentence and refuse to join the League of Nations in the next. Yes, there are moments of delight.

But I was growing toward adolescence and had to admit that Mr. Houghton was not the only one with an irresistible spring in his neck. I, too, felt the compulsive hand of nature and began to find that pointing out contradiction could be costly as well as fun. There was Ruth, for example, a serious and attractive girl. I was an atheist at the time. Grade-two thinking is a menace to religion and knocks down sects like skittles. I put myself in a position to be converted by her with a hypocrisy worthy of grade three. She was a Methodist — or at least, her parents were, and Ruth had to follow suit. But, alas, instead of relying on the Holy Spirit to convert me, Ruth was foolish enough to open her pretty mouth in argument. She claimed that the Bible (King James Version) was literally inspired. I countered by saying that the Catholics believed in the literal inspiration of Saint Jerome's Vulgate,* and the two books were different. Argument flagged

At last she remarked that there were an awful lot of Methodists, and they couldn't be wrong, could they — not all those millions? That was too easy, said I restively (for the nearer you were to Ruth, the nicer she was to be near to) since there were more Roman Catholics than Methodists anyway; and they couldn't be wrong, could they — not all those hundreds of millions? An awful flicker of doubt appeared in her eyes. I slid my arm around her waist and murmured breathlessly that if we were counting heads, the Buddhists were the boys for my money. But Ruth had really wanted to do me good, because I was so nice. She fled. The combination of my arm and those countless Buddhists was too much for her.

That night her father visited my father and left, red-cheeked and indignant. I was given the third degree to find out what had happened. It was lucky we were both of us only fourteen. I lost Ruth and gained an undeserved reputation as a potential libertine.

So grade-two thinking could be dangerous. It was in this knowledge, at the age of fifteen, that I remember making a comment from the heights of grade two, on the limitations of grade three. One evening I found myself alone in the school hall, preparing it for a party. The door of the headmaster's study was open. I went in. The headmaster had ceased to thump Rodin's Thinker down on the desk as an example to the young. Perhaps he had not found any more candidates, but the statuettes were still there, glimmering and gathering dust on top of the cupboard. I stood on a chair and rearranged them. I stood Venus in her bath towel on the filing cabinet, so that now the top drawer caught its breath in a gasp of sexy excitement. "A-ah!" The portentous Thinker I placed on the edge of the cupboard so that he looked down at the bath towel and waited for it to slip.

flag /flæg/ v. begin to lose enthusiasm or energy
restively /ˈrestɪvlɪ/ adv. impatiently, dissatisfiedly or in a bored state
libertine /ˈlɪbəˌtiːn/ n. a dissolute person; usually a man who is morally unrestrained
portentous /pɔːˈtentəs/ a. of momentous or ominous significance; puffed up with vanity
bolster /ˈbəʊlstə/ v. **a.** support and strengthen; **b.** prop up with a pillow or sth.

Grade-two thinking, though it filled life with fun and excitement, did not make for content. To find out the deficiencies of our elders bolsters the young ego but does not make for personal security. I found that grade two was not only the power to point out contradictions. It took the swimmer some distance from the shore and left him there, out of his depth. I decided that Pontius Pilate* was a typical grade-two thinker. "What is truth?" he said, a very common grade-two thought, but one that is used always as the end of an argument instead of the beginning. There is still a higher grade of thought which says, "What is truth?" and sets out to find it.

irreverent /ɪˈrevərənt/ *a.* showing lack of due respect or veneration
loyalties /ˈlɔɪəltɪ/ *n.* **a.** the quality of staying firm in your friendship or support; **b.** feelings of friendship, support, or duty toward someone or something
hallow /ˈhæləʊ/ *v.* set apart as being holy

But these grade-one thinkers were few and far between. They did not visit my grammar school in the flesh though they were there in books. I aspired to them, partly because I was ambitious and partly because I now saw my hobby as an unsatisfactory thing if it went no further. If you set out to climb a mountain, however high you climb, you have failed if you cannot reach the top.

I, too, would be a grade-one thinker. I was irreverent at the best of times. Political and religious systems, social customs, loyalties and traditions, they all came tumbling down like so many rotten apples off a tree. This was a fine hobby and a sensible substitute for cricket, since you could play it all the year round. I came up in the end with what must always remain the justification for grade-one thinking, its sign, seal and charter, I devised a coherent system for living. It was a moral system, which was wholly logical. Of course, as I readily admitted, conversion of the world to my way of thinking might be difficult, since my system did away with a number of trifles, such as big business, centralized government, armies, marriage.

Now you are expecting me to describe how I saw the folly of my ways and came back to the warm nest, where prejudices are so often called loyalties, where pointless actions are hallowed into custom by repetition, where we are content to say we think when all we do is feel.

But you would be wrong. I dropped my hobby and turned professional.

If I were to go back to the headmaster's study and find the dusty statuettes still there, I would arrange them differently. I would dust Venus and put her aside, for I have come to love her and know her for the fair thing she is. But I would put the Thinker, sunk in his desperate thought, where there were shadows before him — and at his back, I would put the leopard, crouched and ready to spring.

Unit Four

Cultural Notes

1. **Sir William Gerald Golding** (1911—1993) was one of the most outstanding contemporary British prose writers. He was especially best known for his novel *Lord of the Flies* (published in 1954 and filmed by Peter Brook in 1963). His reputation came to the highest when he won the Nobel Prize for Literature in 1983. He was also awarded the Booker Prize for literature in 1980 for his novel *Rites of Passage*, the first book of the trilogy To the Ends of the Earth.

2. **The Venus of Milo** was actually one of the most famous ancient Greek statues discovered on the Greek island of Milos at the beginning of the 19th century. This statue is called Aphrodite of Milos. Created sometime between 130 and 100 BC, it is believed to depict Aphrodite, the Greek goddess of love and beauty (Venus to the Romans). It is currently on permanent display at the Louvre Museum in Paris.

3. **Rodin's Thinker** (titled Le Penseur in French, originally named The Poet) is a bronze sculpture on marble pedestal by Auguste Rodin, whose first cast, of 1902, is now in the Musée Rodin in Paris; there are some 20 other original castings, as well as various other versions, studies, and posthumous castings. It depicts a man in sober meditation battling with a powerful internal struggle. It is often used to represent philosophy.

4. **Jawaharlal Nehru** (1889—1964) was the first Prime Minister of India and a central figure in Indian politics for much of the 20th century. He emerged as the paramount leader of the Indian Independence Movement under the tutelage of Mahatma Gandhi and ruled India from its establishment as an independent nation in 1947 until his death in office in 1964. Nehru is considered to be the architect of the modern Indian nation-state; a sovereign, socialist, secular, and democratic republic. He was the father of Indira Gandhi and the maternal grandfather of Rajiv Gandhi, who were to later serve as the third and sixth Prime Ministers of India, respectively.

5. **Gandhi** There are three politically important Gandhis: **Mohandas Gandhi** (1869—1948), commonly known as Mahatma Gandhi, was the preeminent leader of Indian nationalism in British-ruled India. Employing non-violent civil disobedience, Gandhi led India to independence and inspired movements for non-violence, civil rights and freedom across the world. **Indira Gandhi** (1917—1984) was the third Prime Minister of India and a

central figure in Indian politics during the second half of the 20th century. She was elected a record four terms as Prime Minister from 1966—1977 and again from 1980 until her assassination in 1984. **Rajiv Gandhi** (1944—1991), the eldest son of Indira, was the sixth Prime Minister of India (1984—1989). He took office after his mother's assassination on 31 October 1984; he himself was assassinated on 21 May 1991. He became the youngest Prime Minister of India when he took office at the age of 40. The text makes reference to Mahatma Gandhi probably here.

6. **Saint Jerome's Vulgate** refers to a Latin version of the Bible mainly translated by St. Jeromein in the late 4th-century. In 382 this new Latin translation was commissioned by Pope Damasus I. By the 13th century this revision had come to be called the versio vulgata, that is, the "commonly used translation", and ultimately it became the definitive and officially promulgated Latin version of the Bible in the Roman Catholic Church. Its widespread adoption led to the eclipse of earlier Latin translations, which are collectively referred to as the Vetus Latina.

7. **Pontius Pilate,** named **Pontius Pilatus** in Greek, was the fifth Roman prefect (governor) of Judaea (26—36) under the emperor Tiberius and a notorious figure as he presided at the trial of Jesus and gave the order for the crucifixion of Jesus.

Comprehension Exercises

I. Answer the following questions based on the text.

1. In this text the narrator has mentioned and been talking about different grades of thinking. What are they?
2. What were the statuettes the narrator detected in the headmaster's study? What were the narrator's first impressions of them? How many times did the narrator mention these statuettes in this text?
3. What was the headmaster's purpose when he placed these statuettes in his study? Did this arrangement achieve its intended purpose?
4. In the sentence, "If either happened to be prominent in current affairs, no argument could make Mr. Houghton think well of it." What does "either" refer to actually?
5. The narrator mentioned his two teachers, Mr. Houghton and Miss Parsons. What was the narrator's feeling and attitude towards them?

II. Decide whether each of the following statements is true or false according to the text.

1. The narrator found that he himself could not think at all because thinking was just his hobby.
2. The narrator felt that the adults around him could not understand him while he could understand them.
3. In the headmaster's study, there were two statues made by August Rodin. The narrator recognized these small statues at the very first sight but he did not know how to appreciate them.
4. The narrator realized that Mr. Houghton and Miss Parsons were sometimes unconsciously prejudiced and hypocritical.
5. The narrator returned to the headmaster's study and rearranged all the statuettes in honor of the headmaster.

III. Select the most suitable word or phrases and fill in the following blanks in their proper form.

anguish	bolster	crouch	delinquent	depravity
disinterested	exalt	gregarious	hustle	impediment
libertine	opaque	oratory	penal	plonk
portentous	remorselessly	restively	stampede	writhe

1. He believed that he would not be visible from inside the cave if he _____ behind that rock. Yet he did not realize there was a strange thing gazing upon him in the same cave.
2. The chief aims of the _____ system are to deter the potential lawbreaker and to reform the convicted offender.
3. Natasha did not change her position, only her whole body began to ____ with noiseless, convulsive sobs, which choked her.
4. Their play, and ours, appears to have no other purposes than to give pleasure to the players, and apparently, to remove us temporarily from the _____ of life in earnest.
5. When all the other folks thought he did not deserve this sum of money, he _____ it on the table in humiliation.
6. Returning newly from outside, Mr. Brown tells her about his journey and all the moral _____ he saw along the way — faithlessness and immorality — and his stories clearly disturb Lina.
7. In his works, he _____ all those virtues that we, as Chinese, are taught to hold dear throughout our life.

8. Barack Obama is widely acknowledged as a charismatic figure and is noted for his stirring _____.
9. Without electricity and the usual _____ and bustle of a London street it was extremely peaceful.
10. The 12-year-old boy allegedly had blackened eyes, was scarred on his face and there was a severe _____ to his speech.
11. He was seen less and less as a _____ researcher, and more and more as an enthusiastic propagandist.
12. Men are _____ and generally live in groups, and monkeys also live, play and act together and are led by a monkey king, which has an absolute authority over the other monkeys.
13. Syria agreed in early November to withdraw its forces from _____ cities, release political prisoners and start talks with the opposition.
14. There was nothing _____ or solemn about him. He was bubbling with humour.
15. Sustainable growth also requires foreign money to finance capital investment and to _____ the stock market.

IV. Try to paraphrase the following sentences, paying special attention to the underlined parts.

1. I remember how <u>incomprehensible</u> they appeared to me at first, but <u>not, of course, how I appeared to them</u>.

2. I had better explain that I was <u>a frequent visitor</u> to the headmaster's study, because <u>of the latest thing I had done or left undone</u>.

3. Clearly there was <u>something missing</u> in me. Nature had <u>endowed</u> the rest of the human race with a sixth sense and <u>left me out</u>.

4. Mr. Houghton was given to <u>high-minded monologues</u> about the good life, <u>sexless and full of duty</u>.

5. That night her father visited my father and left, red-cheeked and indignant. I was given the third degree to find out what had happened.

V. Discuss with your partner about each of the three statements and write an essay in no less than 250 words about your understanding of one of them.

   1. Thought is often full of unconscious prejudice, ignorance and hypocrisy.

   2. Technically, it (thought) is about as proficient as most businessmen's golf, as honest as most politicians' intentions, or — to come near my own preoccupation — as coherent as most books that get written.

   3. Man is a gregarious animal, and enjoys agreement as cows will graze all the same way on the side of a hill.

VI. List four websites where we can learn more about William Golding and his major literary works and provide a brief introduction to each of them.

   1. _____

   2. _____

   3. _____

   4. _____

Text B

The Art of Living Simply
Richard Wolkomir*

We paddled down Maine's Saco River that September afternoon, five couples in canoes, basking in the summer's last golden sunlight. Grazing deer, fluttering their white tails, watched our flotilla pass. That evening we pitched tents, broiled steaks and sprawled around the campfire, staring sleepily at the stars. One man, strumming his guitar, sang an old Shaker* song: "'Tis the gift to be simple. 'Tis the gift to be free."

Our idyll ended, of course, and we drove back to the world of loan payments, jobs and clogged washing machines. "'Tis the gift to be simple," I found myself humming at odd moments, "'Tis the gift to be free." How I longed for that simplicity. But where could I find it?

"Our life is frittered away by detail. Simplify, simplify." That dictum of Henry David Thoreau*'s, echoing from the days of steamboats and ox-drawn plows, had long haunted me. Yet Thoreau himself was able to spend only two years in the cabin he built beside Walden Pond. And Henry—wifeless, childless, jobless—never had to tussle with such details as variable-rate mortgages.

My life attracted detail, as if my motto were: "Complicate, complicate." And I've found I'm not alone. But one day my thinking about simplicity turned upside down.

I was visiting a physicist in his office tower jutting from his Illinois farmlands. We looked through his window at the laboratory's miles-around particle accelerator, an immense circle in the prairie far below. "It's a kind of time machine," he said, explaining that the

---

paddle /'pædl/ *v.* to move a small light boat through water, using one or more paddles
bask /bɑːsk/ *v.* to enjoy sitting or lying in the heat of the sun or a fire
flotilla /flə'tɪlə/ *n.* a group of small ships
pitch /pɪtʃ/ *v.* to set up (a tent, camp, etc.) in position on open ground, esp. for a certain time only
broil /brɔɪl/ *v.* to grill (chicken, meat, or fish)
sprawl /sprɔːl/ *v.* to lie or sit with your arms or legs stretched out in a lazy or careless way
idyll /'ɪdɪl/ *n.* a place or experience in which everything is peaceful and everyone is perfectly happy
fritter /'frɪtə/ *v.* to waste time, money, or effort on sth. small or unimportant
dictum /'dɪktəm/ *n.* a short phrase that expresses a general rule or truth
haunt /hɔːnt/ *v.* to make someone worry or make them sad
tussle /'tʌsəl/ *v.* to fight or struggle without using any weapons, by pulling or pushing someone rather than hitting them
mortgage /'mɔːgɪdʒ/ *n.* a legal arrangement by which you borrow money from a bank in order to buy a house, and pay back the money over a period of years
jut /dʒʌt/ *v.* to stick out, or make sth. stick out, esp. beyond the surface or edge of sth.
particle accelerator a device in physics used to accelerate charged elementary particles to high energies
prairie /'peəri/ *n.* a wide open area of fairly flat land in North America which is covered in grass or wheat

accelerator enables physicists to study conditions like those shortly after Creation*'s first moment. The universe was simpler then, he noted, a mere dot comprising perhaps only one kind of force and one kind of particle. Now it has many kinds of forces, scores of different particles, and contains everything from stars and galaxies to dandelions, elephants and the poems of Keats*.

Complexity, I began to see from that tower, is part of God's plan.

Deep down, we sense that we speak, disparagingly, of a "simpleton". Nobody wants to be guilty of "simplistic" thinking.

But blinding ourselves to complexity can be dangerous. Once I bought a home. I liked its setting so much I unconsciously avoided probing into its possible defects. After it was mine, I found it needed insulation, roofing, a new heating system, new windows, a new septic system—everything. That old house became an albatross, costing far more than I could afford, the cost in stress was even higher, I had refused to look at the complexities.

Even ordinary finances are rarely simple—what does your insurance policy actually cover? Yet, economics is simplicity itself compared with moral questions.

One afternoon when I was ten, I found myself the leader of an after-school gaggle of boys. I had to divert them quickly, I knew, or my career as leader would be brief. And then I saw Joe.

Joe was an Eiffel Tower* of a kid, an incipient giant. His family had emigrated from Europe, and he had a faint accent.

"Let's get him!" I said.

My little troop of Goths swarmed upon Joe. Somebody snatched his hat and we played catch with it. Joe ran home, and I took his hat as a trophy.

galaxy /ˈgæləksɪ/ *n.* one of the large groups of stars that make up the universe
dandelion /ˈdændɪlaɪən/ *n.* a wild plant with a bright yellow flower
disparage /dɪsˈpærɪdʒ/ *v.* to speak without respect of; make (someone or sth.) sound of little value or importance —*disparagingly adv.*
simpleton /ˈsɪmpəltən/ *n.* (old) someone who has a very low level of intelligence
defect /dɪˈfekt/ *n.* sth. lacking or imperfect; fault
insulation /ˌɪnsjʊˈleɪʃən/ *n.* covering sth. with a material that stops electricity, sound, heat etc. from getting in or out
septic system sewage system
albatross /ˈælbətrɒs/ *n.* sth. that causes problems for you and prevents you from succeeding
a gaggle of a noisy group of
divert /daɪˈvɜːt/ *v.* **a.** to change the direction in which sth. travels **b.** to deliberately take someone's attention from sth. by making them think about other things **c.** (formal) to entertain someone
incipient /ɪnˈsɪpɪənt/ *adj.* starting to happen or exist
Goth /gɒθ/ *adj.* ignorant, uncivilized and brutal man
trophy /ˈtrəʊfɪ/ *n.* sth. that you keep to prove your success in sth., esp. in war or hunting

That night, our doorbell rang. Joe's father, a worried-looking farmer with a thick accent, asked for Joe's hat. I returned it sheepishly. "Please don't upset Joe," he said earnestly. "He has asthma. When he has an attack, it is hard for him to get better."

I felt a lead softball in my chest. The next evening I walked to Joe's house. He was in the garden, tilling the soil, he watched me warily as I walked up. I asked if I could help. "Okay," he said. After that I went often to help him and we became best friends.

I had taken a step toward adulthood. Inside myself I had seen possibilities, like a tangle of wires. This red wire was the possibility for evil, which requires no more than ignoring another's pain. And here was the white wire of sympathy. I could have a hand in connecting all those wires—it was a matter of the decisions I made. I had discovered complexity, and found in it an opportunity to choose, to grow. Its price is responsibility.

Perhaps, that is one reason we yearn for the simple life. In a way, we want to be children, to let someone else carry the awkward backpack of responsibility.

Not long ago I attended a college seminar where a U.S. State Department officer talked about international negotiation. Afterward he asked for questions. One student demanded: "Why don't you just get rid of all these terrible nuclear weapons?" The diplomat looked at her blankly, then said, "That's the problem of our times—some of the world's best minds are struggling with it." "Well, just get rid of them," the student said. After a silence, he sighed and said, "If only it were that simple." Behind that sigh were the teeming complexities of national security, of international politics, of the inability to "disinvent" an existing technology. For me, their exchange had a message: in a complex world, to insist upon simplicity is foolish.

We are like wheat, here on earth to ripen. We ripen intellectually by letting in as much of the universe's complexity as we can. Morally we ripen by making our

sheepish /ˈʃiːpɪʃ/ *adj.* uncomfortable, as from being slightly ashamed or fearful of others —sheepishly *adv.*
asthma /ˈæsmə/ *n.* a medical condition that causes difficulties in breathing
till /tɪl/ *v.* to prepare land for growing crops; cultivate
wary /ˈweərɪ/ showing watchfulness or suspicion —warily *adv.*
tangle /ˈtæŋɡəl/ *n.* **a.** a confused mass **b.** a confused disordered state
seminar /ˈsemɪnɑː/ *n.* a class at a university or college for a small group of students and a teacher to study or discuss a particular subject
teeming /ˈtiːmɪŋ/ *adj.* full of people, animals etc. that are all moving around
disinvent /ˌdɪsɪnˈvent/ *v.* to undo the invention of sth.; to make sth. cease to exist

nutrient /'nju:trɪənt/ *n.* a chemical or food that provides what is needed for plants or animals to live and grow
emit /ɪ'mɪt/ *v.* to send out gas, heat, light, sound
nucleus /'nju:klɪəs/ *n.* the central part of almost all the cells of living things
inscribe /ɪn'skraɪb/ *v.* to carefully cut, print, or write words on sth., esp. on the surface of a stone or coin
mow /məʊ/ *v.* to cut grass using a machine

choices. And we ripen spiritually by opening our eyes to Creation's endless detail.

One afternoon I picked up a fallen leaf from the sugar maple in our yard. Up close it was yellow, with splashes of red. At arm's length it was orange. Its color depends on how I looked at it.

I knew a little about how this leaf had spent its life, transforming sunlight and carbon dioxide into nutrients, and I knew that we animals breathe that oxygen that such plants emit, while they thrive upon the carbon dioxide we exhale. And I knew that each cell of the leaf has a nucleus containing a chemical—DNA*—upon which is inscribed all the instructions for making and operating a sugar maple. Scientists know far more about this than I. But even their knowledge extends only a short way into the sea of complexity that is a sugar maple.

I'm beginning to understand, I think, what simplicity means. It does not mean blinding ourselves to the world's stunning complexity or avoiding the choices that ripen us. By "simplify, simplify," Thoreau meant simplifying ourselves.

To accomplish this, we can:

Focus on deeper things. The simple life is not necessarily living in a cabin, cultivating beans. It is refusing to let our lives be "frittered away by detail". A professor taught me a secret for focusing: Turn off the TV and read great books. They open doors in your brain.

Undertake life's journey one step at a time. I once met a young couple both blind since birth. They had a three-year-old daughter and an infant, both fully

sighted. For those parents, everything was complex: bathing the baby, monitoring their daughter, mowing the lawn. Yet they were full of smiles and laughter. I asked the mother how she kept track of their lively daughter. "I tie little bells in her shoes," she said with a laugh. "What will you do when the infant walks too?" I asked. She smiled. "Everything is so complicated that I don't try to solve a problem until I have to. I take one thing at a time!"

Pare down your desires. English novelist and playwright Jerome Klapka Jerome* caught the spirit of that enterprise when he wrote, "Let your boat of life be light, packed only with what you need—a homely home and simple pleasure, one or two friends, worth the name, someone to love and someone to love you, a cat, a dog and a pipe or two, enough to eat and enough to wear and a little more than enough to drink, for thirst is a dangerous thing."

pare down to reduce sth., esp. by making a lot of small reductions
nibble /ˈnɪbəl/ v. to eat small amounts of food by taking very small bites
snarl /snɑːl/ n. a confused, complicated, or tangled situation; a predicament
slouch /slaʊtʃ/ v. to stand, sit, or walk with your shoulders bent forward that makes you look tired or lazy
shrivel /ˈʃrɪvl/ v. to become wrinkled smaller or cause somebody to become so esp. from drying out or aging
well /wel/ v. to rise or flow to the surface from inside the ground or the body, or cause sth. to do this
bewilder /bɪˈwɪldə/ to confuse, esp. by the presence of lots of different things at the same time —bewilderment n.
savor /ˈseɪvə/ v. to fully enjoy the taste or smell of sth.
brim /brɪm/ v. to fill sth., or be full, to the top edge

Not long ago I flew home to see my father in the hospital. He has a disease that nibbles away the mind. I was a snarl of worries. Treatments? Nursing homes? Finances?

He was slouched in a wheelchair, a shriveled, whitened remnant of the father I had known. As I stood there, hurt and confused, he looked up and saw me. And then I saw something unexpected and wonderful in his eyes: recognition and love. It welled up and filled his eyes with tears. And mine.

That afternoon, my father came back from wherever his illness had taken him. He joked and laughed, once again the man I had known. And then he tired, and we put him to bed. The next day, he did not remember I had come. And the next night he died.

Every death is a door opening on Creation's mystery. The door opens, but we see only darkness. In that awful moment, we realize how vast the universe is, complexity upon complexity, beyond us. But that is the true gift of simplicity: to accept the world's infinite complication, to accept bewilderment.

And then, especially, we can savor simple things. A face we love, perhaps, eyes brimming with love.

It is the simplest of things. But it is more than enough.

Cultural Notes

1. **Richard Wolkomir** is an editor with the McGrawHill Publishing Company in New York. Together with his wife, Joyce Rogers Wolkomir, he writes essays and articles for magazines ranging from *Smithsonian* and *Reader's Digest* to *Wildlife Conservation, Playboy,* and *National Geographic Magazine.*

2. **Shaker** is a name applied to the United Society of Believers in Christ's Second Coming, a sect first heard of about 1750 in Great Britain. The name Shaking Quakers or Shakers came from the peculiar trembling of the secessionists at their meetings. Shaker communities held property in common, practiced asceticism, and honored celibacy above marriage. The movement diminished after 1860.

3. **Henry David Thoreau** (1817—1862) was an American writer, philosopher, and a member of the Transcendentalist Club in Boston and a close associate with Ralph Waldo Emerson. Thoreau's best-known work is *Walden,* which records his experiences in a hand-built cabin at Walden Pond near Concord, Massachusetts, where he spent two years in partial seclusion.

4. **Creation** means the origin of the universe. Big Bang Theory proposes that the universe was once extremely compact, dense, and hot. Some original event, a cosmic explosion called the big bang, occurred about 13.7 billion years ago, and the universe has since been expanding and cooling.

5. **John Keats** (1795—1821) was a British poet and considered among the greatest in English. His works, melodic and rich in classical imagery, include *The Eve of St. Agnes, Ode on a Grecian Urn,* and *To Autumn.*

6. **Eiffel Tower** is a wrought iron tower in Paris. It was designed and built by the French civil engineer Alexandre Gustave Eiffel for the Paris World's Fair of 1889.

7. **Jerome Klapka Jerome** (1859—1927) was an English novelist and playwright. Two books, *Idle Thoughts of an Idle Fellow* (1886) and *Three Men in a Boat* (1889), represent his greatest success as a novelist.

Comprehension Exercises

I. Answer the following questions based on the text.

1. How do you understand Thoreau's dictum about simplicity and the author's motto about complexity?

2. Do you think the author finally understood what Thoreau means by "simplify, simplify"?
3. What does the author mean by "complicate, complicate"? How does he prove the complexity of human morality, life, nature and the universe?
4. How are such topics as morality, growth, choice, responsibility, nuclear weapons, love, etc. relevant to the theme of the essay? How do they contribute to the final conclusion?
5. How does the author adopt the first-person point of view and share with us some episodes in his life?

II. Decide whether each of the following statements is true or false according to the text.

1. The brief escape from the stressful city life made the author long for simplicity and follow Thoreau's example.
2. Compared with its original form, the present universe is far more complicated, comprising many kinds of particles, forces, stars, plants, animals and civilizations.
3. The experience of buying the house further proves the danger of simplifying things, because complexity is the true nature of the universe.
4. Joe came from a rich family in Europe and knew much about Eiffel Tower.
5. Jerome advised to take a little more than enough to drink.
6. The death of the author's father convinces him that the universe is complicated and life is not a simple journey.

III. Select the most suitable word or phrases and fill in the following blanks in their proper form.

bask	defect	disparage	divert	fritter
gaggle	idyll	incipient	paddle	pitch
simpleton	sprawl	teeming	trophy	tussle
wary	inscribe	nibble		

1. We might be able to _____ ourselves across the river to the opposite with no great efforts.
2. They enjoyed their time splashing around in cool, cascading pools or _____ in warm sunshine on the white sand beach.
3. Throughout that period of time, his voice was _____ so high that his words were muffled by his crying.
4. After a whole day's hard work, she came home and _____ herself on the bed, not even moving to cover herself up.

5. Almost at once the area was thronged with wealthy British tourists, who saw in these peaceful, grand valleys the pastoral _____ they had lost in smoky, crowded Britain.

6. They had nothing to do and did not want to _____ away their strength with empty living.

7. At the booking office two men began to _____ over the last ticket for that performance of the Peking Opera.

8. Men often _____ women for being irrational, arbitrary, and more than a little capricious.

9. But the widow was very disappointed to find that her son was as idiotic as a _____, and seemed to know nothing except how to eat and sleep.

10. It's a very interesting story, it had only one _____, which was completely untrue.

11. At the very outset, she was trained as a dancer but unexpectedly she _____ to music teaching.

12. People begin to regain confidence in the national economy as there are not only signs of an _____ national turnaround, but regional figures give further reasons for hope.

13. Entering his office, you cannot fail to find that it was lined with animal heads, which were all _____ of his hunting hobby.

14. As a place of interest, the City of Xi'an is _____ with tourists from all corners of the world for most of the year.

15. It is of great necessity for the parents and teachers alike to teach the children to be _____ of strangers.

16. A marble monument was instituted to commemorate these martyrs by _____ their names on it.

IV. Try to paraphrase the following sentences, paying special attention to the underlined parts.

1. We paddled down Maine's Saco River that September afternoon, five couples in canoes, basking in the summer's lost golden sunlight.

   _____

2. That evening we pitched tents, broiled steaks and sprawled around the campfire, staring sleepily at the stars.

   _____

3. Joe was an Eiffel Tower of a kid, an incipient giant.

4. My little troup of Goths swarmed upon Joe.

5. Behind that sigh were the teeming complexities of national security, of international politics, of the inability to disinvent an existing technology.

V. Discuss with your partner about each of the three statements and write an essay in no less than 250 words about your understanding of one of them.

1. Complexity of part of God's plan.

2. Blinding ourselves to complexity can be dangerous.

3. Every death is a door opening on Creation's mystery.

VI. List four websites where we can learn more about Richard Wolkomir or the simple lifestyle and provide a brief introduction to each of them.

1. _____

2. _____

3. _____

4. _____

Unit Four

Twenty Minutes' Reading

You are required to read the following two sections within 20 minutes.

SECTION A

These days lots of young Japanese do omiai, literally, "meet and look". Many of them do so willingly. In today's prosperous and increasingly conservative Japan, the traditional omiai kekkon, or arranged marriage, is thriving.

But there is a difference. In the original omiai, the young Japanese couldn't reject the partner chosen by his parents and their middleman. After World War II, many Japanese abandoned the arranged marriage as part of their rush to adopt the more democratic ways of their American conquerors. The Western ren'ai kekkon, or love marriage, became popular; Japanese began picking their own mates by dating and falling in love.

But the Western way was often found wanting in an important respect: it didn't necessarily produce a partner of the right economic, social, and educational qualifications. "Today's young people are quite calculating," says Chieko Akiyama, a social commentator.

What seems to be happening now is a repetition of a familiar process in the country's history, the "Japanization" of an adopted foreign practice. The Western ideal of marrying for love is accommodated in a new omiai in which both parties are free to reject the match. "Omiai is evolving into a sort of stylized introduction," Mrs. Akiyama says.

Many young Japanese now date in their early twenties, but with no thought of marriage. When they reach the age — in the middle twenties for women, the late twenties for men — they increasingly turn to omiai. Some studies suggest that as many as 40% of marriages each year are omiai kekkon. It's hard to be sure, say those who study the matter, because many Japanese couples, when polled, describe their marriage as a love match even if it was arranged.

These days, doing omiai often means going to a computer matching service rather than to a nakodo. The nakodo of tradition was an old woman who knew all the kids in the neighbourhood and went around trying to pair them off by speaking to their parents; a successful match would bring her a wedding invitation and a gift of money. But Japanese today find it's less awkward to reject a proposed partner if the nakodo is a computer.

Japan has about five hundred computer matching services. Some big companies, including Mitsubishi, run one for their employees. At a typical commercial service, an applicant pays $80 to $125 to have his or her personal data stored in the computer for two years and $200 or so more if a marriage results. The stored information includes some obvious items, like education and hobbies, and some not-so-obvious ones, like whether a person is the oldest child. (First sons, and to some extent first daughters, face an obligation of caring for elderly parents.)

1. According to the passage, today's young Japanese prefer _____.
   A. a traditional arranged marriage   B. a new type of arranged marriage
   C. a Western love marriage   D. a more Westernized love marriage
2. Which of the following statements is CORRECT?
   A. A Western love marriage tends to miss some Japanese values.
   B. Less attention is paid to the partner's qualification in arranged marriages.
   C. Young Japanese would often calculate their partner's wealth.
   D. A new arranged marriage is a repetition of the older type.
3. According to the passage, the figure 40% (Paragraph Five) is uncertain because _____.
   A. there has been a big increase in the number of arranged marriages
   B. Western love marriage still remains popular among young Japanese
   C. young Japanese start dating very early in their life in a Western tradition
   D. the tendency for arranged marriages could be stronger than is indicated
4. One of the big differences between a traditional nakodo and its contemporary version lies in the way _____.
   A. wedding gifts are presented   B. a proposed partner is refused
   C. formalities are arranged   D. the middleman/woman is chosen
5. What is the purpose of the last paragraph?
   A. To tell the differences between an old and modern nakodo.
   B. To provide some examples for the traditional nakodo.
   C. To offer more details of the computerized nakodo.
   D. To sum up the main ideas and provide a conclusion.

SECTION B

Cordia Harrington was tired of standing up all day and smelling like French fries at night. She owned and operated three McDonald's shops in Illinois, but as a divorced mother of three boys, she yearned for a business that would provide for her children and let her spend more time with them.

Her lucky moment came, strangely enough, after she was nominated in 1992 to be on the McDonald's bun committee. "The company picked me up in a corporate jet to see bakeries around the world," she recalls. "Every time I went to a meeting, I loved it. This was global!"

The experience opened her eyes to business possibilities. When McDonald's decided it wanted a new bun supplier, Harrington became determined to win the contract, even though she had no experience running a bakery.

Harrington studied the bakery business and made sure she was never off executives' radar. "If you have a dream, you can't wait for people to call you," she says. "So I'd visit a mill and send them photos of myself in a baker's hat and jacket, holding a sign that says 'I want to be your baker.'" After four years and 32 interviews, her persistence paid off.

Harrington sealed the deal with a handshake, sold her shops, and borrowed $13.5 million. She was ready to build the fastest, most automated bakery in the world.

The Tennessee Bun Company opened ahead of schedule in 1997, in time for a slump in U.S. fast-food sales for McDonald's. Before Harrington knew it, she was down to her last $20,000, not enough to cover payroll. And her agreement with McDonald's required that she sell exclusively to the company. "I cried myself to sleep many nights," she recalls. "I really did think, I am going to go bankrupt."

But Harrington worked out an agreement to supply Pepperidge Farm as well. "McDonald's could see a benefit if our production went up and prices went down, and no benefit if we went out of business," she says. "That deal saved us."

Over the next eight years, Harrington branched out even more: She started her own trucking business, added a cold-storage company, and now has three bakeries producing fresh buns and frozen dough — all now known as the Bun Companies. Speed is still a priority: It takes 11 people at the main bakery to turn out 60,000 buns an hour for clients across 40 states, South America, and the Caribbean.

Grateful for the breaks she's had, Harrington is passionate about providing opportunities to all 230 employees. "Financial success is the most fun when you can give it away," she says.

The current economy is challenging. Some of her clients' sales have declined, but she's found new clients and improved efficiencies to help sustain the company's double-digit growth.

Cordia Harrington doesn't have to stand on her feet all day anymore. Two of her three sons now work for her. And she's remarried — her husband, Tom, is now her CFO.

"This is more than a job," says Harrington. "It's a mission. I'm always thinking, how can we best serve our employees? If we support them, they'll do their best to look after our clients. That's how it works here."

6. According to the passage, which of the following was most significant in her early career?

   A. Her nomination on the McDonald's bun committee.

   B. Her travel and the visits to bakeries around the world.

   C. A business contract with local bun suppliers.

   D. The interviews and experience in running a bakery.

7. "Harrington...made sure she was never off executives' radar" (Paragraph Four) means that she _____.

   A. herself wanted to be a company executive

   B. meant to hire executives to run the business

   C. meant to keep her management knowledge and skills

   D. focused on the management of the bakery business

8. How did she survive the crisis at the start of her bakery business?

   A. By supplying buns for another company.

   B. By opening her bun company ahead of schedule.

   C. By keeping supplies up for McDonald's.

   D. By making a new agreement with McDonald's.

9. Which of the following statements is INCORRECT in describing her current business?

   A. It is fast growing.   B. It is diversified.

   C. Its clients are all local.   D. It is more efficient.

10. According to the passage, which of the following is fundamental to Harrington's success?

    A. Efficiency and love for the family.

    B. Perseverance and concern for employees.

    C. Business expansion and family support.

    D. Opportunities and speed.

Unit Five

Text A

Once More to the Lake
E. B. White*

One summer, along about 1904, my father rented a camp on a lake in Maine and took us all there for the month of August. The vacation was a success and from then on none of us ever thought there was any place in the world like that lake in Maine. We returned summer after summer—always on August 1st for one month. I have since become a salt-water man, but sometimes in summer there are days when the restlessness of the tides and the fearful cold of the sea water and the incessant wind which blows across the afternoon and into the evening make me wish for the placidity of a lake in the woods. A few weeks ago this feeling got so strong I bought myself a couple of bass hooks and a spinner and returned to the lake where we used to go, for a week's fishing and to revisit old haunts.

I took along my son, who had never had any fresh water up his nose and who had seen lily pads only from train windows. On the journey over to the lake I began to wonder what it would be like. I wondered how time would have marred this unique, this holy spot—the coves and streams, the hills that the sun set behind, the camps and the paths behind the camps. I was sure that the tarred road would have found it out and I wondered in what other ways it would be desolated. It is strange how much you can remember about places like that once you allow your mind to return into the grooves which lead back. You remember one

incessant /ɪnˈsesənt/ *adj*. constant; continuing without stopping
placidity /pləˈsɪdɪti/ *n*. the state of being calm and not easily excited, upset, or disturbed
bass /bæs/ *n*. a fish that can be eaten and lives in both rivers and the sea
spinner /ˈspɪnə/ *n*. a thing used for catching fish that spins when pulled through the water
haunt /hɔːnt/ *n*. a place that someone likes to go to often
pad /pæd/ *n*. here the leaf of a water lily
mar /mɑː/ *v*. to spoil; to make sth. less attractive or enjoyable
cove /kəʊv/ *n*. bay; part of the coast where the land curves round so that the sea is partly surrounded by land
tar /tɑː/ *v*. to cover a surface with tar, a black substance used esp. for making road surfaces
desolate /ˈdesələt/ *v*. to make someone feel very sad and lonely

thing, and that suddenly reminds you of another thing. I guess I remembered clearest of all the early mornings, when the lake was cool and motionless, remembered how the bedroom smelled of the lumber it was made of and of the wet woods whose scent entered through the screen. The partitions in the camp were thin and did not extend clear to the top of the rooms, and as I was always the first up I would dress softly so as not to wake the others, and sneak out into the sweet outdoors and start out in the canoe, keeping close along the shore in the long shadows of the pines. I remembered being very careful never to rub my paddle against the gunwale for fear of disturbing the stillness of the cathedral.

We went fishing the first morning. I felt the same damp moss covering the worms in the bait can, and saw the dragonfly alight on the tip of my rod as it hovered a few inches from the surface of the water. It was the arrival of this fly that convinced me beyond any doubt that everything was as it always had been, that the years were a mirage and there had been no years. The small waves were the same, chucking the rowboat under the chin as we fished at anchor, and the boat was the same boat, the same color green and the ribs broken in the same places, and under the floor-boards the same freshwater leavings and debris—the dead hellgrammite, the wisps of moss, the rusty discarded fishhook, the dried blood from yesterday's catch. We stared silently at the tips of our rods, at the dragonflies that came and wells. I lowered the tip of mine into the water, tentatively, pensively dislodging the fly, which darted two feet away, poised, darted two feet back, and came to rest again a little farther up the rod. There had been no years between the ducking of this dragonfly and the other one—the one that was part of memory.

It seemed to me, as I kept remembering all this, that those times and those summers had been infinitely precious and worth saving. There had been jollity and peace and goodness. The arriving (at the beginning of August) had been so big a

partition /pɑːˈtɪʃən/ *n.* a thin wall that separates one part of a room from another
gunwale /ˈɡʌnəl/ *n.* the upper edge of the side of a boat or small ship
cathedral /kəˈθiːdrəl/ *n.* a church of a particular area under the control of a bishop
hover /ˈhɒvə/ *v.* to float or flutter in the air without moving very far from the same spot
mirage /ˈmɪrɑːʒ/ *n.* **a.** an effect caused by hot air in a desert, which makes you think that you can see objects when they are not actually there **b.** illusion; a dream, hope, or wish that cannot come true
chuck sb. under the chin to gently touch someone under the chin in a friendly way
debris /ˈdebriː/ *n.* pieces of waste material, paper etc.
hellgrammite a large, stout-bodied, net-winged aquatic insect used as fishing bait
wisp /wɪsp/ *n.* **a.** a small separate untidy piece **b.** a small thin twisting bit (of smoke or steam)
tentative /ˈtentətɪv/ *adj.* made or done only as a suggestion to see the effect; not certain —tentatively *adv.*
pensive /ˈpensɪv/ *adj.* thoughtful; thinking a lot about sth., esp. because you are worried or sad —pensively *adv.*
dislodge /dɪsˈlɒdʒ/ *v.* to force or knock sth. out of its position
poise /pɔɪz/ *v.* to put or hold sth. in a carefully balanced position, esp. above sth. else
duck /dʌk/ *v.* to lower your head or body very quickly, esp. to avoid being seen or hit
jollity /ˈdʒɒlɪti/ *n.* fun; cheerful, joking, or celebratory behavior

business in itself, at the railway station the farm wagon drawn up, the first smell of the pine-laden air, the first glimpse of the smiling farmer, and the great importance of the trunks and your father's enormous authority in such matters, and the feel of the wagon under you for the long ten-mile haul, and at the top of the last long hill catching the first view of the lake after eleven months of not seeing this cherished body of water. The shouts and cries of the other campers when they saw you, and the trunks to be unpacked, to give up their rich burden.

 We had a good week at the camp. The bass were biting well and the sun shone endlessly, day after day. We would be tired at night and lie down in the accumulated heat of the little bedrooms after the long hot day and the breeze would stir almost imperceptibly outside and the smell of the swamp drift in through the rusty screens. Sleep would come easily and in the morning the red squirrel would be on the roof, tapping out his gay routine. I kept remembering everything, lying in bed in the mornings—the small steamboat that had a long rounded stern like the lip of a Ubangi*, and how quietly she ran on the moonlight sails, when the older boys played their mandolins and the girls sang and we ate doughnuts dipped in sugar, and how sweet the music was on the water in the shining night, and what it had felt like to think about girls then. After breakfast we would go up to the store and the things were in the same place—the minnows in a bottle, the plugs and spinners disarranged and pawed over by the youngsters from the boys' camp. Outside, the road was tarred and cars stood in front of the store. Inside, all was just as it had always been, except there was more Coca Cola and not so much Moxie* and root beer* and birch beer* and sarsaparilla*. We would walk out with a bottle of pop apiece and sometimes the pop would backfire up our noses and hurt. We explored the streams, quietly, where the turtles slid off the sunny logs and dug their way into the soft bottom; and we lay on the town wharf and fed worms to the tame bass. Everywhere we went I had trouble making out which was I, the one walking at my side, the one walking in my pants.

 One afternoon while we were there at that lake a thunderstorm came up. It was like

---

imperceptible /ˌɪmpəˈseptəbəl/ *adj.* unable to be noticed because of smallness or slightness —**imperceptibly** *adv.*
tap out to hit sth. lightly, esp. with your fingers or foot, in order to make a pattern of sounds
stern /stɜːn/ *n.* the back end of a ship
mandolin /ˈmændəˈlɪn/ *n.* a musical instrument with eight metal strings and a round back, played with a plectrum (small piece of plastic, metal etc.)
doughnut /ˈdəʊnʌt/ *n.* a small round cake, often in the form of a ring
minnow /ˈmɪnəʊ/ *n.* a very small fish that lives in rivers and lakes used as fishing baits
paw /pɔː/ *v.* to touch somebody or sth., or caress somebody, roughly or rudely with the hands
apiece /əˈpiːs/ *adv.* to, for, or from each person or thing; each
backfire /bækˈfaɪə/ *v.* to have an effect opposite to the one intended
tame /teɪm/ *adj.* no longer wild; changed from a wild or uncultivated state to one suitable for domestic use or life

the revival of an old melodrama that I had seen long ago with childish awe. The second-act climax of the drama of the electrical disturbance over a lake in America had not changed in any important respect. This was the big scene, still the big scene. The whole thing was so familiar, the first feeling of oppression and heat and a general air around camp of not wanting to go very far away. In mid-afternoon (it was all the same) a curious darkening of the sky, and a lull in everything that had made life tick; and then the way the boats suddenly swung the other way at their moorings with the coming of a breeze out of the new quarter, and the premonitory rumble. Then the kettle drum, then the snare, then the bass drum and cymbals, then crackling light against the dark, and the gods grinning and licking their chops in the hills. Afterward the calm, the rain steadily rustling in the calm lake, the return of light and hope and spirits, and the campers running out in joy and relief to go swimming in the rain, their bright cries perpetuating the deathless joke about how they were getting simply drenched, and the children screaming with delight at the new sensation of bathing in the rain, and the joke about getting drenched linking the generations in a strong indestructible chain.

When the others went swimming my son said he was going in too. He pulled his dripping trunks from the line where they had hung all through the shower, and wrung them out. Languidly, and with no thought of going in, I watched him, his hard little body, skinny and bare, saw him wince slightly as he pulled up around his vitals the small, soggy, icy garment. As he buckled the swollen belt, suddenly my groin felt the chill of death.

---

melodrama /ˈmelədrɑːmə/ *n.* a play with a sensational or romantic plot

lull /lʌl/ *n.* a short period of time when there is less activity or less noise than usual

tick /tɪk/ *v.* to function well or in the right way

moorings *n.* the ropes, chains, anchors etc. used to fasten a ship or boat to the land or the bottom of the sea

premonitory /prɪˈmɒnɪtərɪ/ *adj.* giving a warning that sth. unpleasant is going to happen

rumble /ˈrʌmbəl/ *n.* a series of long low sounds, esp. a long distance away from you

snare /sneə/ *n.* a trap for catching an animal

cymbal /ˈsɪmbəl/ *n.* a musical instrument in the form of a thin round metal plate, which you play by hitting it with a stick or by hitting two of them together

rustle /ˈrʌsəl/ *v.* to make slight sounds like papers, dry leaves, silk, etc. moving or being rubbed together

perpetuate /pəˈpetʃueɪt/ *v.* to make a situation, attitude etc, esp. a bad one, continue to exist for a long time

drench /drentʃ/ *v.* to make sth. or someone extremely wet

trunks /trʌŋk/ *n.* shorts worn by men for boxing or swimming

wring /rɪŋ/ *v.* to squeeze to remove water

languid /ˈlæŋgwɪd/ *adj.* lacking strength or will; slow and weak —languidly *adv.*

wince /wɪns/ *v.* to suddenly change the expression on your face as a reaction to sth. painful or upsetting

vitals /ˈvaɪtlz/ *n.* the parts of your body that are necessary to keep you alive, e.g. your heart and lungs

soggy /ˈsɒgɪ/ *adj.* unpleasantly wet and soft

groin /grɔɪn/ *n.* the place where the tops of your legs meet the front of your body

Cultural Notes

1. **E. B. White** (1899—1985) was an American writer, famous for his essays and children's literature. Born in Mount Vernon, New York, and educated at Cornell University, White joined the staff of the magazine *The New Yorker* in 1926, when it had just been founded, and remained a regular contributor for many years. White's elegantly written essays gently satirize the complexities and difficulties of modern civilization.
2. **Ubangi**, also called the Oubangui, is a river of central Africa, the chief tributary of the Congo River.
3. **Moxie** is a brand of soft drink originally marketed as a "nerve tonic" in mid twentieth century. In American informal English, Moxie means courage and determination.
4. **Root beer** is an American staple for centuries, quenching the thirst and aiding the digestion and came into commercial marketplace in the late nineteenth century. It is sweet brown carbonated non-alcoholic drink made from the roots or the extracts of various roots and herbs.
5. **Birch beer** is derived from the sap (plant fluid) of the birch tree, a carbonated soft drink made from herbal extracts, usually from birch bark. It was once very popular and has a taste similar to yet distinct from root beer.
6. **Sarsaparilla** is a sweet carbonated drink without alcohol, made from the root of the sassafras plant, similar to root beer.

Comprehension Exercises

I. Answer the following questions based on the text.
1. How does White express his love of the lake and its surroundings?
2. How does White perceive the change of his identity from a son to a father?
3. What does White benefit most from his return to the lake?
4. What makes the thunderstorm a good ending?
5. What does White imply by the last sentence?

II. Decide whether each of the following statements is true or false according to the text.
1. *Once More to the Lake* is autographical and intensely personal.
2. It has been years since White's last visit to the lake. He didn't go there

because no father took him there, because he was trapped by work and family, and also because he became a salt-water man and lived far away from the lake.

3. What White remembered clearest of his past in the lake was to go boating alone in the early morning to the cathedral.
4. The theme of the text is the passage of time and the changes that it brings. Revisiting the lake, White struggles with the illusion that the idyllic world of his childhood and his present existence within it remains the same.
5. Despite his claim that "there had been no years", White confronted several changes that had occurred since his last visit as a child.
6. As the thunderstorm was approaching, White heard the drumming of the kettle, snare, bass and cymbals.

III. Select the most suitable word or phrases and fill in the following blanks in their proper form.

apiece	chunk	dart	debris	desolate	dislodge
duck	hover	imperceptibly	incessant	jollity	languidly
mar	placidity	sneak	tentatively	wisp	

1. _____ rain in that mountainous region made conditions even more intolerable for the local villages.
2. But their heartache is so deep that the _____ and ordinariness of everyday existence seems demeaning and intolerable.
3. But the hope is that Azerbaijan will at least try to avoid international criticism which could greatly _____ the reputation of this country.
4. In this evacuated place, row upon row of houses have now become _____ fields of dried mud and uprooted bush.
5. Under the screen of the night, seven prisoners _____ through the wire one night and head south, toward Lake Baikal.
6. It was devastatingly painful for him to see his father _____ on the brink of death for three months as doctors battled to save her.
7. Visitors to that battlefield still see scenes of devastation, though most of the _____ has been removed.
8. It was exciting for us to spot a thin _____ of smoke straggling up through the trees; we knew there must be some dwellers nearby.
9. The first was a young man who _____ tapped on the door, then stepped briskly, submissively backward when Andrew Patti answered.
10. Holding the high ground, this troop of soldiers successfully resisted repeated efforts by the antagonists to _____ them.

11. The defence secretary tried to _____ the question of whether the United States was winning the war against terrorism.
12. As a jailbird, he was stuck there for a very long time, pining for the _____ of his old days.
13. He was walking slowly, hands behind his back as before, and he seemed to pause when he saw me with his head almost _____ lowered and steps not quite steady.
14. I have made some adjustments every year. I'm trying to deal with the fact that there are so many novels I love written between 1985 and the present that are over 400 pages _____.
15. Coming through the trees and into the clearing, a large puma struts slowly and _____.

IV. Try to paraphrase the following sentences, paying special attention to the underlined parts.

1. I have since become a salt-water man, but sometimes in summer there are days when <u>the restlessness of the tides</u> and the fearful cold of the sea water and <u>the incessant wind</u> which blows across the afternoon and into the evening make me wish for <u>the placidity of a lake</u> in the woods.

2. It was the arrival of this fly that <u>convinced me beyond any doubt</u> that everything was as it always had been, that <u>the years were a mirage</u> and there had been no years.

3. I was sure that <u>the tarred road</u> would have found it out and I wondered in what other ways it would be <u>desolated</u>.

4. We would walk out <u>with a bottle of pop apiece</u> and sometimes the pop would <u>backfire up our nose and hurt</u>.

5. As he <u>buckled the swollen belt</u>, suddenly my <u>groin</u> felt the <u>chill of death</u>.

V. Discuss with your partner about each of the three statements and write an essay in no less than 250 words about your understanding of one of them.

1. The vacation was a success and from then on none of us ever thought there was any place in the world like that lake in Maine.
   _____
   _____

2. It is strange how much you can remember about places like that once you allow your mind to return into the grooves which lead back.
   _____
   _____

3. There had been no years between the ducking of this dragonfly and the other one — the one that was part of memory.
   _____
   _____

VI. List four websites where we can learn more about E. B. White and provide a brief introduction to each of them.

1. _____
   _____
   _____.

2. _____
   _____
   _____.

3. _____
   _____
   _____.

4. _____
   _____
   _____.

Text B

The Almost Perfect State
Don Marquis

NO matter how nearly perfect an Almost Perfect State may be, it is not nearly enough perfect unless the individuals who compose it can, somewhere between death and birth, have a perfectly corking time for a few years. The most wonderful governmental system in the world does not attract us, as a system; we are after a system that scarcely knows it is a system; the great thing is to have the largest number of individuals as happy as may be, for a little while at least, some time before they die.

Infancy is not what it is cracked up to be. The child seems happy all the time to the adult, because the adult knows that the child is untouched by the real problems of life; if the adult were similarly untouched he is sure that he would be happy. But children, not knowing that they are having an easy time, have a good many hard times. Growing and learning and obeying the rules of their elders, of fighting against them, are not easy things to do. Adolescence is certainly far from a uniformly pleasant period. Early manhood might be the most glorious time of all were it not that the sheer excess of life and vigor gets a fellow into continual scrapes. Of middle age the best that can be said is that a middle aged person has likely learned how to have a little fun in spite of his troubles.

It is to old age that we look for reimbursement, the most of us. And most of us look in vain. For the most of us have been wrenched and racked, in one way or another, until old age is the most trying time of all.

In the Almost Perfect State every person shall have at least ten years before he dies of easy, carefree, happy living ··· things will be so arranged economically that this will be possible for each individual.

Personally we look forward to an old age of dissipation and indolence and unreverend disrepute. In fifty years we shall be ninety-two years old. We intend to work rather hard during those fifty years and accumulate enough to live on without working any more for the next ten years, for we have determined to die at the age of one hundred two.

During the last ten years we shall indulge our self in many things that we have been forced by circumstances to forego. We have always been compelled, and we

---

corking /ˈkɔːkɪŋ/ *adj.* excellent; very good

crack up **a.** rhapsodize about **b.** laugh unrestrainedly

scrape /skreɪp/ *n.* an area where the skin is torn or worn off; an indication of damage

reimbursement /ˌriːɪmˈbɜːsmənt/ *n.* compensation paid (to someone) for damages or losses or money already spent etc.

wrench /rentʃ/ *v.* pull or twist it violently, in order to move or remove it

rack /ræk/ *v.* torment emotionally or mentally

dissipation /ˌdɪsɪˈpeɪʃən/ *n.* **a.** breaking up and scattering by dispersion **b.** useless or profitless activity; using or expending or consuming thoughtlessly or carelessly

indolence /ˈɪndələns/ *n.* laziness, inactivity resulting from a dislike of work

disrepute /ˌdɪsrɪˈpjuːt/ *n.* the state of being held in low esteem

forego /fɔːˈɡəʊ/ *v.* decide to do without it; go back further

shall be compelled for many years to come, to be prudent, cautious, staid, sober, conservative, industrious, respectful of established institutions, a model citizen. We have not liked it, but we have been unable to escape it. Our mind, our logical faculties, our observation inform us that the conservatives have the right side of the argument in all human affairs. But the people whom we really prefer as associates, though we do not approve their ideas, are the rebels, the radicals, the wastrels, the vicious, the poets, the idealists, the nuts, the Lucifers, the agreeable good-for-nothings, the sentimentalists, the prophets, the freaks. We have never dared to know any of them, far less become intimate with them.

staid /steɪd/ *adj.* serious, dull, and rather old-fashioned
associate /əˈsəʊʃieɪt/ *n.* a person who joins with others in some activity
wastrels /ˈweɪstrəl/ *n.* someone who dissipates resources self-indulgently
freak /friːk/ *n.* a person very enthusiastic about a thing or activity, caring about nothing else; an abnormal or deformed monstrous person, animal or plant
ribald /ˈrɪbəld/ *adj.* humorously vulgar, offensive vulgar
recline /rɪˈklaɪn/ *v.* **a.** move the upper body backwards and down **b.** lean in a comfortable resting position
bellow /ˈbeləʊ/ *v.* shout angrily in a loud, deep voice
beverage /ˈbevərɪdʒ/ *n.* any liquid suitable for drinking
decanter /dɪˈkæntə/ *n.* a bottle with a stopper; for serving wine or water
caliber /ˈkælɪbə/ *n.* diameter of a tube or gun barrel
pinch /pɪntʃ/ *v.* **a.** squeeze tightly between the fingers **b.** irritate as if by a nip, pinch, or tear
dissolute /ˈdɪsəˌluːt/ *adj.* acting in a wicked and immoral way

Between the years of ninety-two and a hundred and two, however, we shall be the ribald, useless, drunken outcast person we have always wished to be. We shall have a long white beard and long white hair; we shall not walk at all, but recline in a wheel chair and bellow for alcoholic beverages; in the winter we shall sit before the fire with our feet in a bucket of hot water, with a decanter of corn whiskey near at hand, and write ribald songs against organized society; strapped to one arm of our chair will be a forty-five caliber revolver, and we shall shoot out the lights when we want to go to sleep, instead of turning them off; when we want air we shall throw a silver candlestick through the front window and be damned to it; we shall address public meetings to which we have been invited because of our wisdom in a vein of jocund malice. We shall ... but we don't wish to make any one envious of the good time that is coming to us ... we look forward to a disreputable, vigorous, unhonored and disorderly old age.

(In the meantime, of course, you understand you can't have us pinched and deported for our yearnings.)

We shall know that the Almost Perfect State is here when the kind of old age each person wants is possible to him. Of course, all of you may not want the kind we want ... some of you may prefer prunes and morality to the bitter end. Some of you may be dissolute now and may look forward to becoming like one of the nice old fellows in a Wordsworth* poem. But for our part we have always been a hypocrite and we shall have to continue being a hypocrite for a good many years yet, and we yearn to come out in our true colors at last. The point is, that no matter what you want to be, during those last ten years, that you may be in the Almost Perfect State.

Any system of government under which the individual does all the sacrificing for the sake of the general good, for the sake of the community, the State, gets off on its wrong foot. We don't want things that cost us too much. We don't want too much strain all the time.

The best good that you can possibly achieve is not good enough if you have to strain yourself all the time to reach it. A thing is only worth doing, and doing again and again, if you can do it rather easily, and get some joy out of it.

Do the best you can, without straining yourself too much and too continuously, and leave the rest to God. If you strain yourself too much you'll have to ask God to patch you up. And for all you know, patching you up may take time that it was planned to use some other way.

BUT ... overstrain yourself now and then. For this reason: The things you create easily and joyously will not continue to come easily and joyously unless you yourself are getting bigger all the time. And when you overstrain yourself you are assisting in the creation of a new self — if you get what we mean. And if you should ask us suddenly just what this has to do with the picture of the old guy in the wheel chair we should answer: Hanged if we know, but we seemed to sort o' run into it, somehow.

Interplanetary communication is one of the persistent dreams of the inhabitants of this oblate spheroid on which we move, breathe and suffer for lack of beer. There seems to be a feeling in many quarters that if we could get speech with the Martians, let us say, we might learn from them something to our advantage. There is a disposition to concede the superiority of the fellows Out There ⋯ just as some Americans capitulate without a struggle to poets from England, rugs from Constantinople, song and sausage from Germany, religious enthusiasts from Hindustan and cheese from Switzerland, although they have not tested the goods offered and really lack the discrimination to determine their quality. Almost the only

---

oblate /ˈɒbleɪt/ *a.* being flattened at the poles
spheroid /ˈsfɪərɔɪd/ *n.* a shape like but not exactly of a sphere
capitulate /kəˈpɪtjʊˌleɪt/ *v.* surrender under agreed conditions

foreign importations that were ever sneezed at in this country were Swedish matches and Spanish influenza.

But are the Martians ⋯ if Martians there be ⋯ any more capable than the persons dwelling between the Woolworth Building* and the Golden Horn*, between Shwe Dagon* and the First Church, Scientist, in Boston, Mass.? Perhaps the Martians yearn toward earth, romantically, poetically, the Romeos swearing by its light to the Juliets; the idealists and philosophers fabling that already there exists upon it an ALMOST PERFECT STATE—and now and then a wan prophet lifting his heart to its gleams, as a cup to be filled from Heaven with fresh waters of hope and courage. For this earth, it is also a star.

We know they are wrong about us, the lovers in the far stars, the philosophers, poets, the prophets ⋯ or are they wrong?

They are both right and wrong, as we are probably both right and wrong about them. If we tumbled into Mars or Arcturus* of Sirius this evening we should find the people there discussing the shimmy, the jazz, the inconstancy of cooks and the iniquity of retail butchers, no doubt ⋯ and they would be equally disappointed by the way we flitter, frivol, flutter and flivver.

And yet, that other thing would be there too ⋯ that thing that made them look at our star as a symbol of grace and beauty.

Men could not think of THE ALMOST PERFECT STATE if they did not have it in them ultimately to create THE ALMOST PERFECT STATE.

We used sometimes to walk over the Brooklyn Bridge, that song in stone and steel of an engineer who was also a great artist, at dusk, when the tides of shadow flood in from the lower bay to break in a surf of glory and mystery and illusion against the tall towers of Manhattan. Seen from the middle arch of the bridge at twilight, New York with its girdle of shifting waters and its drift of purple cloud and its quick pulsations of unstable light is a miracle of splendor and beauty that lights up the heart like the laughter of a god.

fable /ˈfeɪbl/ *v.* invent or cook up
wan /wɒn/ *adj.* **a.** abnormally deficient in color as suggesting physical or emotional distress; **b.** lacking vitality as from weariness or illness or unhappiness
shimmy /ˈʃɪmɪ/ *n.* lively dancing (usually to ragtime music) with much shaking of the shoulders and hips
iniquity /ɪˈnɪkwɪtɪ/ *n.* absence of moral or spiritual values; an unjust act
flitter /ˈflɪtə/ *v.* move back and forth very rapidly
frivol /ˈfrɪvəl/ *v.* act frivolously
flutter /ˈflʌtə/ *v.* move along rapidly and lightly; skim or dart
girdle /ˈgɜːdəl/ *n.* an encircling or ringlike structure

But, descend. Go down into the city. Mingle with the details. The dirty old shed from which the "L" trains and trolleys put out with their jammed and mangled thousands for flattest Flatbush and the unknown bourne of ulterior Brooklyn is still the same dirty old shed; on a hot, damp night the pasty streets stink like a paperhanger's overalls; you are trodden and over-ridden by greasy little profiteers and their hopping victims; you are encompassed round about by the ugly and the sordid, and the objectionable is exuded upon you from a myriad candid pores; your elation and your illusion vanish like ingenuous snowflakes that have kissed a hot dog sandwich on its fiery brow, and you say: "Beauty? Aw, h—l! What's the use?"

And yet you have seen beauty. And beauty that was created by these people and people like these.··· You have seen the tall towers of Manhattan, wonderful under the stars. How did it come about that such growths came from such soil—that a breed lawless and sordid and prosaic has written such a mighty hieroglyphic against the sky? This glamor out of a pigsty ... how come? How is it that this hideous, half-brute city is also beautiful and a fit habitation for demi-gods? How come?

It comes about because the wise and subtle deities permit nothing worthy to be lost. It was with no thought of beauty that the builders labored; no conscious thought; they were masters or slaves in the bitter wars of commerce, and they never saw as a whole what they were making; no one of them did. But each one had had his dream. And the baffled dreams and the broken visions and the ruined hopes and the secret desires of each one labored with him as he labored; the things that were lost and beaten and trampled down went into the stone and steel and gave it soul; the aspiration denied and the hope abandoned and the vision defeated were the things that lived, and not the apparent purpose for which each one of all the millions sweated and toiled or cheated; the hidden things, the silent things, the winged things, so weak they are easily killed, the unacknowledged things, the rejected beauty, the strangled appreciation, the inchoate art, the submerged spirit—these groped and found each other and gathered themselves together and worked themselves into the tiles and mortar of the edifice and made a town that is a worthy fellow of the sunrise and the sea

mangle /ˈmæŋgəl/ v. alter so as to make unrecognizable
bourne /bɔːn/ n. an archaic term for a boundary
paperhanger /ˈpeɪpəˌhæŋə/ n. a person who hangs wallpaper as an occupation
profiteer /ˌprɒfɪˈtɪə/ n. someone who makes excessive profit (especially on goods in short supply)
encompass /ɪnˈkʌmpəs/ v. include in scope; include as part of something broader
elation /ɪˈleɪʃən/ n. a feeling of great happiness and excitement
prosaic /prəʊˈzeɪɪk/ a. dull and uninteresting
hieroglyphic /ˌhaɪərəˈglɪfɪk/ a. of or concerning a form of writing using picture symbols
baffled /ˈbæfəld/ a. perplexed or bewildered
inchoate /ɪnˈkəʊeɪt/ a. recent or new; vague or not yet properly developed
mortar /ˈmɔːtə/ n. a mixture of sand, water, and cement or lime used to cover walls

winds.

        Humanity triumphs over its details.

conglomerate /kənˈɡlɒmərɪt/ *adj.* composed of heterogeneous elements
high spot the most interesting or memorable part
two-spots a card with two pips; two; deuce

    The individual aspiration is always defeated of its perfect fruition and expression, but it is never lost; it passes into the conglomerate being of the race.

    The way to encourage yourself about the human race is to look at it first from a distance; look at the lights on the high spots. Coming closer, you will be profoundly discouraged at the number of low spots, not to say two-spots. Coming still closer, you will become discouraged once more by the reflection that the same stuff that is in the high spots is also in the two-spots.

Cultural Notes

1. **Donald Robert Perry Marquis** (1878—1937) was a poet, novelist, humorist, journalist, newspaper columnist, and author from New York City. He was born in Illinois in 1878, and did newspaper work in Philadelphia and Atlanta before coming to *The Sun* in 1912. He is remembered best for creating the characters "Archy" and "Mehitabel", supposed authors of humorous verse. Marquis began work for the newspaper *The Evening Sun* in 1912 and edited for the next eleven years a daily column, "The Sun Dial". During 1922 he left *The Evening Sun* for the *New York Tribune*, where his daily column, "The Tower" (later "The Lantern") was a great success. He regularly contributed columns and short stories to the *Saturday Evening Post, Collier's* and *American* magazines and also appeared in *Harper's, Scribner's, Golden Book,* and *Cosmopolitan.*

2. **William Wordsworth** (1770—1850), British poet, credited with ushering in the English Romantic Movement with the publication of *Lyrical Ballads* (1798) in collaboration with Samuel Taylor Coleridge. Wordsworth was one of the most popular of all English poets whose poems are mainly about the beauty of nature and its relationship with all human beings. Many of them describe the countryside of the **Lake District** in north-west England, where he was born and spent most of his life. His best-known works include *Lyrical Ballads* (1798), *Poems* (1807) and *The Prelude,* a long poem about his early life and his intense experiences of nature then, which was published in 1850 after his death.

3. **The Woolworth Building** was designed by architect Cass Gilbert and completed on a piece of land in 1913. With a height of 792 feet (241 meters) this building is one of the oldest skyscrapers in the United States. The land for the building was purchased by F. W. Woolworth in 1910. More than a century after the start of its construction, it remains, at 57 stories, one of the fifty tallest buildings in the United States as well as one of the twenty tallest buildings in New York City. It is a National Historic Landmark and a New York City landmark.

4. **The Golden Horn** is an inlet of the Bosphorus dividing the city of Istanbul and forming the natural harbor that has sheltered Greek, Roman, Byzantine, Ottoman and other ships for thousands of years. It is a scimitar-shaped estuary that joins the Bosphorus just at the point where that strait enters the Sea of Marmara, thus forming a peninsula the tip of which is "Old Istanbul" (ancient Byzantion and Constantinople). Its Greek and English names mean the same, but the significance of the designation "golden" is obscure, while its Turkish name Haliç simply means "estuary". It has witnessed many tumultuous historical incidents, and its dramatic vistas have been the subject of countless works of art.

5. **The Shwedagon Pagoda**, also known in English as the **Great Dagon Pagoda** and the **Golden Pagoda**, is a 99 metre (325 ft) gilded pagoda and stupa located in Yangon, Burma. The pagoda lies to the west of Kandawgyi Lake, on Singuttara Hill, thus dominating the skyline of the city. It is the most sacred Buddhist pagoda for the Burmese with relics of the past four Buddhas enshrined within

6. **Arcturus** (/ɑrkˈtjʊərəs/) is the brightest star in the constellation Boötes and the northern celestial hemisphere. It is the fourth brightest star in the night sky, a relatively close star at only 36.7 light-years from Earth, and, together with Vega and Sirius, one of the most luminous stars in the Sun's neighborhood.

Comprehension Exercises

I. Answer the following questions based on the text.

1. What does the writer endeavor to reveal when talking about "the almost perfect state"?
2. What is the writer's understanding of the most wonderful government?
3. What does the writer mean when he mentions the old age as a time of dissipation,

indolence and unreverend disrepute? Provide your own understanding?

4. In the sentence "Interplanetary communication is one of the persistent dreams of the inhabitants of this oblate spheroid on which we move, breathe and suffer for lack of beer", what does the "oblate spheroid" refer to?

5. Please comment on the statement "Humanity triumphs over its details".

II. Decide whether each of the following statements is true or false according to the text.

1. Even if the adult, just like a child, were similarly untouched, he cannot make sure whether he would be happy.
2. According to the text, the infants feel carefree and happy as the adults have been imagining.
3. If you find that a thing deserving effort is very difficult to achieve, you would get joy out of it and get ready to repeat it.
4. We are always informed to follow the conservatives as they are always right in their position in all human affairs.
5. If you find it is pretty hard to achieve something very important for you, you would give up it even it is concerned about creating a new self.

III. Select the most suitable word or phrases and fill in the following blanks in their proper form if necessary.

associate	bellow	baffle	capitulate	dissipation
dissolute	disrepute	elation	indolent	iniquity
mangle	prosaic	rack	recline	reimbursement
ribald	staid	wrench		

1. All these office workmen may not get _____ for the measure that they have adopted turn out to be less effective.
2. Two policemen pile on top of the thief, _____ his arms behind his back and handcuff him.
3. What pains him is that his 8-year-old infirm son has been _____ by high fever.
4. In the new era, the new government should put stress on mindless _____ of natural resources.
5. The path of diligence is the path to immortality, and the way of _____ is the way to death.
6. It is a disgrace that such people should bring our vocation into _____.
7. Once a model of _____ stability, Dutch political life has been volatile in recent years.

8. During the summer both male and female alligators _____ to catch the attention of the opposite sex.
9. My cousin would _____ on a couch, and I would seize some opportunity of edging up to him.
10. I am also shocked to hear that he should be leading a _____ lifestyle, but that is probably just a nasty rumor.
11. Besieged in a few strongholds, the enemy _____ on the condition that they would be granted to return home voluntarily.
12. In this novel he exposed the various corruptions of capitalism and railed against the _____ of capitalism at his own time.
13. All the school children are told to cherish the communal establishments and they are also told not to _____ public property.
14. His instructor offered a more _____ explanation for the surge in interest.
15. Sam's complete disappearance, as though he had melted into thin air, admittedly has _____ all the experts.

IV. Try to paraphrase the following sentences, paying special attention to the underlined parts.

1. Infancy is not what it is <u>cracked up</u> to be.

2. <u>Early manhood</u> might be the most glorious time of all <u>were it not that the sheer excess of life and vigor</u> gets a fellow into continual scrapes.

3. Personally we look forward to <u>an old age of dissipation and indolence and unreverend disrepute</u>.

4. If you <u>strain yourself</u> too much you'll have to ask God to <u>patch you up</u>.

5. There is <u>a disposition</u> to concede the superiority of the fellows Out There …

V. Discuss with your partner about each of the three statements and write an essay in no less than 250 words about your understanding of one of them.

1. The most wonderful governmental system in the world does not attract us, as a system; we are after a system that scarcely knows it is a system.

2. We have always been compelled, and we shall be compelled for many years to come, to be prudent, cautious, staid, sober, conservative, industrious, respectful of established institutions, a model citizen.

3. The best good that you can possibly achieve is not good enough if you have to strain yourself all the time to reach it.

VI. List four websites where we can learn more about Don Marquis and provide a brief introduction to each of them.

1. _____

2. _____

3. _____

4. _____

Twenty Minutes' Reading

You are required to read the following two sections within 20 minutes.

SECTION A

What is the nature of the scientific attitude, the attitude of the man or woman who studies and applies physics, biology, chemistry, geology, engineering, medicine or any other science? We all know that science plays an important role in the societies in which we live. Many people believe, however, that our progress depends on two different aspects of science. The first of these is the application of the machines, products and systems of applied knowledge that scientists and technologists develop. Through technology, science improves the structure of society and helps man to gain increasing control over his environment.

The second aspect is the application by all members of society of the special methods of thought and action that scientists use in their work.

What are these special methods of thinking and acting? First of all, it seems that a successful scientist is full of curiosity — he wants to find out how and why the universe works. He usually directs his attention towards problems which he notices have no satisfactory explanation, and his curiosity makes him look for underlying relationships even if the data available seem to be unconnected. Moreover, he thinks he can improve the existing conditions and enjoys trying to solve the problems which this involves.

He is a good observer, accurate, patient and objective and applies logical thought to the observations he makes. He utilizes the facts he observes to the fullest extent. For example, trained observers obtain a very large amount of information about a star mainly from the accurate analysis of the simple lines that appear in a spectrum.

He is skeptical—he does not accept statements which are not based on the most complete evidence available—and therefore rejects authority as the sole basis for truth. Scientists always check statements and make experiments carefully and objectively to verify them.

Furthermore, he is not only critical of the work of others, but also of his own, since he knows that man is the least reliable of scientific instruments and that a number of factors tend to disturb objective investigation.

Lastly, he is highly imaginative since he often has to look for relationships in data which are not only complex but also frequently incomplete. Furthermore, he needs imagination if he wants to make hypotheses of how processes work and how events take place.

These seem to be some of the ways in which a successful scientist or technologist thinks and acts.

1. Many people believe that science helps society to progress through _____.
   A. applied knowledge
   B. more than one aspect
   C. technology only
   D. the use of machines
2. Which of the following statements is INCORRECT about curiosity?
   A. It gives the scientist confidence and pleasure in work.
   B. It gives rise to interest in problems that are unexplained.
   C. It leads to efforts to investigate potential connections.
   D. It encourages the scientist to look for new ways of acting.
3. According to the passage, a successful scientist would not _____.
   A. easily believe in unchecked statements
   B. easily criticize others' research work
   C. always use his imagination in work
   D. always use evidence from observation
4. What does the passage mainly discuss?
   A. Application of technology.
   B. Progress in modem society.
   C. Scientists' ways of thinking and acting.
   D. How to become a successful scientist.
5. What is the author's attitude towards the topic?
   A. Critical.   B. Objective.   C. Biased.   D. Unclear.

SECTION B

Over the past several decades, the U.S., Canada, and Europe have received a great deal of media and even research attention over unusual phenomena and unsolved mysteries. These include UFOs as well as sightings and encounters with "nonhuman creatures" such as Bigfoot and the Loch Ness monster. Only recently has Latin America begun to receive some attention as well. Although the mysteries of the Aztec, Mayan, and Inca civilizations have been known for centuries, now the public is also becoming aware of unusual, paranormal phenomena in countries such as Peru.

The Nazca "lines" of Peru were discovered in the 1930s. These lines are deeply carved into a flat, stony plain, and form about 300 intricate pictures of animals such as birds, a monkey, and a lizard. Seen at ground level, the designs are a jumbled senseless mess. The images are so large that they can only be viewed at a height of 1,000 feet — meaning from an aircraft. Yet there were no aircraft in 300 B.C., when it is judged the designs were made. Nor were there then, or are there now, any nearby mountain ranges from which to view them. So how and why did the native people of Nazca create these marvelous designs? One answer appeared in 1969, when the German researcher and writer Erich von Daniken proposed that the lines were drawn by extraterrestrials as runways for their aircraft. The scientific community did not take long to scoff at and abandon von Daniken's theory. Over the years several other theories have been put forth, but none has been accepted by the scientific community.

  Today there is a new and heightened interest in the Nazca lines. It is a direct result of the creation of the Internet. Currently there are over 60 sites dedicated to this mystery from Latin America's past, and even respected scientists have joined the discussion through e-mail and chat rooms.

  Will the Internet help explain these unsolved mysteries? Perhaps it is a step in the right direction.

6. Which of the following statements is INCORRECT?
   A. Latin America has long received attention for unusual phenomena.
   B. Public attention is now directed towards countries like Peru.
   C. Public interest usually focuses on North America and Europe.
   D. Some ancient civilizations have unsolved mysteries.
7. According to the passage, the Nazca lines were found_____.
   A. in mountains   B. in stones   C. on animals   D. on a plain
8. We can infer from the passage that the higher the lines are seen, the _____ the images they present.
   A. smaller   B. larger   C. clearer   D. brighter
9. There has been increasing interest in the Nazca lines mainly because of_____.
   A. the participation of scientists   B. the emergence of the Internet
   C. the birth of new theories   D. the interest in the Internet
10. The author is _____ about the role of the Internet in solving mysteries.
   A. cautious   B. pessimistic   C. uncertain   D. optimistic

Unit Six

Text A

Middle Age, Old Age
W. S. Maugham

I think I have been more than most men conscious of my age. My youth slipped past me unnoticed and I was always burdened with the sense that I was growing old. Because for my years I had seen much of the world and traveled a good deal, because I was somewhat widely read and my mind was occupied with matters beyond my years, I seemed always older than my contemporaries. But it was not till the outbreak of the war in 1914 that I had an inkling that I was no longer a young man. I found then to my consternation that a man of forty was old. I consoled myself by reflecting that this was only for military purposes, but not so very long afterwards I had an experience which put the matter beyond doubt, I had been lunching with a woman whom I had known a long time and her niece, a girl of seventeen. After luncheon we took a taxi to go somewhere or other. The woman got in and then her niece. But the niece sat down on the strapontin leaving the empty seat at the back beside her aunt for me to sit on. It was the civility of youth (as opposed to the rights of sex) to a gentleman no longer young. I realized that she looked upon me with the respect due to age.

It is not a very pleasant thing to recognize that for the young you are no longer an equal. You belong to a different generation. For them your race is run. They can look up to you; they can admire you, but you are apart from them, and in the long run they will always find the companionship of persons of their own age more grateful than yours.

But middle age has its compensations. Youth is bond hand and foot with the shackles of public opinion. Middle age enjoys freedom. I remember that when I left school I said to myself: "Henceforward I can get up when I like and go to bed when I like." That of course was an exaggeration, and I soon found that the trammeled life of the civilized man

---

inkling /ˈɪŋklɪŋ/ *n.* a slight suggestion or vague understanding
consternation /ˌkɒnstəˈneɪʃən/ *n.* a feeling of anxiety or fear
console /kənˈsəʊl/ *v.* try to make them feel more cheerful
strapontin /strəˈpɒntɪn/ *n.* foldstool, or folding chair
trammel /ˈtræməl/ *v.* to hinder or restrain

only permits of a modified independence. Whenever you have an aim you must sacrifice something of freedom to achieve it. But by the time you have reached middle age you have discovered how much freedom it is worth while to sacrifice in order to achieve any aim that you have in view. When I was a boy I was tortured by shyness, and middle age has to great extent brought me a relief from this. I was never of great physical strength and long walks used to tire me, but I went through them because I was ashamed to confess my weakness. I have now no such feeling and I save myself much discomfort. I always hated cold water, but for many years I took cold baths and bathed in cold seas because I wanted to be like everybody else. I used to dive from heights that made me nervous. I was mortified because I played games worse than other people. When I did not know a thing I was ashamed to confess my ignorance. It was not till quite late in life that I discovered how easy it is to say: "I don't know." I find with middle age that no one expects me to walk five and twenty miles, or to play a scratch game of golf, or to dive from a height of thirty feet. This is all to the good and makes life pleasant; but I should no longer care if they did. That is what makes youth unhappy, the vehement anxiety to be like other people, and that is what makes middle age tolerable, the reconciliation with oneself.

mortified /ˈmɔːtɪfaɪd/ *adj.* extremely offended, ashamed or embarrassed
scratch /skrætʃ/ *adj.* that is put together in a hurried way
vehement /ˈviːɪmənt/ *adj.* violent; fervid; intense in emotions or convictions
reconciliation /ˌrekənˌsɪlɪˈeɪʃən/ *n.* getting two things or people to correspond with each other
allotted /əˈlɔtid/ *adj.* given as a share or task
contingency /kənˈtɪndʒənsi/ *n.* **a.** sth. that might happen in the future **b.** a plan or measure that is intended to be used if a possible situation actually occur
scythe /saɪð/ *n.* a tool with a long curved blade at right angles to a long handle, esp. used to cut long grass or grain

Yesterday I was seventy years old. As one enters upon each succeeding decade it is natural, though perhaps irrational, to look upon it as a significant event. When I was thirty my brother said to me: "Now you are a boy no longer, you are a man and you must be a man." When I was forty I said to myself: "It's no good fooling myself, this is middle age and I may just as well accept it." At sixty I said: "Now it's time to put my affairs in order, for this is the threshold of old age and I must settle my accounts." I decided to withdraw from the theatre and I wrote The Summing Up, * in which I tried to review for my own comfort what I had learnt of life and literature, what I had done and what satisfaction it had brought me. But of all anniversaries I think the seventieth is the most momentous. One has reached the three score years and ten which one is accustomed to accept as the allotted span of man, and one can but look upon such years as remain to one as uncertain contingencies stolen while old Time with his scythe has his head turned the other way. At seventy one is no longer on the threshold of old age. One is just an old man.

On the continent of Europe they have an amiable custom when a man who has achieved some distinction reaches that age, his friends, his colleagues, his disciples (if he has any) join together to write a volume of essays in his honor. In England we give our eminent men no such flattering mark of our esteem. At the utmost we give a dinner, and we don't do that unless he is very eminent indeed.

My own birthday passed without ceremony. I worked as usual in the morning and in the afternoon went for a walk in the solitary woods behind my house.

I went back to my house, made myself a cup of tea and read till dinner time. After dinner I read again, played two or three games of patience, listened to the news on the radio and took a detective story to bed with me. I finished it and went to sleep. Except for a few words to my colored maids I had not spoken to a soul all day.

So I passed my seventieth birthday and so I would have wished to pass it. I mused.

Two or three years ago I was walking with Liza and she spoke, I don't know why, of the horror with which the thought of old age filled her.

"Don't forget," I told her, "that when you're old you won't have the desire to do various things that make life pleasant to you now. Old age has its compensations."

"What?" she asked.

"Well, you need hardly ever do anything you don't want to. You can enjoy music, art and literature, differently from when you were young, but in that different way as keenly. You can get a good deal of fun out of observing the course of events in which you are no longer intimately concerned. If your pleasures are not so vivid your pains also have lost their sting."

I could see that all this seemed cold comfort, and even as I spoke I realized that it afforded a somewhat gray prospect. When later I came to think it over, it occurred to me that the greatest compensation of old age is its freedom of spirit. I suppose that is accompanied by a certain indifference to

amiable /ˈeɪmɪəbəl/ *adj.* friendly and pleasant to be with

disciple /dɪˈsaɪpəl/ *n.* someone who believes in the ideas of a great teacher, esp. a religious one, and follows him

esteem /ɪˈstiːm/ *n.* the admiration and respect toward someone

many of the things that men in their prime think important. Another compensation is that it liberates you from envy, hatred and malice. I do not believe that I envy anyone. I have made the most I could of such gifts as nature provided me with; I do not envy the success of others. I am quite willing to vacate the little niche I have occupied so long and let another step into it. I no longer mind what people think of me. They can take me or leave me. I am mildly pleased when they appear to like me and undisturbed if I know they don't. I have long known that there is something in me that antagonizes certain persons; I think it very natural, no one can like everyone; and their ill will interests rather than discomposes me. I am only curious to know what it is in me that is antipathetic to them. Nor do I mind what they think of me as a writer. On the whole I have done what I set out to do, and the rest does not concern me. I have never much cared for the notoriety which surrounds the successful writer and which many of us are simple enough to mistake for fame, and I have often wished that I had written under a pseudonym so that I might have passed through the world unnoticed. I did indeed write my first novel under one, and only put my own name to it because my publisher warned me that the book might be violently attacked and I did not wish to hide myself under a made-up name. I suppose few authors can help cherishing a secret hope that they will not be entirely forgotten the moment they die, and I have occasionally amused myself by weighing the chances I have of survival for a brief period.

> **prime** /praɪm/ *n.* the period of greatest prosperity or productivity; the time of maturity when power and vigor are greatest
> **malice** /ˈmælɪs/ *n.* behaviour that is intended to harm people or their reputations, or embarrass and upset them
> **niche** /nɪtʃ, niːʃ/ *n.* the job or activity which is exactly suitable for someone
> **antagonize** /ænˈtæɡəˌnaɪz/ *v.* provoke the anger or hostility of
> **discompose** /ˌdɪskəmˈpəʊz/ *v.* to disturb the composure of; disconcert
> **antipathetic** /ænˌtɪpəˈθetɪk/ *adj.* strongly opposed or arousing a strong aversion
> **reincarnation** /ˌriːɪnkɑːˈneɪʃən/ *n.* a second or new birth; embodiment in a new form
> **corporeal** /kɔːˈpɔːrɪəl/ *a.* concerning the body as opposed to the mind or spirit

I have been asked on occasion whether I would like to live my life over again. On the whole it has been a pretty good life, perhaps better than most people's, but I should see no point in repeating it. It would be as idle as to read again a detective story that you have read before. But supposing there were such a thing as reincarnation, belief in which is explicitly held by three quarters of the human race, and one could choose whether or no one would enter upon a new life on earth, I have in the past sometimes thought that I should be willing to try the experiment on the chance that I might enjoy experiences which circumstances and my own idiosyncrasies, spiritual and corporeal, have prevented me from enjoying, and learn the many things that I have not had the time or the occasion to learn. But now I should refuse. I have had enough. I neither believe in immortality nor desire it. I

> should like to die quickly and painlessly, and I am content to be assured that with my last breath my soul, with its aspirations and its weaknesses, will dissolve into nothingness. I have taken to heart what Epicurus* wrote to Menoeceus*: "Become accustomed to the belief that death is nothing to us. For all good and evil consists in sensation, but death is deprivation of sensation. And therefore a right understanding that death is nothing to us makes the mortality of life enjoyable, not because it adds to it an infinite span of time, but because it takes away the craving for immortality. For there is nothing terrible in life for the man who has truly comprehended that there is nothing terrible in not living."

> **mortality** /mɔːˈtælɪti/ *n.* the quality or state of being mortal; the ratio of deaths in an area to the population of that area

Cultural Notes

1. **W. Somerset Maugham** (1874—1965) was an English novelist, playwright, and short-story writer. He abandoned a short career in medicine when his first novel, *Liza of Lambeth* (1897), had some success. His plays, mainly Edwardian social comedies, brought him financial security. His reputation rests primarily on the novels *Of Human Bondage* (1915), *The Moon and Sixpence* (1919), *Cakes and Ale* (1930), and *The Razor's Edge* (1944), all of which were adapted for film and some for television. His short stories often portray the confusion of Europeans in alien surroundings. His works, regarded less highly today than formerly, are characterized by a clear, unadorned style, cosmopolitan settings, and a shrewd understanding of human nature.

2. **Epicurus** (341—270 BCE) was an ancient Greek philosopher and the founder of Epicureanism. Of his 300 written works, only a few fragments and letters remain. Epicurus held that the purpose of philosophy was to attain the happy, tranquil life, characterized by peace and freedom from fear as well as the absence of pain. He taught that pleasure and pain are the measures of what is good and evil; death is the end of both body and soul and should therefore not be feared; the gods do not reward or punish humans; the universe is infinite and eternal; and events in the world are ultimately based on the motions and interactions of atoms moving in empty space.

3. **Menoeceus** refers to a figure from ancient Greek mythology, a descendant of the Sparti and the father of Jocasta and Creon, who sacrificed himself to end a plague in Thebes. In the war of the Seven Argives against Thebes, Teiresias

declared that the Thebans should conquer, if Menoeceus would sacrifice himself for his country. Menoeceus accordingly killed himself outside the gates of Thebes.

Comprehension Exercises

I. Answer the following questions based on the text.

1. When did the author begin to have a vague idea that he himself was no longer young?
2. What was the author's feeling when he was over forty?
3. What are the major compensations of old age according to the text? Try to say something about them.
4. What kind of suggestion can we get from this utterance: "If your pleasures are not so vivid your pains also have lost their sting."
5. What was the author's attitude towards death and mortality at the end of the excerpt?

II. Decide whether each of the following statements is true or false according to the text.

1. The author did not realize he was old because he had read more books and seen more things than his contemporaries.
2. The girl of seventeen left the empty seat at the back of the taxi for the author to take, for he was the only man in the taxi.
3. According to the text, the allotted life span is commonly believed to be sixty years.
4. When the writer reached seventy, friends, his colleagues, his students joined together to write a volume of essays in his honor.
5. Later on, the writer found out that the greatest compensation of old age is its freedom of spirit.

III. Select the most suitable word or phrases and fill in the following blanks in their proper form.

allotted	amiable	antagonize	antipathetic
aspirations	console	consternation	corporeal
disciple	discomposed	esteem	inkling
malice	morbidity	mortality	mortify
prime	vehement		

1. Actually I came across few high school students who have no _____ about computing technology.
2. To his family's _____, he should become a publisher of comic books when he returned to Indonesia after his four-year-study of biology in America in 1978.
3. The only _____ for the baseball team is that they look likely to get another chance.
4. In a statement at the time of making his comments, Mr. Frost apologized and said he was _____ by the offence that he had caused.
5. She suddenly became very _____ and agitated, jumping around and shouting.
6. To their great contentment, all the settlers are _____ the available farmland after the government came to power.
7. Roberts is an immensely _____, engaging personality who easily relates to people and seems to genuinely care for other people.
8. Socrates was a great philosopher and a major intellectual figure with many a _____ throughout Athens at his own time, among them Xenophon and Plato.
9. For the past decade, this brilliant engineer has been held in high _____ by colleagues in the construction industry.
10. We cannot fail to notice that some athletes are still trying to come back although they are well past their _____.
11. Last week, he said he bore no _____ to Mary despite the life-changing injuries he had actually brought upon her.
12. These newly employed are told to be always respectful of any officials, follow their instructions even if they are wrong, and do not _____ them.
13. He was _____ when he heard the bad news that three people were criticized for his own fault.
14. It seemed that this old lady, holding fast on the traditional idea of education, was _____ to modern ways of education.
15. Descartes insisted — as part of his proof of the 'cogito' — that the mind or spiritual things must be utterly distinct from _____ things.

IV. Try to paraphrase the following sentences, paying special attention to the underlined parts.

1. <u>My youth slipped past me unnoticed</u> and I was always burdened with the sense that I was growing old.

2. But the niece sat down on the strapontin leaving the empty seat at the back

beside her aunt for me to sit on. It was the civility of youth (as opposed to the rights of sex) to a gentleman no longer young.

3. When I was a boy I was tortured by shyness, and middle age has to great extent brought me a relief from this.

4. On the continent of Europe they have an amiable custom when a man who has achieved some distinction reaches that age, his friends, his colleagues, his disciples join together to write a volume of essays in his honor. In England we give our eminent men no such flattering mark of our esteem.

5. I have long known that there is something in me that antagonizes certain persons; I think it very natural, no one can like everyone; and their ill will interests rather than discomposes me.

V. Discuss with your partner about each of the three statements and write an essay in no less than 250 words about your understanding of one of them.

1. But middle age has its compensations. Youth is bond hand and foot with the shackles of public opinion.

2. Whenever you have an aim you must sacrifice something of freedom to achieve it. But by the time you have reached middle age you have discovered how much freedom it is worth while to sacrifice in order to achieve any aim that you have in view.

3. For all good and evil consists in sensation, but death is deprivation of sensation.

VI. List four websites where we can learn more about W. S. Maugham and his major literary works and provide a brief introduction to each of them.

1. _____
_____.

2. _____
_____.

3. _____
_____.

4. _____
_____.

Text B

Men Are Very Delicate
Barbara Cawthorne Crafton*

I think I have to fire a man. I have tried warnings and changes in the job description and other changes in the work location and God knows what else. But it has become clear that he has no intention of working at the level of excellence of which he is capable and which his colleagues <u>maintain</u>, that he may be less than <u>candid</u> in his reporting of the work he does do, and that his fellow employees see all this and are wondering how long it's going to go on. So do my superiors, who also, then, wonder about *me*.

He has had <u>detractors</u> for years. People have been telling on this guy ever since I became his supervisor. I have suspected that some of the <u>snitching</u> is racist, and I still think that. I have suspected that some of the misgivings I myself have had about his work may be racist, too, the impatience of a <u>WASP</u> who hits the ground running with a person of another, more leisurely culture, one that was producing masterpieces of literature and sculpture when my ancestors were sitting around a campfire painting themselves blue. But dammit, I say to myself, I didn't paint myself blue, and he didn't write those

maintain /meɪnˈteɪn/ *v.* to hold; to keep up
candid /ˈkændɪd/ *adj.* open; frank; ingenuous; outspoken
detractor /dɪˈtræktə/ *n.* one who criticize or belittles the worth of sth. or somebody
snitching /snɪtʃ/ *n.* the act of giving away information about somebody
WASP White Anglo-Saxon Protestant

poems. We're just trying to do a job here, and I don't think he's trying very hard. I have kept him on too long for the good of the group already.

He has a wife and two children. Can I put a father out of his job? When should I do it? Before Christmas so his unemployment can start the first of January? Or should I let him get through the holidays in innocence? What if he argues with me? What if he begs me to keep him on? What if he hates me? What if he drew my name for the office Christmas party?

I have known for a long time that one of my biggest enemies is my own desire to make men feel good. I threw spelling bees so that boys could win them. I remember one that I did not throw, and I am *still* cut by the hate in the glance Patrick Reeves shot me thirty years ago as I spelled "foreign" correctly and won. I have felt responsible for men's inadequacies all my life, it seems, and have expended a fair amount of energy shoring them up, patching them together so well that the stitches barely show. I have felt responsible for helping them to conceal the areas in which they fall short, creating distractions from these unpleasantnesses by serving as a loud cheerleader for the smallest of their virtues.

This makes me a very kind boss. I love everything they do. If I don't love it, I feel it's somehow my fault. In a way that I now think emasculating, I have wanted to pick up after them, cleaning up their messes, following them with an invisible whisk broom and dust pan into which I sweep their mistakes so that nobody else will see them. In doing this, I deny them the opportunity to learn from the consequences of their errors, the painful but educational road people have to travel to advance. I have to fight myself—hard—to avoid showing these hurtful kindnesses.

I am not alone in this. Generations of women have made sure men looked smart and strong, and have made sure *they* didn't appear too smart and strong in the presence of the Other Kind. The male ego, we were told, simply couldn't tolerate the threat. It was only recently that we gave ourselves political permission to stop doing this. At last, we said,

throw /θrəʊ/ *v.* to lose deliberately
spelling bee a contest in which you are eliminated if you fail to spell a word correctly
cut /kʌt/ *v.* hurt
inadequacy /ɪnˈædɪkwɪəsi/ *n.* a lack of competence
shore (up) /ʃɔː/ *v.* to support by placing against sth. solid or rigid
emasculate /mæskjʊleɪt/ *v.* to deprive of masculine vigor or spirit; to weaken
whisk broom a small short-handled broom used to brush clothes
ego /ˈiːɡəʊ/ *n.* your consciousness of your own identity

we can be what we are. What shocked me—continues to shock me—is how reflexive a thing it is for me, still, to try and smooth their paths. I still feel an obligation to support men in their work.

reflexive /rɪˈfleksɪv/ *adj.* automatic
up to one's ears busy
hunt-and-peck an act of typing on a keyboard using only one or two fingers of each hand
stereotypical /ˌsterɪəˈtɪpɪkəl/ *adj.* lacking spontaneity or originality or individuality
spare /speə/ *v.* **a.** to use frugally or carefully **b.** to refrain from harming
threshold /ˈθreʃhəʊld/ *n.* an amount, level, or limit on a scale
frazzled /ˈfræzəld/ *adj.* exhausted
trauma /ˈtrɔːmə/ *n.* any physical damage to the body caused by violence or accident or fracture etc.
tuck /tʌk/ *v.* to insert; to fit into
ambidextrousness /ˌæmbɪˈdekstrəsnɪs/ *n.* the ability to use both hands with equal ease; versatility
snatch /snætʃ/ *n.* **a.** a small piece, fragment, or quantity. **b.** a broken part

I type for a colleague when something has to get finished and all the secretaries are up to their ears. I made my living as a secretary once upon a time, and I'm fast. He uses a slow hunt-and-peck. I offer to help, and am proud of my speed. I love him. And I feel happy to have helped him meet his deadline. But I am also aware that what I have just done is a very stereotypical thing. I've put aside my work to help him finish his. I'll get mine done somehow. I always do.

Why aren't there more famous women composers and rocket scientists? One reason is that men are usually the ones who decide who's going to be famous. The other one is that men can usually find women to help arrange their worlds so they can do their work. Nobody does that for us. Men are encouraged from childhood to be single-minded about their work, not to allow any distractions. And women are encouraged from childhood to set things up for them so that they don't have any. Don't make so much noise; your father is working. And when do we do our work? Late at night, when everyone is sleeping. Or early in the morning, before anyone else is up.

As a result of being spared like this, men have a low threshold for distraction. They are *delicate*. They are made nervous by having to do more than one thing at a time. They feel frazzled and angry if they have to answer three phone calls, and have a hard time settling back to work after the trauma. Women, on the other hand, develop the skill of doing many things at once. They tuck the phone in between their shoulders and their ears, hold a baby on one hip, stir a pot on the stove, all the while thinking about an idea for a story. They don't think it's unfair to have to do this. They think it's normal.

Women are just more complex than men about work. We've learned how to be that way. We've learned to love our ambidextrousness, our snatches of solitary time, and to make the most of them. For years I got up at five so I could write with no kids around. The kids are grown up now, but I still do that. It has become my most creative time. I wouldn't give it up for anything. It's not particularly fair that it was necessary, but there you are. Men do their jobs brilliantly when they have little else to do. I should think they would. If they contended with the additional jobs many women have, they'd measure success differently. And they'd be stronger.

The goddess Kali*, friend of Hindu women, is depicted with nine arms. That's about how many you need. She's not as affirming to men as we tend to be; she rains down death and destruction on those who treat women unjustly, and she doesn't care who they are. I don't know about that. There's got to be a middle ground between our colluding in men's privileging themselves and wanting to kill them. Marrying later may help—more brides today go into marriage with established careers and work habits than used to be the case. They have negotiating skills that ought to help them get a fair shake. Their husbands carry their babies around in canvas slings and shop at the same time. That's progress. But even now, even with babies in slings, the burden of home and child care is not equitably distributed in most marriages.

But it's an imperfect world. Things usually *aren't* equitable. Somebody usually has to give. It's usually the woman, and it usually makes her mad if she has time to think about it, and then she usually gets over being mad and makes the best of it, and grows in complexity as a result. Life is short, and most people don't want to fight their way through it. So couples point out to each other from time to time that things aren't fair, and a fairness that fits is found. It may be a little lopsided, and it's irritating when people pretend it's perfectly symmetrical. It's not. But it fits. That's the important thing.

---

contend /kən'tend/ *v.* to compete for sth.; engage in a contest
affirm /ə'fɜ:m/ *v.* **a.** to declare or assert positively **b.** to make firm; to confirm, or ratify
collude /kə'lu:d/ *v.* to act together secretly to achieve a goal
privilege /'prɪvɪlɪdʒ/ *n.* a special right or advantage limited to a few people of a particular kind; *v.* to grant a privilege to
shake /ʃeɪk/ *n.* treatment; chance
sling /slɪŋ/ an object made of ropes, straps, or cloth that is used for carrying things
equitable /'ekwɪtəbəl/ *adj.* just, fair. —equitably *adv.*
get over to deal with successfully
lopsided /'lɒp'saɪdɪd/ *adj.* turned or twisted toward one side
symmetrical /sɪ'metrɪkəl/ *adj.* having similarity in size, shape, and relative posit

Cultural Notes

1. **Barbara Cawthorne Crafton** is an Episcopal priest living in New York City. Her work has taken her from Trinity Church on Wall Street to the New York waterfront. She is now on the staff of Seamen's Church Institute, serving merchant sailors. Crafton has published essays in magazines and newspapers, including *New Woman, Family Circle,* and the "Hers" column of the *New York Times*. The selection here comes from Crafton's book *The Sewing Room: Uncommon Reflections on Life, Love and Work* (1993).

2. **Kali** is a complex Hindu goddess. She is sometimes identified as the wife of Shiva. She is death and destruction, but, to some she is the instrument of rebirth, too. In Tantric Hinduism, she comes to be the Supreme divinity.

Comprehension Exercises

I. Answer the following questions based on the text.

1. Why does the author want to fire her employee?
2. Why does the author hesitate to fire her employee?
3. Why aren't there more famous women composers and rocket scientists?
4. In what way does the author mean "men are very delicate"?
5. How are women different from men according to the author?

II. Decide whether each of the following statements is true or false according to the text.

1. The man the author wants to fire works as hard as his colleagues after receiving some warnings.
2. The author is a kind, helpful and considerate boss.
3. The author is a WASP.
4. The author feels satisfied with what she did for men in her work.
5. The author was once an efficient secretary.
6. With social progress, the burden of home and child care is now equitably distributed in most marriages now.

III. Select the most suitable word or phrases and fill in the following blanks in their proper form.

affirm	candid	collude	detractor	dexterous
emasculate	equitable	frazzled	inadequacy	patch
pick	privilege	reflexive	shore	sling
snatch	snitch	stereotype	threshold	

1. His wonderful performance after many years of retirement will definitely silence many of his _____ who view that he is already at his wit's end.
2. When asked about her marriage, Natalie is _____ about the problems she is having with Steve.
3. Kids pick up this practice fast. In school if you _____ on others, you become an outcast. That is just awful.
4. Not a few experts hold that our predominant reliance on cyberspace stands in stark contrast to the dire _____ of our cyber security.
5. Meanwhile, Australian foreign minister Alexander Downer arrived in Indonesia to _____ up rocky bilateral relations.
6. One of the mechanics took off the damaged tyre, and took it back to the station to be _____.
7. The boys here are the _____ of the high school's football players and their team is bound to be the champion.
8. To ensure the security of all the other countries, it was quite necessary to get this country's military power largely _____ after its defeat in the Second World War.
9. These feminists have been thinking about how to combat and eradicate the existing _____ of women as sexy model in mass media.
10. Most of us are well aware we are on the _____ of a new era in technology.
11. The bartenders at these establishments are of a different breed, usually older gentlemen dressed smartly and exuding an aura of calm and sophistication that can soothe even the most _____ tourist.
12. One often-heard complaint is that corrupt officials _____ with developers to sell off farmland without giving farmers the proper compensation.
13. The senior citizen had to admit that they generally become less _____ as they were no longer young.
14. Let us never forget the central role education plays in promoting _____ and sustainable development.
15. "This is a propaganda carried out by the opposition to _____ mud at the government," observed this politician.

16. It requires fathers, husbands, sons and brothers to _____ and support the rights of women.

IV. Try to paraphrase the following sentences, paying special attention to the underlined parts.

1. I have <u>tried warnings</u> and changes in <u>the job description</u> and other changes in the work location and <u>God knows what else</u>.

2. He has <u>had detractors</u> for years. People have been <u>telling on</u> this guy ever since I became his supervisor.

3. When should I do <u>it</u>? Before Christmas so <u>his unemployment can start the first of January</u>.

4. I <u>have felt responsible for men's inadequacies</u> all my life, it seems, and have expended a fair amount of energy <u>shoring them up, patching them together</u> so well that <u>the stitches barely show</u>.

5. In a way that I now think <u>emasculating</u>, I have wanted to <u>pick up after them, cleaning up their messes</u>, following them with an invisible whisk broom and dust ban into which I sweep their mistakes so that nobody else will see them.

V. Discuss with your partner about each of the three statements and write an essay in no less than 250 words about your understanding of one of them.

1. Men are usually the ones who decide who's going to be famous.

2. Men are encouraged from childhood to be single-minded about their work, not to allow any distractions. And women are encouraged from childhood to set things up for them so that they don't have any.

3. But it's an imperfect world. Things usually aren't equitable. Somebody usually has to give.

   _____
   _____

VI. List four websites where we can learn more about Barbara Cawthorne Crafton and provide a brief introduction to each of them.

   1. _____
      _____
      _____.

   2. _____
      _____
      _____.

   3. _____
      _____
      _____.

   4. _____
      _____
      _____.

Twenty Minutes' Reading

You are required to read the following two sections within 20 minutes.

Graduation speeches are a bit like wedding toasts. A few are memorable. The rest tend to trigger such thoughts as, "Why did I wear such uncomfortable shoes?"

But graduation speeches are less about the message than the messenger. Every year a few colleges and universities in the US attract attention because they've managed to book high-profile speakers. And, every year, the media report some of these speakers' wise remarks.

Last month, the following words of wisdom were spread:

"You really haven't completed the circle of success unless you can help somebody else move forward." (Oprah Winfrey, Duke University).

"There is no way to stop change; change will come. Go out and give us a future worthy of the world we all wish to create together." (Hillary Clinton, New York University).

"This really is your moment. History is yours to bend." (Joe Biden, Wake Forest University).

Of course, the real "get" of the graduation season was first lady Michelle Obama's appearance at the University of California, Merced. "Remember that you are blessed," she told the class of 2009, "Remember that in exchange for those blessings, you must give something back... As advocate and activist Marian Wright Edelman says, 'Service is the rent we pay for living ... it is the true measure, the only measure of success'."

Calls to service have a long, rich tradition in these speeches. However, it is possible for a graduation speech to go beyond cliché and say something truly compelling. The late writer David Foster Wallace's 2005 graduation speech at Kenyon College in Ohio talked about how to truly care about other people. It gained something of a cult after it was widely circulated on the Internet. Apple Computer CEO Steve Jobs' address at Stanford University that year, in which he talked about death, is also considered one of the best in recent memory.

But when you're sitting in the hot sun, fidgety and freaked out, do you really want to be lectured about the big stuff? Isn't that like trying to maintain a smile at your wedding reception while some relative gives a toast that amounts to "marriage is hard work"? You know he's right; you just don't want to think about it at that particular moment. In fact, as is the case in many major life moments, you can't really manage to think beyond the blisters your new shoes are causing.

That may seem anticlimactic. But it also gets to the heart of one of life's greatest, saddest truths: that our most "memorable" occasions may elicit the fewest memories. It's probably not something most graduation speakers would say, but it's one of the first lessons of growing up.

1. According to the passage, most graduation speeches tend to recall _____ memories.
   A. great   B. trivial   C. unforgettable   D. unimaginative
2. "But graduation speeches are less about the message than the messenger" is explained_____.
   A. in the final paragraph   B. in the last but one paragraph
   C. in the first paragraph   D. in the same paragraph
3. The graduation speeches mentioned in the passage are related to the following themes EXCEPT_____.
   A. death   B. success   C. service   D. generosity
4. It is implied in the passage that at great moments people fail to_____.
   A. remain clear-headed   B. keep good manners
   C. remember others' words   D. recollect specific details

5. What is "one of the first lessons of growing up"?
   A. Attending a graduation ceremony.
   B. Listening to graduation speeches.
   C. Forgetting details of memorable events.
   D. Meeting high-profile graduation speakers.

SECTION B

Cultural rules determine every aspect of food consumption. Who eats together defines social units. For example, in some societies, the nuclear family is the unit that regularly eats together. The anthropologist Mary Douglas has pointed out that, for the English, the kind of meal and the kind of food that is served relate to the kinds of social links between people who are eating together. She distinguishes between regular meals, Sunday meals when relatives may come, and cocktail parties for acquaintances. The food served symbolizes the occasion and reflects who is present. For example, only snacks are served at a cocktail party. It would be inappropriate to serve a steak or hamburgers. The distinctions among cocktails, regular meals, and special dinners mark the social boundaries between those guests who are invited for drinks, those who are invited to dinner, and those who come to a family meal. In this example, the type of food symbolizes the category of guest and with whom it is eaten.

In some New Guinea societies, the nuclear family is not the unit that eats together. The men take their meals in a men's house, separately from their wives and children. Women prepare and eat their food in their own houses and take the husband's portion to the men's house. The women eat with their children in their own houses. This pattern is also widespread among Near Eastern societies.

Eating is a metaphor that is sometimes used to signify marriage. In many New Guinea societies, like that of the Lesu on the island of New Ireland in the Pacific and that of the Trobriand Islanders, marriage is symbolized by the couple's eating together for the first time. Eating symbolizes their new status as a married couple. In U.S. society, it is just the reverse. A couple may go out to dinner on a first date.

Other cultural rules have to do with taboos against eating certain things. In some societies, members of a clan, a type of kin (family) group, are not allowed to eat the animal or bird that is their totemic ancestor. Since they believe themselves to be descended from that ancestor, it would be like eating that ancestor or eating themselves.

There is also an association between food prohibitions and rank, which is found in its most extreme form in the caste system of India. A caste system consists of ranked groups, each with a different economic specialization. In India, there is an association between caste and the idea of pollution. Members of highly ranked groups can be polluted by coming into contact with the bodily secretions, particularly saliva, of individuals of lower-ranked castes. Because of the fear of pollution, Brahmans and other high-ranked individuals will not share food with, not eat from the same plate as, not even accept food from an individual from a low-ranking caste.

6. According to the passage, the English make clear distinctions between_____.
   A. people who eat together
   B. the kinds of food served
   C. snacks and hamburgers
   D. family members and guests
7. According to the passage, who will NOT eat together?
   A. The English.
   B. Americans on their first date.
   C. Men and women in Near Eastern societies.
   D. Newly-weds on the island of New Ireland.
8. According to the passage, eating together indicates all the following EXCEPT_____.
   A. the type of food
   B. social relations
   C. marital status
   D. family ties
9. The last paragraph suggests that in India_____decides how people eat.
   A. pollution
   B. food
   C. culture
   D. social status
10. Which of the following can best serve as the topic of the passage?
    A. Different kinds of food in the world.
    B. Relations between food and social units.
    C. Symbolic meanings of food consumption.
    D. Culture and manners of eating.

Unit Seven

Beauty

Susan Sontag*

For the Greeks, beauty was a virtue: a kind of excellence. Persons then were assumed to be what we now have to call—lamely, enviously—whole persons. If it did occur to the Greeks to distinguish between a person's "inside" and "outside," they still expected that inner beauty would be matched by beauty of the other kind. The well-born young Athenians who gathered around Socrates* found it quite paradoxical that their hero was so intelligent, so brave, so honorable, so seductive—and so ugly. One of Socrates' main pedagogical acts was to be ugly—and teach those innocent, no doubt splendid-looking disciples of his how full of paradoxes life really was.

They may have resisted Socrates' lesson. We do not. Several thousand years later, we are more wary of the enchantments of beauty. We not only split off—with the greatest facility—the "inside" (character, intellect) from the "outside" (looks); but we are actually surprised when someone who is beautiful is also intelligent, talented, good.

It was principally the influence of Christianity that deprived beauty of the central place it had in classical ideals of human excellence. By limiting excellence (*virtus* in Latin) to moral virtue only, Christianity set beauty adrift—as an alienated, arbitrary, superficial enchantment.

lamely /ˈleɪmlɪ/ *adv.* in a way that does not sound very confident
paradox /ˈpærədɒks/ *n.* a situation that seems to have contradictory or inconsistent qualities. —paradoxical *adj.*
seductive /sɪˈdʌktɪv/ *adj.* **a.** tending to seduce, or lead astray **b.** tempting; enticing; interesting
pedagogical /pedəˈgɒdʒɪkəl/ *adj.* of or characteristic of teachers or teaching
disciple /dɪˈsaɪpəl/ *n.* a pupil or follower of any teacher or school of religion, learning, art, etc.
wary /ˈweərɪ/ cautious
facility /fəˈsɪlɪtɪ/ *n.* **a.** ease of doing or making **b.** a ready ability
adrift /əˈdrɪft/ *adj.* **a.** floating freely without being steered **b.** without any particular aim or purpose
alienate /ˈeɪlɪəneɪt/ *v.* to make it difficult for someone to belong to a particular group
arbitrary /ˈɑːbɪtrərɪ/ *adj.* not fixed by rules but left to one's judgment or choice

And beauty has continued to lose prestige. For close to two centuries it has become a convention to attribute beauty to only one of the two sexes: the sex which, however Fair, is always Second. Associating beauty with women had put beauty even further on the defensive, morally.

A beautiful woman, we say in English. But a handsome man. "Handsome" is the masculine equivalent of—and refusal of—a compliment which has accumulated certain demeaning overtones, by being reserved for women only. That one can call a man "beautiful" in French and in Italian suggests that Catholic countries—unlike those countries shaped by the Protestant version of Christianity—still retain some vestiges of the pagan admiration for beauty. But the difference, if one exists, is of degree only. In every modern country that is Christian or post-Christian, women are the beautiful sex—to the detriment of the notion of beauty as well as of women.

To be called beautiful is thought to name something essential to women's character and concerns. (In contrast to men—whose essence is to be strong, or effective, or competent.) It does not take someone in the throes of advanced feminist awareness to perceive that the way women are taught to be involved with beauty encourages narcissism, reinforces dependence and immaturity. Everybody (women and men) knows that. For it is "everybody", a whole society, that has identified being feminine with caring about how one *looks*. (In contrast to being masculine—which is identified with caring about what one is and *does* and only secondarily, if at all, about how one looks.) Given these stereotypes, it is no wonder that beauty enjoys, at best, a rather mixed reputation.

It is not, of course, the desire to be beautiful that is wrong but the obligation to be—or to try. What is accepted by most women as a flattering idealization of their sex is a way of making women feel inferior to what they actually are—or normally grow to be. For the ideal of beauty is administered as a form of self-oppression. Women are taught to see their bodies in parts, and to evaluate each part separately. Breasts, feet, hips, waistline, neck, eyes, nose, complexion, hair, and so on—each in

prestige /preˈstiːʒ/ *n.* **a.** the power to impress. **b.** reputation; renown
compliment /ˈkɒmplɪmənt/ *n.* **a.** an act or expression of courtesy or respect **b.** sth. said in admiration, praise, or flattery
demean /dɪˈmiːn/ *v.* to lower in status or character; degrade; humble
overtone /ˈəʊvətəʊn/ *n.* an implication; nuance
vestige /ˈvestɪdʒ/ *n.* a trace or sign of sth. that once existed but has passed away
pagan /ˈpeɪɡən/ *n.* not Christian, Moslem, or Jewish
detriment /ˈdetrɪmənt/ *n.* damage; injury; harm
in the throes of in the act of struggling with a problem, a decision, task, etc.
narcissism /ˈnɑːsɪsɪzəm/ *n.* excessive self-love
stereotype /ˈsterɪəʊtaɪp/ *n.* a fixed or conventional notion or conception of a person, group, idea, etc.
administer /ədˈmɪnɪstə/ *v.* to give out or dispense punishment or justice

turn is submitted to an anxious, fretful, often despairing scrutiny. Even if some pass muster, some will always be found wanting. Nothing less than perfection will do.

In men, good looks is a whole, something taken in at a glance. It does not need to be confirmed by giving measurements of different regions of the body; nobody encourages a man to dissect his appearance, feature by feature. As for perfection, that is considered trivial—almost unmanly. Indeed, in the ideally good-looking man a small imperfection or blemish is considered positively desirable. According to one movie critic (a woman) who is a declared Robert Redford* fan, it is having that cluster of skin-colored moles on one cheek that saves Redford from being merely a "pretty face." Think of the depreciation of women—as well as of beauty—that is implied in that judgment.

"The privileges of beauty are immense," said Cocteau*. To be sure, beauty is a form of power. And deservedly so. What is lamentable is that it is the only form of power that most women are encouraged to seek. This power is always conceived in relation to men; it is not the power to do but the power to attract. It is a power that negates itself. For this power is not one that can be chosen freely—at least, not by women—or renounced without social censure.

To preen, for a woman, can never be just a pleasure. It is also a duty. It is her work. If a woman does real work—and even if she has clambered up to a leading position in politics, law, medicine, business, or whatever—she is always under pressure to confess that she still works at being attractive. But in so far as she is keeping up as one of the Fair Sex, she brings under suspicion her very capacity to be objective, professional, authoritative, thoughtful. Damned if they do—women are. And damned if they don't.

One could hardly ask for more important evidence of the dangers of considering persons as split between what is "inside" and what is "outside" than that interminable half-comic half-tragic tale, the oppression of women. How easy

fretful /ˈfretfəl/ *adj.* irritable and discontented; peevish
scrutiny /ˈskruːtɪni/ *n.* a close examination; minute inspection
pass muster to be accepted as good enough
dissect /dɪˈsekt/ *v.* **a.** to cut up the body in order to study it **b.** to examine carefully
trivial /ˈtrɪvɪəl/ *adj.* not serious, important, or valuable
blemish /ˈblemɪʃ/ *n.* a small mark on the surface of an object that spoils its appearance
depreciation /dɪpriːʃɪˈeɪʃən/ *n.* a reduction in the value or price of sth.
lamentable /ˈlæməntəbəl/ *adj.* very unsatisfactory or disappointing; terrible
negate /nɪˈgeɪt/ *v.* **a.** to prevent sth. from having any effect **b.** to state that sth. does not exist or is untrue
renounce /rɪˈnaʊns/ *v.* to give up by a formal public statement
censure /ˈsenʃə/ *n.* a condemning as wrong; strong disapproval
preen /priːn/ *v.* **a.** to clean and trim (the feathers) with the beak **b.** to make oneself trim; dress up or adorn oneself
clamber /ˈklæmbə/ *v.* to climb with effort or clumsily
confess /kənˈfes/ *v.* **a.** to admit a fault **b.** to acknowledge an opinion or view. **c.** to declare one's faith in
interminable /ɪnˈtɜːmɪnəbəl/ *adj.* forever; endless

it is to start off by defining women as caretakers of their surfaces, and then to <u>disparage</u> them (or find them adorable) for being "superficial". It is a crude trap, and it has worked for too long. But to get out of the trap requires that women get some critical distance from that excellence and privilege which is beauty, enough distance to see how much beauty itself has been <u>abridged</u> in order to prop up the mythology of the "feminine." There should be a way of saving beauty *from* women—and *for them*.

> **disparage** /dɪsˈpærɪdʒ/ *v.* to speak slightly of; show disrespect for; belittle
> **abridge** /əˈbrɪdʒ/ to reduce in scope, extent, etc.; to lessen or curtail rights, authority, etc.

Cultural Notes

1. **Susan Sontag** (1933—2004) was an American essayist, novelist, human rights activist and leading commentator on modern culture. Her innovative essays on such diverse subjects as camp, pornographic literature, fascist aesthetics, photography, AIDS, and revolution have gained a wide attention. Sontag also writes screenplays and directed films. She has a great impact on experimental art in the 1960s and 1970s, and has introduced many new stimulating ideas to American culture.

2. **Socrates** (470 BC—399 BC) was a classical Greek philosopher. He is best known for the creation of Socratic Irony and the Socratic Method. Specifically, he is renowned for developing the practice of a philosophical type of pedagogy in which the teacher asks students questions to elicit the best answer and fundamental insight. Socrates is credited with exerting a powerful influence upon the founders of Western philosophy, most particularly Plato and Aristotle, and while Socrates' principal contribution to philosophy is in the field of ethics, he also makes important and lasting contributions to the fields of epistemology and logic. His willingness to call everything into question and his determination to accept nothing less than an adequate account of the nature of things make him the first clear exponent of critical philosophy.

3. **Charles Robert Redford, Jr.** (1936—) is among the biggest American movie stars of the 1970s. In spite of an increasingly rare onscreen presence in subsequent years, he remains a powerful motion-picture industry force as an Academy Award-winning director as well as a highly visible champion of American independent filmmaking.

4. **Jean Maurice Eugène Clément Cocteau** (1889—1963) was a French poet, novelist, dramatist, playwright and filmmaker. Like Victor Hugo and Charles

Baudelaire, he intended his artistic work to serve a dual purpose—to be entertaining and political. His versatile, unconventional approach and enormous output brought him international acclaim.

Comprehension Exercises

I. I. Answer the following questions based on the text.
1. What does Sontag want to say most in the text?
2. Why is beauty associated with women and why does it enjoy a mixed reputation?
3. How does beauty mean differently to the Greeks, Socrates and Christians?
4. How was Socrates different from other Greeks?
5. What might be an ideal woman like, according to Sontag?
6. What does Sontag suggest women to do?

II. Decide whether each of the following statements is true or false according to the text.
1. Susan Sontag disagrees with Socrates.
2. Susan Sontag means that people don't have to be wary of the enchantment of beauty.
3. It is possible for someone to be beautiful, intelligent and good at once.
4. Christian culture is hostile to both beauty and women.
5. Catholic countries are more prejudiced against beauty than Protestant countries.
6. Susan Sontag favors feminism.
7. Susan Sontag believes that external beauty does not matter for a woman.
8. Susan Sontag believes that women are taught in a wrong way.

III. Select the most suitable word or phrases and fill in the following blanks in their proper form if necessary.

adrift	arbitrary	blemish	demean	facility
fretful	lamely	muster	overtone	paradoxical
pedagogical	prestige	renounce	seductive	throes
trivial	vestige	wary		

1. And here I have _____ related to you the uneventful chronicle of two foolish children in a flat who most unwisely sacrificed for other the greatest treasures of their house.

2. _____, the less you have to do the more you may resent the work that does come your way.

3. And her response to all of us alternated between _____ charm and sudden hostility.

4. The school district provides training to help teachers improve their _____ methods.

5. Such talents can give these smart students a _____ for certain skills that allow them to excel, while more hardworking students never manage to reach a comparable level.

6. Amy had the growing sense that she was _____ and isolated from the rest of the world after her 20 years' absence.

7. It is very terrible to learn that _____ arrests and detention without trial are common in this remote place.

8. It was his responsibility for foreign affairs that gained him international _____ .

9. The female get-togethers have become characterized by a strange sort of competitiveness in which the women alternately boast about their children and _____ their husbands.

10. "My life is my work and my work is my life" implies an extremely high level of devotion. There is an _____ of sacrifice and selflessness.

11. He and others wonder how this _____ of the old country will accommodate the arrival of modern public health standards.

12. It was my first time in America and I was in the heady _____ of my first lovelorn experience, savouring the most delicious freedom I had ever known.

13. After a period of practice, he was able to pass _____ as a qualified teacher.

14. The survivor's sleep may be _____, concentration becomes impaired, and assumptions about personal safety are replaced by uncertainty.

15. But in all Israel there was none to be so much praised as Absalom for his beauty: from the sole of his foot even to the crown of his head there was no _____ in him.

IV. Try to paraphrase the following sentences, paying special attention to the underlined parts.

1. Persons then were <u>assumed</u> to be what we now have to call—<u>lamely, enviously</u>—<u>whole persons</u>.

_____

_____

2. We not only split off — with the greatest facility — the "inside" (character, intellect) from the "outside" (looks); but we are actually surprised when someone who is beautiful is also intelligent, talented, good.

3. By limiting excellence to moral virtue only, Christianity set beauty adrift — as an alienated, arbitrary, superficial enchantment.

4. "Handsome" is the masculine equivalent of — and refusal of — a compliment which has accumulated certain demeaning overtones, by being reserved for women only.

5. But to get out of the trap requires that women get some critical distance from that excellence and privilege which is beauty, enough distance to see how much beauty itself has been abridged in order to prop up the mythology of the "feminine".

V. Discuss with your partner about each of the three statements and write an essay in no less than 250 words about your understanding of one of them.

1. Beauty is a virtue, a kind of excellence.

2. It is indubitable that human life is really full of paradoxes.

3. To be sure, beauty is a form of power.

VI. List four websites where we can learn more about Susan Sontag and provide a brief introduction to each of them.

1. _____

2. _____
_____.

3. _____
_____.

4. _____
_____.

Text B

Cinderella's Stepsisters
Toni Morrison*

Let me begin by taking you back a little. Back before the days at college. To nursery school, probably, to a once-upon-a-time time when you first heard, or read, or, I suspect, even saw "Cinderella*." Because it is Cinderella that I want to talk about; because it is Cinderella who causes me a feeling of urgency. What is unsettling about that fairy tale is that it is essentially the story of household—a world, if you please—of women gathered together and held together in order to abuse another woman. There is, of course, a rather vague absent father and a nick-of-time prince with a foot fetish. But neither has much personality. And there are the surrogate "mothers", of course (god- and step-), who contribute both to Cinderella's grief and to her release and happiness. But it is her stepsisters who interest me. How crippling it must have been for those young girls to grow up with a mother, to watch and imitate that mother, enslaving another girl.

I am curious about their fortunes after the story ends. For contrary to recent adaptations, the stepsisters were not ugly, clumsy, stupid girls with outsize feet. The Grimm collection* describes them as "beautiful and fair in appearance". When

abuse /ə'bju:z/ *v.* to treat in a harmful, injurious, or offensive way; to speak insultingly, harshly, and unjustly to or about
nick-of-time the critical moment, the exact instant at which sth. has to take place
fetish /'fetɪʃ/ *n.* (in psychology) an object whose presence is necessary for sexual satisfaction
surrogate /'sʌrəgɪt/ *n.* a substitute
crippling /'krɪplɪŋ/ *adj.* having a severe adverse effect on; weakening seriously

we are introduced to them they are beautiful, elegant, women of status, and clearly women of power. Having watched and participated in the violent dominion of another woman, will they be any less cruel when it comes their turn to enslave other children, or even when they are required to take care of their own mother?

It is not a wholly medieval problem. It is quite a contemporary one: feminine power when directed at other women has historically been wielded in what has been described as a "masculine" manner. Soon you will be in a position to do the very same thing. Whatever your background—rich or poor—whatever the history of education in your family—five generations or one—you have taken advantage of what has been available to you at Barnard* and you will therefore have both the economic and social status of the stepsisters *and* you will have their power.

dominion /dəˈmɪnjən/ *n.* the power or right to rule
medieval /ˌmedɪˈiːvəl/ *adj.* of, pertaining to, characteristic of, or in the style of the Middle Ages; (*Informal*) extremely old-fashioned; primitive
feminine /ˈfemɪnɪn/ *adj.* pertaining to a woman or girl; belonging to the female sex; female
wield /wiːld/ *v.* to exercise (power, authority, influence, etc.), as in ruling or dominating
agency /ˈeɪdʒənsɪ/ *n.* an organization, company, or bureau that provides some service for another; a governmental bureau, or an office that represents it
stay one's hand to cease action; to stop or halt; check
deflect /dɪˈflekt/ *v.* to turn aside or cause to turn aside; turn aside and away from an initial or intended course
decency /ˈdiːsənsɪ/ *n.* the quality of being socially acceptable
killing floor /ˈwɪðə/ the slaughtering room of an abattoir, a slaughter house
wither /ˈwɪðə/ *v.* to cause (esp. plant) to become reduced in size, color, etc.
deserving /dɪˈzɜːvɪŋ/ *adj.* qualified for or having a claim to reward, assistance, etc.
expendable /ɪksˈpendəbəl/ *adj.* not strictly necessary; dispensable

I want not to *ask* you but to *tell* you not to participate in the oppression of your sisters. Mothers who abuse their children are women, and another woman, not an agency, has to be willing to stay their hands. Mothers who set fire to school buses are women, and another woman, not an agency, has to tell them to stay their hands. Women who stop the promotion of other women in careers are women, and another woman must come to the victim's aid. Social and welfare workers who humiliate their clients may be women, and other women colleagues have to deflect their anger.

I am alarmed by the violence that women do to each other: professional violence, competitive violence, emotional violence. I am alarmed by the willingness of women to enslave other women. I am alarmed by a growing absence of decency on the killing floor of professional women's worlds. You are the women who will take your place in the world where *you* can decide who shall flourish and who shall wither; you will make distinctions between the deserving poor and the undeserving poor; where you can yourself determine which life is expendable and which is indispensable. Since you will have the power to do it, you may also be persuaded that you have the right to do it. As educated women the distinction between the two is first-order business.

first-order first-class
rainbow /ˈreɪnbəʊ/ *n.* a visionary goal; any brightly multicolored arrangement or display
status quo the existing state or condition, also status in quo
diminish /dɪˈmɪnɪʃ/ *v.* to make or cause to seem smaller, less important; lessen; reduce
emanate /ˈeməneɪt/ *v.* to flow out, issue, or proceed, as from a source or origin; come forth; originate
abstraction /əbˈstrækʃn/ *n.* an abstract or general idea or term; the act of considering sth. as a general quality or characteristic, apart from concrete realities, specific objects, or actual instances

    I am suggesting that we pay as much attention to our nurturing sensibilities as to our ambition. You are moving in the direction of freedom and the function of freedom is to free somebody else. You are moving toward self-fulfillment, and the consequences of that fulfillment should be to discover that there is something just as important as you are and that just-as-important thing may be Cinderella—or your stepsister.

    In your rainbow journey toward the realization of personal goals, don't make choices based only on your security and your safety. Nothing is safe. That is not to say that anything ever was, or that anything worth achieving ever should be. Things of value seldom are. It is not safe to have a child. It is not safe to challenge the status quo. It is not safe to choose work that has not been done before, or to do old work in a new way. There will always be someone there to stop you. But in pursuing your highest ambitions, don't let your personal safety diminish the safety of your stepsister. In wielding the power that is deservedly yours, don't permit it to enslave your stepsisters. Let your might and your power emanate from that place in you that is nurturing and caring.

    Women's rights is not only an abstraction, a cause; it is also a personal affair. It is not only about "us"; it is also about me and you. Just the two of us.

Cultural Notes

1. **Toni Morrison** (1931—   ) is the first African American woman to receive the Nobel Prize for Literature (1993). She is widely recognized for her epic power, unerring ear for dialogue, and her poetically-charged and richly-expressive depictions of Black America. In her novels she focuses on the experience of black Americans, particularly emphasizing black women's experience in a racist and male-dominated society and their search for cultural identity. She uses fantasy and mythic elements along with realistic depiction of racial, gender and class conflict. "Cinderella's Stepsisters" is a speech given at **Barnard** College.

2. "**Cinderella**" is a fairy tale or folk tale written by the Grimm Brothers

(Jacob and Wilhelm) and collected in **The Grimm Fairy Tales**. In the story, the titular heroine is maltreated by a malevolent stepmother, but marries a prince and achieves happiness through the benevolent intervention of a fairy godmother.

Comprehension Exercises

I. I. Answer the following questions based on the text.
1. Why is Morrison interested in the story of Cinderella?
3. What is professional violence, competitive violence or emotional violence, according to Morrison?
4. What is the first-order business to educated women, according to Morrison?
5. Why does Morrison say that women's rights is a personal affair?
6. What does Morrison mean by the last sentence?

II. Decide whether each of the following statements is true or false according to the text.
1. There is a detailed description of man characters in "Cinderella".
2. Having watched and participated in the violent dominion of another woman, Cinderella's stepsisters will be as cruel when it comes their turn to enslave other children, or even when they are required to take care of their own mother.
3. The problem is that feminine power has always been used in a masculine manner when directed at women.
4. In professional women's worlds, the competition is fierce and violent, even at the price of decency.
5. According to Morrison, nurturing sensibilities are as important as ambition.

III. Select the most suitable word or phrases and fill in the following blanks in their proper form if necessary.

abstraction	abuse	agency	crippling	decency
deflect	deserving	diminish	dominion	emanate
expendable	flourish	medieval	nick-of-time	status
surrogate	wield	wither		

1. However, if our continuing _____ of natural resources continues at this rate unchecked, we can be anything but optimistic about our species' future.
2. If you decided to go ahead with it, and if you had not time to tell me

personally, you might ask your _____ Mary to phone me.

3. The lack of competitiveness is _____ all the firms across Italy's most productive region, the northeast.
4. Four of the ____ Towers have been converted into places of accommodation, each sleeping four to six people.
5. The insurgents _____ most influence in areas which are mostly poor and dominated by tribespeople.
6. They have been trying to _____ public attention from the charge that their candidate, the President, was improperly involved in the notorious affair.
7. My belief comes from nothing but the unyielding faith in the _____ and generosity of the hospitable local people.
8. It was an exasperating thing for me to see my body gradually _____ away before my own eyes.
9. To be frankly, I'd love to keep the glorious honor to myself, but I think he is _____ of it as he has contributed so much to our company.
10. But in the 1990s, companies fired these _____ women in an attempt to protect male lifetime employment.
11. I am certain that the passing of time will never _____ our friendship no matter how far and how long we are away from each other.
12. I can still remember the days when the heady aroma of wood smoke _____ from the stove with my grandmother enjoying a cup of hot and heavy tea.
13. Knowledge is to summarize and abstract human experience, characterized with _____ and universality.
14. There are not a few people who are strongly opposed to any form of reforms in Croatia and are content with the _____ quo.
15. It's from that story we have the idea that mankind is responsible or has _____ over the animals and the earth.

IV. Try to paraphrase the following sentences, paying special attention to the underlined parts.

1. There is, of course, <u>a rather vague absent father</u> and a <u>nick-of-time prince with a foot fetish</u>.

   _____
   _____

2. Social and welfare <u>workers who humiliate their clients</u> may be women, and other women colleagues have to <u>deflect their anger</u>.

   _____
   _____

3. I am alarmed by the growing absence of decency on the killing floor of professional women's worlds.

4. You are the women who will take your place in the world where you can decide who shall flourish and who shall wither; you will make distinctions between the deserving poor and the undeserving poor; where you can yourself determine which life is expendable and which is indispensible.

5. Let your might and power emanate from that place in you that is nurturing and caring.

V. Discuss with your partner about each of the three statements and write an essay in no less than 250 words about your understanding of one of them.

1. When directed at other women, feminine power has historically been wielded in what has been described as a "masculine" manner.

2. In pursuing your highest ambitions, don't let your personal safety diminish the safety of your stepsister.

3. In wielding the power that is deservedly yours, don't permit it to enslave your stepsisters.

VI. List four websites where we can learn more about Toni Morrison and provide a brief introduction to each of them.

1. _____

2. _____

3. _____
_____
_____.
4. _____
_____
_____.

Twenty Minutes' Reading

You are required to read the following two sections within 20 minutes.

 **SECTION A**

Do you realize that every time you take a step, the bones in your hip are subjected to forces between four and five times your body weight? When you are running, this force is increased further still. What happens if through disease a hip-joint ceases to be able to resist such forces? For many years hip-joints and other body joints have been replaceable either partially or completely. It is after all a simple ball and socket joint; it has certain loads imposed on it; it needs reliability over a defined life; it must contain materials suitable for the working environment. Any engineer will recognize these as characteristic of a typical engineering problem, which doctors and engineers have worked together to solve, in order to bring a fresh lease of life to people who would otherwise be disabled.

This typifies the way in which engineers work to help people and create a better quality of life. The fact that this country has the most efficient agricultural industry in the world is another good example. Mechanical engineers have worked with farmers and biologists to produce fertilizers, machinery and harvesting systems. This team effort has now produced crops uniformly waist high or less so that they are better suited to mechanical harvesting. Similar advances with other crops have released people from hard and boring jobs for more creative work, whilst machines harvest crops more efficiently with less waste. Providing more food for the rapidly increasing population is yet another role for the mechanical engineer.

1. According to the passage, when would most weight be imposed on hip-joints?
   A. When one is walking   B. When one is running
   C. When one is standing   D. When one is lying down

2. Engineers regard the replacement of hip-joints as a(n) _____ Problem.
   A. mechanical   B. medical   C. health   D. agricultural
3. According to the passage, how do engineers contribute to increasing efficiency of the agricultural industry?
   A. By working with farmers.
   B. By working in teams.
   C. By growing crops of the same height.
   D. By making agricultural machinery.
4. According to the context, "This team effort" in Paragraph Two refers to _____.
   A. mechanical engineers   B. doctors and engineers
   C. biologists, doctors and farmers   D. farmers, biologists and engineers

SECTION B

Nowadays, a cell phone service is available to everyone, everywhere. Probably thousands of people have already been using it, but I just discovered it, so I'm going to claim it and also name it: Fake Foning.

The technology has been working well for me at the office, but there are infinite applications. Virtually in any public space.

Say you work at a big university with lots of talky faculty members buzzing about. Now, say you need to use the restroom. The trip down the hall will take approximately one hour, because a person can't walk into those talky people without getting pulled aside for a question, a bit of gossip, a new read on a certain line of Paradise Lost.

So, a cell phone. Any cell phone. Just pick it up. Don't dial. Just hold that phone to your face and start talking. Walk confidently down the hall engaged in fake conversation, making sure to tailor both the topic and content to the person standing before you whom you are trying to evade.

For standard colleague avoidance, I suggest fake chatting about fake business:

"Yes, I'm glad you called, because we really need to hammer out the details. What's that? Yes, I read Page 12, but if you look at the bottom of 4, I think you can see the problem begins right there."

Be animated. Be engaged in your fake fone conversation. Make eye contact with the people passing, nod to them, gesture keen interest in talking to them at a later time, point to your phone, shrug and move on.

Shoppers should consider fake foning anytime they spot a talky neighbor in the produce department pinching (用手捏) unripe peaches. Without your phone at your face, you'd be in for a 20-minute speech on how terrible the world is.

One important caution about fake foning. The other day I was fake foning my way past a colleague, and he was actually following me to get my attention. I knew he wanted to ask about a project I had not yet finished. I was trying to buy myself some time, so I continued fake foning with my doctor. "So I don't need the operation? Oh, doctor, that is the best news."

And then: Brrrrrng! Brrrrrmg! Brrrrrmg! My phone started ringing, right there while it was planted on my face. My colleague looked at me, and I looked at him, and naturally I gasped. "What is the matter with this thing?" I said, pulling the phone away to look at it, and then putting it back to my ear.

"Hello? Are you still there?"

Oops.

5. Which of the following statements is INCORRECT?
   A. Cell phone service is popular among people.
   B. Cell phone has much use in office.
   C. Fake foning is a new cell phone service.
   D. Fake foning is a new discovery.

6. What is fake foning?
   A. A strategy to avoid people.
   B. A device newly produced.
   C. A service provided everywhere.
   D. A skill of communication.

7. In the author's opinion, in order to make fake foning look real one has to _____.
   A. talk about interesting matters
   B. behave politely to people passing by
   C. hold the phone while walking
   D. appear absorbed in conversation

8. What does the last example show?
   A. One effective way is to fake fone one's doctor.
   B. One has to be careful while fake foning.
   C. Fake foning may not deceive people.
   D. Fake foning is always quite successful.

9. After his phone suddenly began ringing, the author _____.
   A. immediately started talking to the caller
   B. immediately started talking to his colleague
   C. put the phone away and stopped talking
   D. continued with his fake conversation

10. What is the tone of the passage?
    A. Critical.   B. Humorous.   C. Serious.   D. Unclear.

Unit Eight

In Praise of Idleness
Bertrand Russell*

Like most of my generation, I was brought up on the saying: "Satan finds some mischief for idle hands to do." Being a highly virtuous child, I believed all that I was told, and acquired a conscience which has kept me working hard down to the present moment. But although my conscience has controlled my actions, my opinions have undergone a revolution. I think that there is far too much work done in the world, that immense harm is caused by the belief that work is virtuous, and that what needs to be preached in modern industrial countries is quite different from what always has been preached. Everyone knows the story of the traveler in Naples who saw twelve beggars lying in the sun (it was before the days of Mussolini*), and offered a lira to the laziest of them. Eleven of them jumped up to claim it, so he gave it to the twelfth. This traveler was on the right lines. But in countries which do not enjoy Mediterranean sunshine idleness is more difficult, and a great public propaganda will be required to inaugurate it. I hope that, after reading the following pages, the leaders of the YMCA* will start a campaign to induce good young men to do nothing. If so, I shall not have lived in vain.

Before advancing my own arguments for laziness, I must dispose of one which I cannot accept. Whenever a person who already has enough to live on proposes to engage in some everyday kind of job, such as school-teaching or typing, he or she is told that such conduct takes the bread out of other people's mouths, and is therefore wicked. If this argument were valid, it would only be necessary for us all to be idle in order that we should all have our mouths full of bread. What people who say such things forget is that what a man earns he usually spends, and in spending he gives employment. As long as a man spends his income, he puts just as much bread into people's mouths in spending as he takes out of other people's mouths in earning. The real villain, from this point of view, is the man who saves.

mischief /ˈmɪstʃɪf/ *n.* **a.** reckless or malicious behavior that causes discomfort or annoyance in others **b.** the quality or nature of being harmful or evil

preach /priːtʃ/ *v.* **a.** deliver a sermon **b.** speak, plead, or argue in favor of

lira /ˈlɪrə/ *n.* the basic unit of money in Turkey or in Italy in the past

inaugurate /ɪnˈɔːgjuˌreɪt/ *v.* **a.** commence officially **b.** open ceremoniously or dedicate formally

If he merely puts his savings in a stocking, like the proverbial French peasant, it is obvious that they do not give employment. If he invests his savings, the matter is less obvious, and different cases arise.

One of the commonest things to do with savings is to lend them to some Government. In view of the fact that the bulk of the public expenditure of most civilized Governments consists in payment for past wars or preparation for future wars, the man who lends his money to a Government is in the same position as the bad men in Shakespeare who hire murderers. The net result of the man's economical habits is to increase the armed forces of the State to which he lends his savings. Obviously it would be better if he spent the money, even if he spent it in drink or gambling.

But, I shall be told, the case is quite different when savings are invested in industrial enterprises. When such enterprises succeed, and produce something useful, this may be conceded. In these days, however, no one will deny that most enterprises fail. That means that a large amount of human labor, which might have been devoted to producing something that could be enjoyed, was expended on producing machines which, when produced, lay idle and did no good to anyone. The man who invests his savings in a concern that goes bankrupt is therefore injuring others as well as himself. If he spent his money, say, in giving parties for his friends, they (we may hope) would get pleasure, and so would all those upon whom he spent money, such as the butcher, the baker, and the bootlegger. But if he spends it (let us say) upon laying down rails for surface cars in some place where surface cars turn out not to be wanted, he has diverted a mass of labor into channels where it gives pleasure to no one. Nevertheless, when he becomes poor through failure of his investment he will be regarded as a victim of undeserved misfortune, whereas the gay spendthrift, who has spent his money philanthropically, will be despised as a fool and a frivolous person.

All this is only preliminary. I want to say, in all seriousness, that a great deal of harm is being done in the modern world by belief in the virtuousness of work, and that the road to happiness and prosperity lies in an organized diminution of work.

---

bulk /bʌlk/ *n.* the main part
net result the final result of something
bootlegger /ˈbuːtˌlegə/ *n.* someone who makes or sells; smuggler of illegal liquor
surface car refers to a car (as a streetcar) for transportation on land as opposed to a subway or elevated car
divert /daɪˈvɜːt/ *v.* **a.** turn aside; turn away from **b.** send on a course or in a direction different from the planned or intended one
spendthrift /ˈspendθrɪft/ *n.* someone who spends money prodigally or wastefully
philanthropically /ˌfɪlənˈθrɒpɪkəli/ *adv.* in a philanthropic manner; in a humanitarian way
preliminary /prɪˈlɪmɪnəri/ *adj.* rudimentary; happening before sth. that is more important
diminution /ˌdɪmɪˈnjuːʃən/ *n.* reduction in size, importance, or intensity

First of all: what is work? Work is of two kinds: first, altering the position of matter at or near the earth's surface relatively to other such matter; second, telling other people to do so. The first kind is unpleasant and ill paid; the second is pleasant and highly paid. The second kind is capable of indefinite extension: there are not only those who give orders, but those who give advice as to what orders should be given. Usually two opposite kinds of advice are given simultaneously by two organized bodies of men; this is called politics. The skill required for this kind of work is not knowledge of the subjects as to which advice is given, but knowledge of the art of persuasive speaking and writing, i.e. of advertising.

Throughout Europe, though not in America, there is a third class of men, more respected than either of the classes of workers. There are men who, through ownership of land, are able to make others pay for the privilege of being allowed to exist and to work. These landowners are idle, and I might therefore be expected to praise them. Unfortunately, their idleness is only rendered possible by the industry of others; indeed their desire for comfortable idleness is historically the source of the whole gospel of work. The last thing they have ever wished is that others should follow their example.

From the beginning of civilization until the Industrial Revolution, a man could, as a rule, produce by hard work little more than was required for the subsistence of himself and his family, although his wife worked at least as hard as he did, and his children added their labor as soon as they were old enough to do so. The small surplus above bare necessaries was not left to those who produced it, but was appropriated by warriors and priests. In times of famine there was no surplus; the warriors and priests, however, still secured as much as at other times, with the result that many of the workers died of hunger. This system persisted in Russia until 1917, and still persists in the East; in England, in spite of the Industrial Revolution, it remained in full force throughout the Napoleonic wars*, and until a hundred years ago, when the new class of manufacturers acquired power. In America, the system came to an end with the Revolution, except in the South, where it persisted until the Civil War. A system which lasted so long and ended so recently has naturally left a profound impress upon men's thoughts and opinions. Much that we take for granted about the desirability of work is derived from this system, and, being pre-industrial, is not adapted to the modern

simultaneously /ˌsaɪməlˈteɪniəsli/ *adv.* at the same instant

gospel /ˈgɒspəl/ *n.* **a.** an unquestionable truth; **b.** the written body of teachings of a religious group that are generally accepted by that group; **c.** a doctrine that is believed to be of great importance

appropriate /əˈprəʊprɪɪt/ *v.* take sth. for yourself with no right to do this; take possession of by force, as after an invasion

world. Modern technique has made it possible for leisure, within limits, to be not the prerogative of small privileged classes, but a right evenly distributed throughout the community. The morality of work is the morality of slaves, and the modern world has no need of slavery.

prerogative /prɪˈrɒgətɪv/ *n.* a right reserved exclusively by a particular person or group
part with give up what is not strictly needed
subsist /səbˈsɪst/ *v.* live (on); sustain; support oneself
compulsion /kəmˈpʌlʃən/ *n.* an uncontrollably strong desire to do something
munitions /mjuːˈnɪʃənz/ *n.* military equipment and supplies, especially bombs, shells, and guns

It is obvious that, in primitive communities, peasants, left to themselves, would not have parted with the slender surplus upon which the warriors and priests subsisted, but would have either produced less or consumed more. At first, sheer force compelled them to produce and part with the surplus. Gradually, however, it was found possible to induce many of them to accept an ethic according to which it was their duty to work hard, although part of their work went to support others in idleness. By this means the amount of compulsion required was lessened, and the expenses of government were diminished. To this day, 99 percent of British wage-earners would be genuinely shocked if it were proposed that the King should not have a larger income than a working man. The conception of duty, speaking historically, has been a means used by the holders of power to induce others to live for the interests of their masters rather than for their own. Of course the holders of power conceal this fact from themselves by managing to believe that their interests are identical with the larger interests of humanity. Sometimes this is true; Athenian slave-owners, for instance, employed part of their leisure in making a permanent contribution to civilization which would have been impossible under a just economic system. Leisure is essential to civilization, and in former times leisure for the few was only rendered possible by the labors of the many. But their labors were valuable, not because work is good, but because leisure is good. And with modern technique it would be possible to distribute leisure justly without injury to civilization.

Modern technique has made it possible to diminish enormously the amount of labor required to secure the necessaries of life for everyone. This was made obvious during the war. At that time all the men in the armed forces, and all the men and women engaged in the production of munitions, all the men and women engaged in spying, war propaganda, or Government offices connected with the war, were withdrawn from productive occupations. In spite of this, the general level of well-being among unskilled wage-earners on the side of the Allies was higher than before or since. The significance of this fact was concealed by finance: borrowing made it appear as if the future was nourishing the present. But that, of course, would have been impossible; a man cannot eat a loaf of bread that does not yet exist. The war showed conclusively that, by the scientific organization of production, it is possible to keep modern populations in fair comfort on a small part of the working capacity of the modern world. If, at the end of the war, the scientific organization, which had been created in order to liberate men for fighting and munition work, had been preserved, and the hours of the week had been cut down to four, all would have been well. Instead of that the old chaos was restored, those whose work was demanded were made to work long hours, and the rest were left to starve as unemployed. Why? Because work is a duty, and a man should not receive wages in proportion to what he has produced, but in proportion to his virtue as exemplified by his industry.

Cultural Notes

1. **Bertrand Arthur William Russell** (1872—1970) was a British philosopher, logician, essayist and social critic best known for his work in mathematical logic and analytic philosophy. Over the course of his long career, Russell made significant contributions, not just to logic and philosophy, but to a broad range of subjects including education, history, political theory and religious studies. In addition, many of his writings on a variety of topics in both the sciences and the humanities have influenced generations of general readers. Russell was awarded the Order of Merit in 1949 and the Nobel Prize for Literature in 1950. Noted for his many spirited anti-war and anti-nuclear protests, Russell remained a prominent public figure until his death at the age of 97. This text was written in 1932 and first provided by the Massachusetts Green Party.

2. **Benito Amilcare Andrea Mussolini** (1883—1945) was an Italian politician who led the National Fascist Party, ruling the country from 1922 to his ousting in 1943. Mussolini has been credited with being one of the key figures in the creation of fascism. Mussolini was Dictator of Italy from 1930 to 1943, having destroyed all political opposition through his secret police and having outlawed workers to go on strike.

3. **YMCA** is an abbreviation for "Young Men's Christian Association".

4. **The Napoleonic Wars** (1803—1815) were a series of wars declared against Napoleon's French Empire by opposing coalitions. After the French Revolution of 1789, French power rose quickly as Napoleon's armies

conquered much of Europe but collapsed rapidly after France's disastrous invasion of Russia in 1812. Napoleon's empire ultimately suffered complete military defeat resulting in the restoration of the Bourbon monarchy in France. Despite a final victory against Napoleon, five of seven coalitions saw defeat at the hands of France. But after the retreat from Russia, in spite of incomplete victories, France was beaten by the sixth coalition at Leipzig and the seventh coalition at Waterloo. The wars resulted in the dissolution of the Holy Roman Empire.

Comprehension Exercises

I. Answer the following questions based on the text.

1. What is the author's basic tone in this text?
2. What did Russell mean in saying "Satan finds some mischief for idle hands to do"?
3. The author puts forward two kinds of work. What are they? Besides, the author has also pointed out the existence of a third class of people. What kind of people are they?
4. The author says "But although my conscience has controlled my actions, my opinions have undergone a revolution." What is this revolution for the author?
5. What is Russell's actual attitude towards the idleness? Was he simply singing high praise for it?

II. Decide whether each of the following statements is true or false according to the text.

1. According to this text, the author did no longer believe in the virtue of work.
2. This text has been attempting to persuade young men to idle away their life.
3. The author holds that it is good for one to lend his money to the government.
4. In times of famine when there was no surplus, the warriors and priests could secure food and things no more, and they would die of hunger.
5. The men holding power are always pretending that their own interests are identical with the larger interests of humanity.

III. Select the most suitable word or phrases and fill in the following blanks in their proper form.

appropriate	bulk	compulsion	diminution	divert
philanthropically		mischief	preaching	munitions
spendthrift	inaugurate	prerogative	subsist	preliminary
simultaneously	part	gospel		

1. And there is no question that it will be used around the world to stir up political _____.
2. Our parents as well as our teachers are constantly _____ about the importance of study for our future.
3. The ambassador said it was a historic event and that he was certain it would _____ a new era and a new relationship between the two countries.
4. These tourists come from all over the world, though the _____ is from the Indian subcontinent.
5. All these politicians are endeavoring to _____ the attention of the people from the real issues.
6. There's no reason to believe that a couple of minutes spent in virtual reality can turn a long-time _____ into a permanent miser.
7. It plans to hold _____ discussions this week to prepare for ministerial-level contact in Seoul.
8. He insisted that it was critically important for Bhutan to complete the process of becoming a constitutional monarchy, despite the reluctance of many Bhutanese to see a _____ of the monarch's powers.
9. He claimed the Scotland National Party was trying to run a high-carbon and a low-carbon economy _____.
10. All the other roommates hold that Brown is selfish for he is always _____ the biggest bookcase and desk.
11. As the presidential nominee, it's Obama's _____, of course, to shape the convention any way he wants.
12. What deserved special notice was that the prisoners in that region _____ on one mug of the worst quality porridge three times a day.
13. We come into this world, we grow, we make friends, we look for opportunities and ultimately, we have to _____ with our friends and family members.
14. Many universities argued that students learned more when they were in classes out of choice rather than out of _____.
15. U.S. officials also believe there may be as many as 180 underground _____ factories in the country.

IV. Try to paraphrase the following sentences, paying special attention to the underlined parts.

1. Before <u>advancing my own arguments for laziness</u>, I must <u>dispose of</u> one which I cannot accept.

2. The man who <u>invests his savings in a concern</u> that goes bankrupt is therefore injuring others as well as himself.

3. Unfortunately, their idleness is only rendered possible by the <u>industry</u> of others; indeed their desire for <u>comfortable idleness</u> is historically <u>the source of the whole gospel of work</u>.

4. <u>The small surplus above bare necessaries</u> was not left to those who produced it, but was <u>appropriated</u> by warriors and priests.

5. It is obvious that, in primitive communities, peasants, <u>left to themselves</u>, would not have <u>parted with</u> the <u>slender surplus</u> upon which the warriors and priests <u>subsisted</u>, but would have either produced less or consumed more.

V. Discuss with your partner about each of the three statements and write an essay in no less than 250 words about your understanding of one of them.

1. Whenever a person who already has enough to live on proposes to engage in some everyday kind of job, such as school-teaching or typing, he or she is told that such conduct takes the bread out of other people's mouths, and is therefore wicked.

2. Leisure is essential to civilization, and in former times leisure for the few was only rendered possible by the labors of the many.

3. Modern technique has made it possible to diminish enormously the amount

of labor required to secure the necessaries of life for everyone.

VI. List four websites where we can learn more about Bertrand Russell and provide a brief introduction to each of them.

1. _____.

2. _____.

3. _____.

4. _____.

Text B

To Err Is Human
Lewis Thomas*

Everyone must have had at least one personal experience with a computer error by this time. Bank balances are suddenly reported to have jumped from $ 379 into the millions, appeals for charitable contributions are mailed over and over to people with crazy-sounding names at your address, department stores send the wrong bills, utility companies write that they're turning everything off, that sort of thing. If you manage to get in touch with someone and complain, you then get instantaneously typed, guilty letters from the same computer, saying, "Our computer was in error, and an adjustment is being made in your account."

These are supposed to be the sheerest, blindest accidents. Mistakes are not believed

balance /'bæləns/ *n.* money which remains or is left over
appeal /ə'piːl/ *n.* an earnest request for aid, support, sympathy, mercy, etc.; entreaty; petition; plea
charitable /'tʃærɪtəbəl/ *adj.* of, for, or concerned with charity; generous in donations or gifts to relieve the needs of indigent, ill, or helpless persons, or of animals
utility /juː'tɪlɪtɪ/ *n.* a public service, as a telephone or electric-light system, a streetcar or railroad line, or the like

to be part of the normal behavior of a good machine. If things go wrong, it must be a personal, human error, the result of fingering, tampering, a button getting stuck, someone hitting the wrong key. The computer, at its normal best, is infallible.

I wonder whether this can be true. After all, the whole point of computers is that they represent an extension of the human brain, vastly improved upon but nonetheless human, superhuman maybe. A good computer can think clearly and quickly enough to beat you at chess, and some of them have even been programmed to write obscure verse. They can do anything we can do, and more besides.

tamper /ˈtæmpə/ *v.* to touch or make changes to sth. without permission
infallible /ɪnˈfæləbl/ *adj.* not fallible; exempt from liability to error, as persons, their judgment, or pronouncements; absolutely trustworthy or sure
spool /spuːl/ *n.* any cylindrical piece or device on which sth. is wound; the material or quantity of material wound on such a device
equivalent /ɪˈkwɪvələnt/ *adj.* equal in value, measure, force, effect, significance, etc.
property /ˈprɒpəti/ *n.* a quality, power, or effect that belongs naturally to sth.
embed /ɪmˈbed/ *v.* to fix into a surrounding mass; to incorporate or contain as an essential part or characteristic
nodule /ˈnɒdjuːl/ *n.* (*Botany*) a small knoblike outgrowth, as those found on the roots of many leguminous plants
knack /næk/ *n.* a special skill, talent, or aptitude; a trick or ruse

It is not yet known whether a computer has its own consciousness, and it would be hard to find out about this. When you walk into one of those great halls now built for the huge machines, and stand listening, it is easy to imagine that the faint, distant noises are the sound of thinking, and the turning of the spools gives them the look of wild creatures rolling their eyes in the effort to concentrate, choking with information. But real thinking, and dreaming, are other matters.

On the other hand, the evidences of something like an unconscious, equivalent to ours, are all around, in every mail. As extensions of the human brain, they have been constructed with the same property of error, spontaneous, uncontrolled, and rich in possibilities.

Mistakes are at the very base of human thought, embedded there, feeding the structure like root nodules. If we were not provided with the knack of being wrong, we could never get anything useful done. We think our way along by choosing between right and wrong alternatives, and the wrong choices have to be made as frequently as the right ones. We get along in life this way. We are built to make mistakes, coded for error.

We learn, as we say, by "trial and error". Why do we always say that? Why not "trial and rightness" or "trial and triumph"? The old phrase puts it that way because that is, in real life, the way it is done.

A good laboratory, like a good bank or a corporation or government, has to run like a computer. Almost everything is done flawlessly, by the book, and all the numbers add up to the predicted sums. The days go by. And then, if it is a lucky day, and a lucky laboratory, somebody makes a mistake: the wrong buffer, something in one of the blanks, a decimal misplaced in reading counts, the warm room off by a degree and a half, a mouse out of his box, or just a misreading of the day's protocol. Whatever, when the results come in, something is obviously screwed up, and then the action can begin.

by the book according to the correct or established form; in the usual manner
buffer /ˈbʌfə/ *n.* an apparatus at the end of a railroad car, railroad track, etc., for absorbing shock
decimal /ˈdesɪməl/ *adj.* pertaining to tenths or to the number 10
protocol /ˈprəʊtəkɒl/ *n.* plan for carrying out a scientific study or a patient's treatment regimen; (Computers) a set of rules governing the format of messages that are exchanged between computers
screw up to mismanage; make an error
harangue /həˈræŋ/ *v.* to make a long or intense verbal attack; to deliver a long and vehement speech
amiable /ˈeɪmɪəbəl/ *adj.* of a pleasant nature; good-tempered; friendly
faculty /ˈfækəltɪ/ *n.* **a.** the power or ability to do sth. particular **b.** a natural power or ability, esp. of the mind
endowment /ɪnˈdaʊmənt/ *n.* the natural qualities that a person is endowed with
stipulate /ˈstɪpjʊleɪt/ *v.* to make an express demand or arrangement as a condition of agreement

The misreading is not the important error: it opens the way. The next step is the crucial one. If the investigator can bring himself to say, "But even so, look at that!" then the new finding, whatever it is, is ready for snatching. What is needed, for progress to be made, is the move based on the error.

Whenever new kinds of thinking are about to be accomplished, or new varieties of music, there has to be an argument beforehand. With two sides debating in the same mind, haranguing, there is an amiable understanding that one is right and the other wrong. Sooner or later the thing is settled, but there can be no action at all if there are not the two sides, and the argument. The hope is in the faculty of wrongness, the tendency toward error. The capacity to leap across mountains of information to land lightly on the wrong side represents the highest of human endowments.

It may be that this is a uniquely human gift, perhaps even stipulated in our genetic instructions. Other creatures do not seem to have DNA* sequences for making mistakes as a routine part of daily living, certainly not for programmed error as a guide for action.

We are at our human finest, dancing with our minds, when there are more choices than two. Sometimes there are ten, even twenty different ways to go, all but one bound to be the wrong, and the richness of selection in such situations can lift us

onto totally new ground. This process is called exploration and is based on human fallibility. If we had only a single center in our brains, capable of responding only when a correct decision was to be made, instead of the jumble of different credulous, easily conned clusters of neurons that provide for being flung off into blind alleys, up trees, down dead ends, out into blue sky, along wrong turnings, around bends, we could only stay the way we are today, stuck fast.

The lower animals do not have this splendid freedom. They are limited most of them, to absolute infallibility. Cats, for all their good side, never make mistakes. I have never seen a maladroit, clumsy, or blundering cat. Dogs are sometimes fallible, occasionally able to make charming minor mistakes, but they get this way by trying to mimic their masters. Fish are flawless in everything they do. Individual cells in a tissue are mindless machines, perfect in their performance, as absolutely inhuman as bees.

We should have this in mind as we become dependent on more complex computers for the arrangement of our affairs. Give the computers their heads, I say; let them go their way. If we can learn to do this, turning our heads to one side and wincing while the work proceeds, the possibilities for the future of mankind, and computerkind, are limitless. Your average good computer can make calculations in an instant which would take a lifetime of slide rules for any of us. Think of what we could gain from the near infinity of precise, machine-made miscomputation which is now so easily within our grasp. We would begin the solving of some of our hardest problems. How, for instance, should we go about organizing ourselves for social living on a planetary scale, now that we have become, as a plain fact of life, a single community? We can assume, as a working hypothesis, that all the right ways of doing this are unworkable. What we need, then, for moving ahead, is a set of wrong alternatives much longer and more interesting than the short list of mistaken courses that any of us can think

jumble /ˈdʒʌmbəl/ n. a disorderly mixture
con /kɒn/ v. to swindle; trick; to persuade by deception, cajolery, etc.
stick fast to be hopelessly bogged
maladroit /ˌmæləˈdrɔɪt/ adj. lacking in adroitness; unskillful; awkward; bungling; tactless
mimic /ˈmɪmɪk/ v. to imitate or copy in action, speech, etc., often playfully or derisively
wince /wɪns/ v. to draw back, as with fear or pain
slide rule an instrument for calculating numbers
hypothesis /haɪˈpɒθəsɪs/ n. a proposition, or set of propositions, set forth as an explanation for the occurrence of some specified group of phenomena, either asserted merely as a provisional conjecture to guide investigation (working hypothesis) or accepted as highly probable in the light of established facts

stun /stʌn/ *v.* **a.** to make unconscious by hitting the head **b.** to cause to lose the sense of balance **c.** to shock into helplessness **d.** to delight

in the clear absolved of blame or guilt; free

up right now. We need, in fact, an infinite list, and when it is printed out we need the computer to turn on itself and select, at random, the next way to go. If it is a big enough mistake, we could find ourselves on a new level, stunned, out in the clear, ready to move again.

Cultural Notes

1. **Lewis Thomas** (1913—1993) was an American physician and educator. Educated at Princeton and Harvard, he served as president of Memorial Sloan-Kettering Cancer Center from 1973 to 1980. The short essays which he began writing for fun in 1971 established him as a serious writer of prose who combined his knowledge and insights into science, especially microbiology and immunology, with meditative reflections on nature and the human body in a style widely recognized as clear, graceful and witty. The title "To Err Is Human" is a parody of a poem line: "To err is human, to forgive divine" taken from *An Essay on Criticism* written by Alexander Pope (1688—1744).

2. **DNA,** or deoxyribonucleic acid, is a nucleic acid that contains the genetic instructions used in the development and functioning of all known living organisms and some viruses. The main role of DNA molecules is the long-term storage of information. DNA is often compared to a set of blueprints, since it contains the instructions needed to construct other components of cells, such as proteins and RNA molecules. The DNA segments that carry this genetic information are called genes, but other DNA sequences have structural purposes, or are involved in regulating the use of this genetic information.

Comprehension Exercises

I. Answer the following questions based on the text.

1. What is the author's tone of voice throughout the text? How could you prove this?
2. How would you summarize the author's opinions in your own words?
3. How does the author define a computer?
4. How is a human being different from an animal being?
5. Why does the author use "To Err Is Human" as the title for this article?

II. Decide whether each of the following statements is true or false according to the text.

1. Computers are largely untrustworthy, so are human beings.
2. It is very common to be fooled by a computer.
3. Wrong choices promote human progress.
4. It is certain that a computer has its own consciousness.
5. It is only human beings that seem to have DNA sequences for making mistakes as a routine part of daily living.
6. Absolute infallibility belongs to lower animals.

III. Select the most suitable word or phrases and fill in the following blanks in their proper form.

appeal	balance	charitable	decimal	embed
endowment	equivalent	harangue	hook	infallible
jumble	knack	maladroit	property	protocol
stipulate	tamper	utility		

1. What should be established I think is an artistic, harmonious _____ between the reader's mind and the author's mind.
2. But I know that his _____ donations are something that are tremendously important to him.
3. Considering his rent includes all the _____ such as electricity, heating system, and other public services, he is not overcharged by the landlady.
4. He said security officials had detected no serious attempts to _____ with the votes and this election was trustworthy.
5. People tend to think it must be so because the computer says it's so. And therefore it is commonly believed to be always _____.
6. By human scale, the ant city was the _____ of two hundred underground stories.
7. The farmer was the person who started it all when he decided to have sheep on his _____.
8. I think that hatred of and competition against the other is deeply _____ in our present society.
9. Herbert's _____ for blurring the lines between the political and personal has always served him well.
10. I have to warn you that hotels.com is on the _____ for selling you a room that fell short of its description.
11. Obviously, when you win a game like that, you are excited, but there is a _____.

12. An argument ensued, with various band members joining in and _____ the trouble-makers for over two hours.
13. Singapore regulations _____ that at least 12% of a listed company must be in public hands.
14. He's making a new film by _____ together bits of his other movies and he would definitely fail this time.
15. When he was interviewed by the press for the first time in his life, he was rather sheepish and _____.

IV. Try to paraphrase the following sentences, paying special attention to the underlined parts.

1. If things go wrong, it must be a personal, human error, the result of <u>fingering</u>, <u>tampering</u>, a button <u>getting stuck</u>, someone hitting the wrong key.

2. As <u>extensions</u> of the human brain, they have been constructed with the same <u>property of error</u>, spontaneous, uncontrolled, and rich in possibilities.

3. Mistakes are <u>at the very base of</u> human thought, <u>embedded there, feeding the structure</u> like root nodules.

4. With two sides <u>debating</u> in the same mind, <u>haranguing</u>, there is an amiable understanding that one is right and the other is wrong.

5. If it is a big enough mistake, we could find ourselves <u>on a new level, stunned, out in the clear</u>, ready to move again.

V. Discuss with your partner about each of the three statements and write an essay in no less than 250 words about your understanding of one of them.

1. Computers are an extension of human brains.

2. What is needed, for progress to be made, is the move based on the error.

3. What we need, then, for moving ahead, is a set of wrong alternatives much longer and more interesting than the short list of mistaken courses that any of us can think up right now.

VI. List four websites where we can learn more about Lewis Thomas and provide a brief introduction to each of them.

1.

2.

3.

4.

Twenty Minutes' Reading

You are required to read the following two sections within 20 minutes.

SECTION A

It was late in the afternoon, and I was putting the final touch on a piece of writing that I was feeling pretty good about. I wanted to save it, but my cursor had frozen. I tried to shut the computer down, and it seized up altogether. Unsure of what else to do, I yanked (用力猛拉) the battery out.

Unfortunately, Windows had been in the midst of a delicate and crucial undertaking. The next morning, when I turned my computer back on, it informed me that a file had been corrupted and Windows would not load. Then, it offered to repair itself by using the Windows Setup CD.

I opened the special drawer where I keep CDs. But no Windows CD in there. I was forced to call the computer company's Global Support Centre. My call was answered by a woman in some unnamed, far-off land. I find it annoying to make small talk with someone when I don't know what continent they're standing on. Suppose I were to comment on the beautiful weather we've been having when there was a monsoon at the other end of the phone? So I got right to the point.

"My computer is telling me a file is corrupted and it wants to fix itself, but I don't have the Windows Setup CD."

"So you're having a problem with your Windows Setup CD." She has apparently been dozing and, having come to just as the sentence ended, was attempting to cover for her inattention.

It quickly became clear that the woman was not a computer technician. Her job was to serve as a gatekeeper, a human shield for the technicians. Her sole duty, as far as I could tell, was to raise global stress levels.

To make me disappear, the woman gave me the phone number for Windows' creator, Microsoft. This is like giving someone the phone number for, I don't know, North America. Besides, the CD worked; I just didn't have it. No matter how many times I repeated my story, we came back to the same place. She was calm and resolutely polite.

When my voice hit a certain decibel (分贝), I was passed along, like a hot, irritable potato, to a technician.

"You don't have the Windows Setup CD, ma'am, because you don't need it," he explained cheerfully.

"Windows came preinstalled on your computer!"

"But I do need it."

"Yes, but you don't have it." We went on like this for a while. Finally, he offered to walk me through the use of a different CD, one that would erase my entire system. "Of course, you'd lose all your e-mail, your documents, your photos." It was like offering to drop a safe on my head to cure my headache. "You might be able to recover them, but it would be expensive." He sounded delighted. "And it's not covered by the warranty (产品保证书)!" The safe began to seem like a good idea, provided it was full.

I hung up the phone and drove my computer to a small, friendly repair place I'd heard about. A smart, helpful man dug out a Windows CD and told me it wouldn't be a problem. An hour later, he called to let me know it was ready. I thanked him, and we chatted about the weather, which was the same outside my window as it was outside his.

1. Why did the author shut down her computer abruptly?
   A. She had saved what she had written.
   B. She couldn't move the cursor.
   C. The computer refused to work.
   D. The computer offered to repair itself.
2. Which of the following is the author's opinion about the woman at the Global Support Centre?
   A. She sounded helpful and knowledgeable.
   B. She was there to make callers frustrated.
   C. She was able to solve her computer problem.
   D. She was quick to pass her along to a technician.
3. According to the passage, the solution offered by the technician was _____.
   A. effective   B. economical   C. unpractical   D. unacceptable
4. "It was like offering to drop a safe on my head to cure my headache" in the last but one paragraph means that _____.
   A. the technician's proposal would make things even worse
   B. the technician's proposal could eventually solve the problem
   C. files stored on her computer were like a safe
   D. erasing the entire system was like curing a headache
5. It can be inferred from the passage that the differences between the Global Support Centre and the local repair shop lie in all the following EXCEPT _____.
   A. efficiency   B. location   C. setup CDs   D. attitude

SECTION B

Not long ago, a mysterious Christmas card dropped through our mail slot. The envelope was addressed to a man named Raoul, who, I was relatively certain, did not live with us. The envelope wasn't sealed, so I opened it. The inside of the card was blank. Ed, my husband, explained that the card was both from and to the newspaper deliveryman. His name was apparently Raoul, and Raoul wanted a holiday tip. We were meant to put a check inside the card and then drop the envelope in the mail. When your services are rendered at 4 a.m., you can't simply hang around, like a hotel bellboy expecting a tip. You have to be direct.

So I wrote a nice holiday greeting to this man who, in my imagination, fires *The New York Times* from his bike aimed at our front door, causing more noise with mere newsprint than most people manage with sophisticated black market fireworks. With a start, I realized that perhaps the reason for the 4 a.m. wake-up noise was not ordinary rudeness but carefully executed spite: I had not tipped Raoul in

Christmases past. I honestly hadn't realized I was supposed to. This was the first time he'd used the card tactic. So I got out my checkbook. Somewhere along the line, holiday tipping went from an optional thank-you for a year of services to a Mafia-style protection racket (收取保护费的黑社会组织).

Several days later, I was bringing our garbage bins back from the curb when I noticed an envelope taped to one of the lids. The outside of the envelope said MICKEY. It had to be another tip request, this time from our garbage collector. Unlike Raoul, Mickey hadn't enclosed his own Christmas card from me. In a way, I appreciated the directness. "I know you don't care how merry my Christmas is, and that's fine," the gesture said. "I want $30, or I'll 'forget' to empty your garbage bin some hot summer day."

I put a check in the envelope and taped it back to the bin. The next morning, Ed noticed that the envelope was gone, though the trash hadn't yet been picked up: "Someone stole Mickey's tip!" Ed was quite certain. He made me call the bank and cancel the check.

But Ed had been wrong. Two weeks later, Mickey left a letter from the bank on our steps. The letter informed Mickey that the check, which he had tried to cash, had been cancelled. The following Tuesday morning, when Ed saw a truck outside, he ran out with his wallet. "Are you Mickey?"

The man looked at him with scorn. "Mickey is the garbageman. I am the recycling." Not only had Ed insulted this man by hinting that he was a garbageman, but he had obviously neglected to tip him. Ed ran back inside for more funds. Then he noticed that the driver of the truck had been watching the whole transaction. He peeled off another twenty and looked around, waving bills in the air. "Anyone else?"

Had we consulted the website of the Emily Post Institute, this embarrassing breach of etiquette (礼节) could have been avoided. Under "trash/recycling collectors" in the institute's Holiday Tipping Guidelines, it says: "$10 to $30 each." You may or may not wish to know that your pet groomer, hairdresser, mailman and UPS guy all expect a holiday tip.

6. The newspaper deliveryman put a blank card inside the envelope because _____.
   A. he forgot to write a few words on it
   B. he wanted the couple to send it back
   C. he used it to ask for a Christmas tip
   D. he was afraid of asking for a tip in person

7. From the passage, we learn that the author _____.
   A. didn't like Raoul's way of delivering the paper
   B. didn't realize why Raoul delivered the paper that way

    C. didn't know that Raoul came very early in the morning
    D. didn't feel it necessary to meet Raoul when he came
 8. According to the passage, the author felt _____ to give Raoul a holiday tip.
    A. excited   B. delighted   C. embarrassed   D. forced
 9. Which of the following is CORRECT about Mickey, the garbage collector?
    A. He wrote a letter to the couple afterwards.
    B. He failed to collect the money from the bank.
    C. He wanted the couple to send him a Christmas card.
    D. He collected both the cheek and the garbage that day.
10. Ed's encounter with the recycling team shows that _____.
    A. Ed was desperate to correct his mistake
    B. Ed only wanted to give money to Raoul
    C. Ed was unwilling to tip the truck driver
    D. Ed no longer wanted to give them money

Unit Nine

Text A

On National Prejudice
Oliver Goldsmith*

As I am one of that sauntering tribe of mortals who spend the greatest part of their time in taverns, coffeehouses, and other places of public resort, I have thereby an opportunity of observing an infinite variety of characters, which to a person of a contemplative turn is a much higher entertainment than a view of all the curiosities of art or nature. In one of these my late rambles I accidentally fell into a company of half a dozen gentlemen, who wereengaged in a warm dispute about some political affair, the decision of which, as they were equally divided in their sentiments, they thought proper to refer to me, which naturally drew me in for a share of the conversation.

Amongst a multiplicity of other topics, we took occasion to talk of the different characters of the several nations of Europe; when one of the gentlemen, cocking his hat, and assuming such an air of importance as if he had possessed all the merit of the English nation in his own person, declared, that the Dutch were a parcel of avaricious wretches; the French a set of flattering sycophants; that the Germans were drunken sots, and beastly gluttons; and the Spaniard proud, haughty, and surly tyrants; but

saunter /ˈsɔːntə/ *v.* to walk with a leisurely gait; stroll
mortal /ˈmɔːtl/ *n.* a human being
tavern /ˈtævən/ *n.* a public house, inn
resort /rɪˈzɔːt/ *n.* a place to which people frequently go for relaxation
turn /tɜːn/ *n.* character, disposition
ramble /ˈræmbəl/ *n.* a walk without a definite route, taken merely for pleasure
amongst /əˈmʌŋst/ *prep.* among
cock /kɒk/ *v.* to set or turn up or to one side, often in an assertive, jaunty, or significant manner
merit /ˈmerɪt/ *n.* sth. that deserves or justifies a reward or commendation; a commendable quality
avaricious /ˌævəˈrɪʃəs/ *adj.* greedy for wealth
sycophant /ˈsɪkəfənt/ *n.* a flatterer
sot /sɒt/ *n.* a habitual drunkard
glutton /ˈɡlʌtn/ *n.* **a.** a person who eats and drinks voraciously. **b.** a person with a remarkable desire for sth.
haughty /ˈhɔːtɪ/ *adj.* disdainfully proud; snobbish; scornfully arrogant

that in bravery, generosity, clemency, and in every other virtue, the English excelled all the world.

This very learned and judicious remark was received with a general smile of approbation by all the company—all, I mean, but your humble servant, who, endeavouring to keep my gravity as well as I could, and reclining my head upon my arm, continued for some time in a posture of affected thoughtfulness, as if I had been musing on something else, and did not seem to attend to the subject of conversation; hoping by this to avoid the disagreeable necessity of explaining myself, and thereby depriving the gentleman of his imaginary happiness.

clemency /ˈklemənsɪ/ *n.* mercy
excel /ɪkˈsel/ *v.* to surpass others or be superior in some respect or area
judicious /dʒuːˈdɪʃəs/ *adj.* discreet, prudent or politic
approbation /ˌæprəˈbeɪʃən/ *n.* approval; commendation
gravity /ˈɡrævɪtɪ/ *n.* dignity; serious conduct
muse /mjuːz/ *v.* to think or meditate in silence
suffrage /ˈsʌfrɪdʒ/ *n.* **a.** the right to vote **b.** a vote given in favor of a proposal
forward /ˈfɔːwəd/ *adj.* **a.** well-advanced **b.** ready, prompt, or eager
maxim /ˈmæksɪm/ *n.* a principle or rule of conduct
peremptory strain /pəˈremptərɪ streɪn/ haughty air
scruple /ˈskruːpl/ *v.* to hesitate
frugal /ˈfruːɡəl/ *adj.* **a.** economical in use or expenditure **b.** meager; scanty
staid /steɪd/ *adj.* sober, grave
sedate /sɪˈdeɪt/ *adj.* calm, quiet, or composed
impetuous /ɪmˈpetʃʊəs/ *adj.* impulsive
elated /ɪˈleɪtɪd/ *adj.* very happy or proud
despond /dɪsˈpɒnd/ *v.* to be depressed by loss of hope
adversity /ədˈvɜːsɪtɪ/ *n.* **a.** adverse fortune or fate **b.** an adverse event or circumstance
jealous /ˈdʒeləs/ *adj.* hostile, resentful
observe /əbˈzɜːv/ *v.* **a.** to follow **b.** to say or mention casually; remark **c.** to notice or perceive

But my pseudo-patriot had no mind to let me escape so easily. Not satisfied that his opinion should pass without contradiction, he was determined to have it ratified by the suffrage of every one in the company; for which purpose, addressing himself to me with an air of inexpressible confidence, he asked me if I was not of the same way of thinking. As I am never forward in giving my opinion, especially when I have reason to believe that it will not be agreeable; so, when I am obliged to give it, I always hold it for a maxim to speak my real sentiments. I therefore told him that, for my own part, I should not have ventured to talk in such a peremptory strain unless I had made the tour of Europe, and examined the manners of these several nations with great care and accuracy; that perhaps a more impartial judge would not scruple to affirm, that the Dutch were more frugal and industrious, the French more temperate and polite, the Germans more hardy and patient of labour and fatigue, and the Spaniards more staid and sedate, than the English; who, though undoubtedly brave and generous, were at the same time rash, headstrong, and impetuous; too apt to be elated with prosperity, and to despond in adversity.

I could easily perceive, that all the company began to regard me with a jealous eye before I had finished my answer, which I had no sooner done, than the patriotic gentleman observed, with a contemptuous sneer, that he was greatly surprised how some people could have the conscience to live in a country which they did not love, and to enjoy the protection of a government to which in their hearts they were inveterate enemies. Finding that by this modest declaration of my sentiments I had forfeited the good opinion of my companions, and given them occasion to call my political principles in question, and well knowing that it was in vain to argue with men who were so very full of themselves, I threw down my reckoning and retired to my own lodgings, reflecting on the absurd and ridiculous nature of national prejudice and prepossession.

Among all the famous sayings of antiquity, there is none that does greater honour to the author, or affords greater pleasure to the reader, (at least if he be a person of a generous and benevolent heart,) than that of the philosopher who, being asked what countryman he was, replied, that he was "a citizen of the world". How few are there to be found in modern times who can say the same, or whose conduct is consistent with such a profession! We are now become so much Englishmen, Frenchmen, Dutchmen, Spaniards, or Germans, that we are no longer citizens of the world; so much the natives of one particular spot, or members of one party society, that we no longer consider ourselves as the general inhabitants of the globe, or members of that grand society which comprehends the whole human kind.

Did these prejudices prevail only among the meanest and lowest of the people, perhaps they might be excused, as they have few, if any, opportunities of correcting them by reading, traveling, or conversing with foreigners; but the misfortune is, that they infect the minds, and influence the conduct, even of our gentlemen; of those, I mean, who have every title to this appellation but an exemption from prejudice, which, however, in my opinion, ought to be regarded as the characteristical mark of a gentleman; for let a man's birth be ever so high, his station ever so exalted, or his fortune ever so large, yet if he is not free from national and other prejudices, I should make bold to tell him, that he had a low and vulgar mind, and had no just claim to the character of a gentleman. And, in fact, you will always find that those are most apt to boast of national merit, who have little or no merit of their own to depend on; than which, to be sure, nothing is more natural; the slender vine twists around the sturdy oak, for no other reason in the world

inveterate /ɪnˈvetərɪt/ *adj.* firmly established over a long period; of long standing; deep-rooted

forfeit /ˈfɔːfɪt/ *v.* to lose or be deprived of for some crime, fault, etc.

reckoning /ˈrekənɪŋ/ *n.* bill in the public house

prepossess /priːpəˈzes/ *v.* **a.** to occupy beforehand **b.** to prejudice or bias, esp. favorably — prepossession. *n.*

comprehend /kɒmprɪˈhend/ *v.* **a.** to grasp mentally; understand **b.** to include; comprise

station /ˈsteɪʃən/ *n.* social standing, position, or rank

exalt /ɪɡˈzɔːlt/ *v.* to raise in status, dignity, power, honor, wealth, etc.

sturdy /ˈstɜːdɪ/ *adj.* physically strong; vigorous; hardy

but because it has not strength sufficient to support itself.

    Should it be alleged in defence of national prejudice, that it is the natural and necessary growth of love to our country, and that therefore the former cannot be destroyed without hurting the latter, I answer that this is a gross fallacy and delusion. That it is the growth of love to our country, I will allow; but that it is the natural and necessary growth of it, I absolutely deny. Superstition and enthusiasm, too, are the growth of religion; but who ever took it in his head to affirm, that they are the necessary growth of this noble principle? They are, if you will, the bastard sprouts of this heavenly plant, but not its natural and genuine branches, and may safely enough be lopped off, without doing any harm to the parent stock; nay, perhaps, till once they are lopped off, this goodly tree can never flourish in perfect health and vigour.

    Is it not very possible that I may love my own country, without hating the natives of other countries? that I may exert the most heroic bravery, the most undaunted resolution, in defending its laws and liberty, without despising all the rest of the world as cowards and poltroons? Most certainly it is; and if it were not—But why need I suppose what is absolutely impossible? —But if it were not, I must own I should prefer the title of the ancient philosopher, viz, a citizen of the world, to that of an Englishman, a Frenchman, a European, or to any other appellation whatever.

gross /grəʊs/ *adj.* **a.** big **b.** total, entire
fallacy /ˈfæləsɪ/ *n.* an error in reasoning; defect in argument
enthusiasm /ɪnˈθjuːzɪæzəm/ *n.* **a.** intense interest; zeal; fervor **b.** (archaic) religious fanaticism
lop off to trim (a tree, etc.) by cutting off branches, twigs, or stems
nay /neɪ/ *adv.* no
undaunted /ʌnˈdɔːntɪd/ *adj.* not faltering or hesitating because of fear or discouragement; intrepid
resolution /ˌrezəˈluːʃən/ *n.* **a.** a resolute quality of mind **b.** a formal statement of opinion or determination
poltroon /pɒlˈtruːn/ *n.* spiritless coward
own /əʊn/ *v.* **a.** to possess **b.** to admit; recognize; acknowledge
viz /vɪz/ *adv.* that is; namely

Cultural Notes

Oliver Goldsmith (1728—1774) was an Anglo-Irish writer, poet, and physician known for his novel *The Vicar of Wakefield* (1766), his pastoral poem "The Deserted Village" (1770), and his plays *The Good-natur'd Man* (1768) and *She Stoops to Conquer* (1771). He belonged to the circle of Samuel Johnson, Edmund Burke, Joshua Reynolds, and was one of "The Club." His carelessness, intemperance, and habit of gambling constantly brought him into debt. Broken in health and mind, he died in 1774.

Unit Nine

Comprehension Exercises

I. Answer the following questions based on the text.
1. What does Goldsmith want to express most in the text?
2. How does Goldsmith define English nationality?
3. What is Goldsmith's standard for a real gentleman?
4. How does Goldsmith define the relationship between religion and superstition?
5. How did the English gentleman think of the Spaniard?

II. Decide whether each of the following statements is true or false according to the text.
1. Goldsmith does not love England.
2. Goldsmith loves drinking and constantly goes to the taverns.
3. Goldsmith compares religion to a heavenly plant.
4. Goldsmith would rather be called a citizen of the world than an Englishman.
5. Goldsmith was very disputatious.
6. The English gentlemen were prejudiced against almost all the European nations other than the English.

III. Select the most suitable word or phrases and fill in the following blanks in their proper form.

adversity	approbation	avaricious	clemency	despond
glutton	haughty	impetuous	inveterate	judicious
merit	ramble	resort	sauntering	scruple
suffrage	sycophant	turn		

1. He frequents the streets and the dance halls of the big city, recording what he sees and hears while _____ aimlessly.
2. As the first national seaside _____, this place would also become a cool summertime retreat for wealthy visitors from all other parts of this country.
3. All his friends know well that he was of a mild yet melancholy _____ of mind.
4. He was sure that it must have been a casual encounter during some country _____; he was not greatly curious about it.
5. All of these approaches have their respective _____, and deserve a fair hearing in the months ahead.
6. These two brothers were so alike. One was so selfish as to sacrifice his own

life for the national interest while his brother was so _____ as to stop at nothing in order to meet his personal demands.

7. A dictator has always been surrounded by _____, who would never tell him what he may not like in earnest.

8. He is like a _____ at a feast, with his mouth stuffed full, trying to squeeze something else into an already crammed mouth. There just isn't room for more.

9. Emma Thompson, headmistress of the school Jenny attended, had been a _____ woman with a casual scorn for Jews.

10. They are hopeful that their appeals for _____ will be answered by the Board of Pardons and Paroles in this state.

11. The president authorizes the _____ use of military force to protect the citizens of this country and their interest from any injury.

12. When he heard my poetic lines for the first time he was as surprised as he was pleased, and with his _____ my road to literature was widened.

13. When Catherine perceived that he held it rather a punishment than a gratification to endure our company, she made no _____ of proposing to depart with him presently.

14. His blood's type was B, which means he was inclined to be irritable and _____, and his intentions did not always come across.

15. The supporters of the Presidential candidate _____ when they miserably learned the final results of the election.

IV. Try to paraphrase the following sentences, paying special attention to the underlined parts.

1. In one of these <u>my late rambles</u> I accidentally <u>fell into a company</u> of half a dozen gentlemen, who were engaged in a warm dispute about some political affair, the decision of which, as they were <u>equally divided in their sentiments</u>, they thought proper to <u>refer to</u> me, which naturally drew me in for a share of conversation.

_____

_____

2. <u>Amongst a multiplicity of</u> other topics, we <u>took occasion to</u> talk of the different characters of the several nations of Europe.

_____

_____

3. This very **learned and judicious remark** was received with **a general smile of approbation** by all the company.

   _____

4. I therefore told him that, <u>for my own part</u>, I should not have ventured to talk in such as a <u>peremptory strain</u> unless I had made the tour of Europe, and examined the manners of these several nations with great care and accuracy.

   _____

5. Finding that by this <u>modest declaration</u> of my sentiments I had <u>forfeited</u> the good opinion of my companions, and given them occasion to <u>call my political principles in question</u>.

   _____

V. Discuss with your partner about each of the three statements and write an essay in no less than 250 words about your understanding of one of them.

1. In bravery, generosity, clemency, and in every other virtue, the English excelled the world.

   _____

2. If one is not free from national and other prejudices, he has a low and vulgar mind, and has no just claim to the character of a gentleman.

   _____

3. Those most apt to boast of national merit have little or no merit of their own to depend on.

   _____

VI. List four websites where we can learn more about Oliver Goldsmith and provide a brief introduction to each of them.

1. _____

2. _____

3. _____.

4. _____.

Text B

Politics and the English Language
George Orwell

Most people who bother with the matter at all would admit that the English language is in a bad way, but it is generally assumed that we cannot by conscious action do anything about it. Our civilization is decadent and our language — so the argument runs — must inevitably share in the general collapse. It follows that any struggle against the abuse of language is a sentimental archaism, like preferring candles to electric light or hansom cabs to aeroplanes. Underneath this lies the half-conscious belief that language is a natural growth and not an instrument which we shape for our own purposes.

Now, it is clear that: it is not due simply to the bad influence of this or that individual writer. But an effect can become a cause, reinforcing the original cause and producing the same effect in an intensified form, and so on indefinitely. A man may take to drink because he feels himself to be a failure, and then fail all the more completely because he drinks. It is rather the same thing that is happening to the English language. It becomes ugly and inaccurate because our thoughts are foolish, but the slovenliness of our language makes it easier for us to have foolish thoughts. The point is that the process is reversible. Modern English, especially written English, is full of bad habits which spread by imitation and which can be avoided if one is willing to take the necessary trouble. If one gets rid of these habits one can think more clearly, and to think clearly is a

decadent /ˈdekədənt/ *a.* having low moral standards and being more concerned with your own pleasure than serious matters
archaism /ˈɑːkɪˌɪzəm/ *n.* the adoption or imitation of something archaic, such as a word or an artistic or literary style
hansom /ˈhænsəm/ *n.* in former times, a hansom or a hansom cab was a horse-drawn carriage with two wheels and a fixed hood
slovenliness /ˈslʌvnlɪnɪs/ *n.* **a.** a lack of order and tidiness; not cared for **b.** habitual uncleanliness
reversible /rɪˈvɜːsəbəl/ *adj.* capable of reversing or being reversed

necessary first step towards political regeneration: so that the fight against bad English is not frivolous and is not the exclusive concern of professional writers.

As I have tried to show, modern writing at its worst does not consist in picking out words for the sake of their meaning and inventing images in order to make the meaning clearer. It consists in gumming together long strips of words which have already been set in order by someone else, and making the results presentable by sheer humbug. The attraction of this way of writing is that it is easy. It is easier —even quicker, once you have the habit — to say In my opinion it is not an unjustifiable assumption that than to say I think. If you use ready-made phrases, you not only don't have to hunt about for words; you also don't have to bother with the rhythms of your sentences, since these phrases are generally so arranged as to be more or less euphonious. When you are composing in a hurry — when you are dictating to a stenographer, for instance, or making a public speech — it is natural to fall into a pretentious, Latinized style. Tags like a consideration which we should do well to bear in mind or a conclusion to which all of us would readily assent will save many a sentence from coming down with a bump. By using stale metaphors, similes and idioms, you save much mental effort, at the cost of leaving your meaning vague, not only for your reader but for yourself. This is the significance of mixed metaphors. The sole aim of a metaphor is to call up a visual image. When these images clash — as in The Fascist octopus has sung its swan song, the jackboot is thrown into the melting pot — it can be taken as certain that the writer is not seeing a mental image of the objects he is naming; in other words he is not really thinking. A scrupulous writer, in every sentence that he writes, will ask himself at least four questions, thus: What am I trying to say? What words will express it? What image or idiom will make it clearer? Is this image fresh enough to have an effect? And he will probably ask himself two more: Could I put it more shortly? Have I said anything that is avoidably ugly? But you are not obliged to go to all this trouble. You can shirk it by simply throwing your mind open and letting the ready-made phrases come crowding in. They will construct your sentences for you — even think your thoughts for you, to a certain extent — and at need they will perform the important service of partially concealing your meaning even from

frivolous /ˈfrɪvələs/ *adj.* not serious in content or attitude or behavior
exclusive /ɪkˈskluːsɪv/ *adj.* used or owned by only one person or group, and not shared with anyone else
gum /ɡʌm/ *v.* to stick together or in place with gum
humbug /ˈhʌmˌbʌɡ/ *n.* **a.** pretentious or silly talk or writing; **b.** something intended to deceive; **c.** deliberate trickery intended to gain an advantage
euphonious /juːˈfəʊnɪəs/ *adj.* (of speech or dialect) pleasing in sound; not harsh or strident; pleasing to the ear
stenographer /stəˈnɒɡrəfə/ *n.* a person who types and writes shorthand, usually in an office
with a bump suddenly; surprisingly
scrupulous /ˈskruːpjʊləs/ *adj.* characterized by extreme care and great effort
shirk /ʃɜːk/ *v.* avoid (one's assigned duties); avoid dealing with

yourself. It is at this point that the special connection between politics and the debasement of language becomes clear.

In our time it is broadly true that political writing is bad writing. Where it is not true, it will generally be found that the writer is some kind of rebel, expressing his private opinions and not a "party line." Orthodoxy, of whatever color, seems to demand a lifeless, imitative style. The political dialects to be found in pamphlets, leading articles, manifestos, White Papers* and the speeches of undersecretaries do, of course, vary from party to party, but they are all alike in that one almost never finds in them a fresh, vivid, home-made turn of speech. When one watches some tired hack on the platform mechanically repeating the familiar phases — bestial atrocities, iron heel, bloodstained tyranny, free peoples of the world, stand shoulder to shoulder — one often has a curious feeling that one is not watching a live human being but some kind of dummy: a feeling which suddenly becomes stronger at moments when the light catches the speaker's spectacles and turns them into blank discs which seem to have no eyes behind them. And this is not altogether fanciful. A speaker who uses that kind of phraseology has gone some distance towards turning himself into a machine. The appropriate noises are coming out of his larynx, but his brain is not involved as it would be if he were choosing his words for himself. If the speech he is making is one that he is accustomed to make over and over again, he may be almost unconscious of what he is saying, as one is when one utters the responses in church. And this reduced state of consciousness, if not indispensable, is at any rate favorable to political conformity.

In our time, political speech and writing are largely the defense of the indefensible. Things like the continuance of British rule in India, the Russian purges and deportations, the dropping of the atom bombs on Japan, can indeed be defended, but only by arguments which are too brutal for most people to face, and which do not square with the professed aims of political parties. Thus political language has to

---

debasement /dɪˈbeɪsmənt/ *n.* the action of reducing the value or quality of something; changing to a lower state (a less respected state)
orthodoxy /ˈɔːθəˌdɒksɪ/ *n.* an accepted view about sth.; a belief or orientation agreeing with conventional standards
undersecretary /ˌʌndəˈsekrətrɪ/ *n.* a secretary immediately subordinate to the head of a department of government
hack /hæk/ *n.* **a.** a mediocre and disdained writer; **b.** a politician who belongs to a small clique that controls a political party for private rather than public ends
dummy /ˈdʌmɪ/ *n.* **a.** a person who does not talk **b.** an ignorant or foolish person **c.** a figure representing the human form
fanciful /ˈfænsɪfʊl/ *adj.* not based on fact; dubious
phraseology /ˌfreɪzɪˈɒlədʒɪ/ *n.* the manner in which sth. is expressed in words
larynx /ˈlærɪŋks/ *n.* the top part of the passage that leads from your throat to your lungs and contains your vocal cords
indispensable /ˌɪndɪˈspensəbəl/ *adj.* **a.** essential **b.** absolutely necessary
purge /pɜːdʒ/ *n.* an act of removing by cleansing; ridding of sediment or other undesired elements
deportation /ˌdiːpɔːˈteɪʃən/ *n.* the act of expelling a person from their native land
square with *v. phr.* accord with

consist largely of euphemism, question-begging and sheer cloudy vagueness. Defenseless villages are bombarded from the air, the inhabitants driven out into the countryside, the cattle machinegunned, the huts set on fire with incendiary bullets: this is called pacification. Millions of peasants are robbed of their farms and sent trudging along the roads with no more than they can carry: this is called transfer of population or rectification of frontiers. People are imprisoned for years without trial, or shot in the back of the neck or sent to die of scurvy in Arctic lumber camps: this is called elimination of unreliable elements. Such phraseology is needed if one wants to name things without calling up mental pictures of them. Consider for instance some comfortable English professor defending Russian totalitarianism. He cannot say outright, "I believe in killing off your opponents when you can get good results by doing so." Probably, therefore, he will say something like this:

bombard /bɒmˈbɑːd/ *v.* throw bombs at or attack with bombs
incendiary /ɪnˈsendɪərɪ/ *adj.* capable of catching fire spontaneously or causing fires or burning
rectification /ˌrektɪfɪˈkeɪʃən/ *n.* the act of offering an improvement to replace a mistake; setting right
scurvy /ˈskɜːvɪ/ *n.* a disease that is caused by a lack of vitamin C
totalitarianism /təʊˌtælɪˈteərɪənɪzəm/ *n.* a form of government in which the ruler is an absolute dictator (not restricted by a constitution or laws or opposition etc.)
concede /kənˈsiːd/ *v.* **a.** admit, make a clean breast of **b.** give over; surrender or relinquish to the physical control of another
deplore /dɪˈplɔː/ *v.* **a.** express strong disapproval of **b.** regret strongly
curtailment /kəˈteɪlmənt/ *n.* **a.** the act of withholding or withdrawing **b.** the reduction of expenditures in order to become financial stable
concomitant /kənˈkɒmɪtənt/ *n.* an event or situation that happens at the same time as or in connection with another
inflated /ɪnˈfleɪtɪd/ *adj.* pretentious (especially with regard to language or ideals)
cuttlefish /ˈkʌtəlˌfɪʃ/ *n.* a sea animal that has a soft body and a hard shell inside
squirt /skwɜːt/ *v.* cause to come out in a squirt
schizophrenia /ˌskɪtsəʊˈfriːnɪə/ *n.* a serious mental illness and people who suffer from it are unable to relate their thoughts and feelings to what is happening around them and often withdraw from society

While freely conceding that the Soviet regime exhibits certain features which the humanitarian may be inclined to deplore, we must, I think, agree that a certain curtailment of the right to political opposition is an unavoidable concomitant of transitional periods, and that the rigors which the Russian people have been called upon to undergo have been amply justified in the sphere of concrete achievement.

The inflated style is itself a kind of euphemism. A mass of Latin words falls upon the facts like soft snow, blurring the outlines and covering up all the details. The great enemy of clear language is insincerity. When there is a gap between one's real and one's declared aims, one turns as it were instinctively to long words and exhausted idioms, like a cuttlefish squirting out ink. In our age there is no such thing as "keeping out of politics." All issues are political issues, and politics itself is a mass of lies, evasions, folly, hatred and schizophrenia. When the general atmosphere

unjustifiable /ʌnˈdʒʌstɪˌfaɪəbəl/ *adj.* incapable of being justified or explained
/prɪˈzjuːməblɪ/ *adv.* by reasonable assumption; very likely
cavalry /ˈkævəlrɪ/ *n.* troops trained to fight on horseback
bugle /ˈbjuːgəl/ *n.* a brass instrument often used for military calls and fanfares
anaesthetize /əˈniːsθətaɪz/ *v.* make unconscious by means of anesthetic drugs
tinker with make some small changes to sth., in an attempt to improve it or repair it

is bad, language must suffer. I should expect to find — this is a guess which I have not sufficient knowledge to verify — that the German, Russian and Italian languages have all deteriorated in the last ten to fifteen years, as a result of dictatorship.

But if thought corrupts language, language can also corrupt thought. A bad usage can spread by tradition and imitation, even among people who should and do know better. The debased language that I have been discussing is in some ways very convenient. Phrases like a not unjustifiable assumption, leaves much to be desired, would serve no good purpose, a consideration which we should do well to bear in mind, are a continuous temptation, a packet of aspirins always at one's elbow. Look back through this essay, and for certain you will find that I have again and again committed the very faults I am protesting against. By this morning's post I have received a pamphlet dealing with conditions in Germany. The author tells me that he "felt impelled" to write it. I open it at random, and here is almost the first sentence that I see: "[The Allies] have an opportunity not only of achieving a radical transformation of Germany's social and political structure in such a way as to avoid a nationalistic reaction in Germany itself, but at the same time of laying the foundations of a cooperative and unified Europe." You see, he "feels impelled" to write — feels, presumably, that he has something new to say — and yet his words, like cavalry horses answering the bugle, group themselves automatically into the familiar dreary pattern. This invasion of one's mind by ready-made phrases (lay the foundations, achieve a radical transformation) can only be prevented if one is constantly on guard against them, and every such phrase anaesthetizes a portion of one's brain.

I said earlier that the decadence of our language is probably curable. Those who deny this would argue, if they produced an argument at all, that language merely reflects existing social conditions, and that we cannot influence its development by any direct tinkering with words and constructions. As far as the general tone or spirit of a language goes, this may be true, but it is not true in detail. Silly words and expressions have often disappeared, not through any evolutionary process but owing to the conscious action of a minority. Two recent examples were explore every avenue and leave no stone unturned, which were killed by the jeers of a few journalists. There is a long list of flyblown metaphors which could similarly be got rid of if enough people would interest themselves in the job; and it should also be possible to laugh the not unformation* out of existence, to reduce the amount of Latin and Greek in the average sentence, to drive out foreign phrases and strayed scientific words, and, in general, to make pretentiousness unfashionable. But all these are minor points. The defense of

flyblown /ˈflaɪˌbləʊn/ *adj.* **a.** spoiled and covered with eggs and larvae of flies **b.** foul and run-down and repulsive **c.** especially of reputation
stray /streɪ/ *v.* **a.** wander from a direct course or at random **b.** move about aimlessly or without any destination **c.** lose clarity or turn aside especially from the main subject of attention or course of argument in writing, thinking, or speaking
salvage /ˈsælvɪdʒ/ *v.* **a.** save from ruin, destruction, or harm **b.** collect discarded or refused material
obsolete /ˈɒbsəˌliːt/ *adj.* old; no longer in use or valid or fashionable
scrap /skræp/ *v.* dispose of (something useless or old)
prefabricated /priːˈfæbrɪkeɪtɪd/ *adj.* manufactured in standard sizes to be shipped and assembled elsewhere

the English language implies more than this, and perhaps it is best to start by saying what it does not imply.

To begin with it has nothing to do with archaism, with the salvaging of obsolete words and turns of speech, or with the setting up of a "standard English" which must never be departed from. On the contrary, it is especially concerned with the scrapping of every word or idiom which has outworn its usefulness. It has nothing to do with correct grammar and syntax, which are of no importance so long as one makes one's meaning clear, or with the avoidance of Americanisms, or with having what is called a "good prose style". On the other hand it is not concerned with fake simplicity and the attempt to make written English colloquial. Nor does it even imply in every case preferring the Saxon word to the Latin one, though it does imply using the fewest and shortest words that will cover one's meaning. What is above all needed is to let the meaning choose the word, and not the other way about. In prose, the worst thing one can do with words is to surrender to them. When you think of a concrete object, you think wordlessly, and then, if you want to describe the thing you have been visualizing you probably hunt about till you find the exact words that seem to fit it. When you think of something abstract you are more inclined to use words from the start, and unless you make a conscious effort to prevent it, the existing dialect will come rushing in and do the job for you, at the expense of blurring or even changing your meaning. Probably it is better to put off using words as long as possible and get one's meaning as clear as one can through pictures or sensations. Afterwards one can choose — not simply accept — the phrases that will best cover the meaning, and then switch round and decide what impression one's words are likely to make on another person. This last effort of the mind cuts out all stale or mixed images, all prefabricated phrases, needless repetitions, and humbug and vagueness generally. But one can often be in doubt

> **equivalent** /ɪˈkwɪvələnt/ *n.* a person or thing equal to another in value or measure or force or effect or significance etc
> **outright** /ˈaʊtraɪt/ *adj.* without reservation or exception
> **worn-out** *adj.* **a.** used until no longer useful **b.** drained of energy or effectiveness; extremely tired; completely exhausted
> **jackboot** /ˈdʒækbuːt/ *n.* heavy boots that come up to the knee, such as the ones worn by some soldiers
> **inferno** /ɪnˈfɜːnəʊ/ *n.* **a.** (Christianity) the abode of Satan and the forces of evil; where sinners suffer eternal punishment **b.** any place of pain and turmoil
> **refuse** /ˈrefjuːs/ *n.* waste; junk

about the effect of a word or a phase, and one needs rules that one can rely on when instinct fails. I think the following rules will cover most cases:

1. Never use a metaphor, simile or other figure of speech which you are used to seeing in print.
2. Never use a long word where a short one will do.
3. If it is possible to cut a word out, always cut it out.
4. Never use the passive where you can use the active.
5. Never use a foreign phrase, a scientific word or a jargon word if you can think of an everyday English equivalent.
6. Break any of these rules sooner than say anything outright barbarous.

These rules sound elementary, and so they are, but they demand a deep change of attitude in anyone who has grown used to writing in the style now fashionable.

Political language — and with variations this is true of all political parties, from conservatives to Anarchists — is designed to make lies sound truthful and murder the respectable, and to give an appearance of solidity to pure wind. One cannot change this all in a moment, but one can at least change one's own habits, and from time to time one can even, if one jeers loudly enough, send some worn-out and useless phrase — some jackboot, Achilles' heel,* hotbed, melting pot, acid test, veritable inferno or other lump of verbal refuse — into the dustbin where it belongs. (1946)

Cultural Notes

1. **George Orwell** (1903—1950) was the penname of Eric Arthur Blair who was an English novelist and journalist. His work is marked by clarity, intelligence and wit, awareness of social injustice, opposition to totalitarianism, and belief in democratic socialism. Considered perhaps the 20th century's best chronicler of English culture, Orwell wrote literary criticism, poetry, fiction and polemical journalism. He is best known for the dystopian novel *Nineteen Eighty-Four* (1949) and the allegorical novella *Animal Farm* (1945), which together have sold more copies than any two

books by any other 20th-century author. His book *Homage to Catalonia* (1938), an account of his experiences in the Spanish Civil War, is widely acclaimed, as are his numerous essays on politics, literature, language and culture. In 2008, The Times ranked him second on a list of "The 50 greatest British writers since 1945". This selection is based on his 1946 article.

2. **White books** refers to an official government report in any of a number of countries, including Britain, Australia, New Zealand, and Canada, which sets out the government's policy on a matter that is or will come before Parliament.

3. **the not un– formation** was a phraseology made up by George Orwell and he went further to offer examples to this formation in a footnote: "One can cure oneself of the *not un-* formation by memorizing this sentence: *A not unblack dog was chasing a not unsmall rabbit across a not ungreen field.*"

4. **Achilles:** In Greek mythology, Achilles was a Greek hero of the Trojan War, one of the central characters and the greatest warrior of Homer's *Iliad*. Later legends state that Achilles was invulnerable in all of his body except for his heel. **An Achilles' heel** is a deadly weakness in spite of overall strength, which can actually or potentially lead to downfall. While the mythological origin refers to a physical vulnerability, this idiomatic phrase is always used to refer to other attributes or qualities that can lead to downfall.

Comprehension Exercises

I. Answer the following questions based on the text.

1. What is the relationship between politics and the English language according to the author?
2. Please speculate and comment upon this statement: "In our time, political speech and writing are largely the defense of the indefensible."
3. What are the benefits for the use of stale metaphors, similes and metaphor according to the text?
4. The author tells us that a scrupulous writer will ask himself at least four questions. Does the author favor this kind of writer or not? Why?
5. What is the author's attitude toward the use of euphemism in political discourse?

II. Decide whether each of the following statements is true or false according to the text.

1. The decline of a language must ultimately have political and economic causes.
2. The fight against bad English is the professional writers' concern.
3. The author does not hold that the political writings of his time are generally bad writings.
4. According to the text, thought and language can corrupt each other.
5. Political language, no matter what political parties are controlling it, is deceptively truthful.

III. Select the most suitable word or phrases and fill in the following blanks in their proper form.

curtail	bombard	decadent	deplore	exclusive
fanciful	frivolous	indispensable	inflated	orthodoxy
presumably	rectification	scrupulous	squirt	shirk
slovenly	tinker	unjustifiable		

1. In particular, after the Opium War in 1840, China endured many trials and tribulations because of the _____ rule of feudalism and the ravaging aggression of imperialist powers.
2. Among the habits which children should shun are _____, rudeness, laziness, lying, stealing and slandering.
3. The group says it wants politicians to stop wasting public money on what it believes are _____ projects.
4. Science and chemistry concern all of us and must not remain the _____ field of experts.
5. Mr. Black, our language teacher, praised Tom O'Casey for his ____ attention to detail.
6. "I always take my responsibility and I'll never _____ from that," he told BBC Radio Cumbria.
7. These days, the dish has become almost _____ at wedding banquets, festivals and family celebrations.
8. Serious readers might dismiss these questions as _____, but concern about flesh-eating ghosts is manifestly evident in today's popular culture.
9. More than 30 categories of books were ruled as obscene publications, six publishing houses were ordered to suspend operations for _____.
10. Obama could (and probably will) revisit this decision, but for now it

represents a dramatic break with Clinton-era _____.

11. When you interview somebody in person, you get to have a conversation with them, not just _____ them with questions.
12. Muslim and Jewish leaders have issued statements _____ the violence and urging the United Nations to take action.
13. The main risk is that a major recession in the United States could sharply _____ exports from developing countries.
14. For all the afternoon, he had been _____ away at the broken machine, but to no avail.
15. The experienced detective came to his conclusion that this small knife is _____ the murder weapon.

IV. Try to paraphrase the following sentences, paying special attention to the underlined parts.

1. Most people who <u>bother with</u> the matter at all would admit that the English language is in a bad way, but it is <u>generally assumed</u> that we cannot <u>by conscious action</u> do anything about it.

2. It consists in <u>gumming together long strips of words</u> which have already been set in order by someone else, and <u>making the results presentable by sheer humbug</u>.

3. If you use <u>ready-made phrases</u>, you not only don't have to <u>hunt about for</u> words; you also don't have to bother with the rhythms of your sentences, since these phrases are generally so arranged as to be <u>more or less euphonious</u>.

4. You can <u>shirk</u> it by <u>simply throwing your mind open</u> and letting the ready-made phrases come <u>crowding in</u>.

5. And this <u>reduced state of consciousness</u>, if not <u>indispensable</u>, is at any rate favorable to <u>political conformity</u>.

V. Discuss with your partner about each of the three statements and write an essay in no less than 250 words about your understanding of one of them.

1. Our civilization is decadent and our language — so the argument runs — must inevitably share in the general collapse.

2. But an effect can become a cause, reinforcing the original cause and producing the same effect in an intensified form, and so on indefinitely.

3. The political dialects to be found in pamphlets, leading articles, manifestos, White Papers and the speeches of undersecretaries do, of course, vary from party to party, but they are all alike in that one almost never finds in them a fresh, vivid, home-made turn of speech.

VI. List four websites where we can learn more about George Orwell or about the relationship between politics and language and provide a brief introduction to each of them.

1.
2.
3.
4.

Twenty Minutes' Reading

You are required to read the following two sections within 20 minutes.

SECTION A

When the sun is up in Amsterdam, the largest city in the Netherlands sits quietly on the Amstel River. You can rent a bicycle, visit the Van Gogh or Anne Frank museum, or take a water taxi.

But when the sun goes down, the partying begins. In the big clubs and in coffee shops, tourists gather to hang out, talk politics and smoke.

Several areas of the city clearly show the two worlds that rule Amsterdam. And they're all within a short cab ride of each other.

For example, Dam Square attracts daytime sightseers to its festivals, open markets, concerts and other events. Several beautiful and very popular hotels can be found there. And there is the Royal Palace and the Magna Plaza shopping mall.

But as evening descends on Dam Square so do the party-seekers. Hip pop or funk music begins blaring from Club Paradiso and Club Melkweg. These are two of the most popular clubs in Europe. So if you come, be ready to dance. The clubs don't shut down until 4 am.

And while you are there, check out the various inexpensive ways to tour the city. Don't worry about getting lost. Although Dutch is the official language, most people in Amsterdam speak English and are happy to help you with directions.

And you'll notice that half the people in the streets are on bicycles. They rent for US$17 to $20 for a whole day.

Amsterdam also has a good canal system. From anywhere between US$2 and $9.50, you can use the canal bus or a water taxi to cruise the "Venice of the North".

You can take in the picturesque canal house architecture: the rows of neat, narrow four-story dwellings of brownstone with large windows are well worth seeing. Many of them are several centuries old.

You might also want to jump out of the canal bus at the Museum Quarter and start walking. Masterpieces by Dutch artists such as Rembrandt, Brueghel, Van Gogh and others are on display at the Van Gogh Museum, Rembrandt House and others.

The city has an appreciation of its historic past. One place to visit is the Anne Frank House in Nine Streets. It was there that the young Jewish girl wrote her famous diary during World War II. Visitors can view Anne's original diary and climb behind the bookcase to the room where she and her family hid from the Nazis for two years.

1. At the beginning of the passage, the author indicates that _____.
   A. Amsterdam is generally known as a quiet city
   B. parties go on all day long in Amsterdam
   C. Amsterdam presents two different pictures
   D. Amsterdam attracts many daytime visitors
2. Which tourist attraction is cited for elaboration in Paragraphs Four and Five?
   A. Royal Palace.   B. Dam Square.
   C. Club Paradiso.   D. Magna Plaza.
3. According to the passage, the local people have all the following characteristics EXCEPT _____.
   A. they are party goers   B. they show hospitality
   C. they can speak English   D. they are fond of cycling
4. Which of the following adjectives can best describe Amsterdam as a tourist city?
   A. Modern.   B. Delightful.   C. Quiet.   D. Historic.

SECTION B

In an article some Chinese scholars are described as being "tantalized by the mysterious dragon bone hieroglyphics". Tantalized is one of many English words that have their origins in myths and legends of the past (in this case, Greek and Roman ones). The meaning of the verb tantalize is a very particular one: "to promise or show something desirable to a person and then take it away; to tease by arousing hope." Many (but not all) English dictionaries give you a brief indication of a word's origins in brackets before or after the explanation of the meaning. For tantalize the following explanation is given: [> Tantalus]. This means that you should look up the name Tantalus to find out the word's origins, and if you do, you will find out that in Greek mythology, Tantalus was a king who was punished in the lower world with eternal hunger and thirst; he was put up to his chin in water that always moved away when he tried to drink it and with fruit on branches above him placed just a little bit out of his reach. Can you see why his name was changed into a verb meaning "to tease or torment by arousing desire"?

Another example is the word siren, familiar to us as the mechanical device that makes such an alarming sound when police cars, ambulances, or fire engines approach. This word also has its origins in Greek mythology. The traveler Odysseus (Ulysses to the Romans) made his men plug their ears so that they wouldn't hear the dangerous voices of the sirens, creatures who were half bird and half woman and who lured sailors to their deaths on sharp rocks. So the word came to be associated both with a loud sound and with danger!

When someone speaks of a "jovial mood" or a "Herculean effort", he or she is using words with origins in mythology. Look these words up to find their meaning and relationship to myths.

Many common words, such as the names for the days of the week and the months of the year, also come from mythology. Wednesday derives from the ancient Norse king of the gods, Woden, and Thursday was originally Thor's day, in honour of Thor, the god of thunder. As a matter of fact, all the planets, except the one we live on, bear names that come from Roman mythology, including the planet that is farthest away from the sun and for that reason was called after the Roman god of the dead. This god has also given his name to one of the chemical elements. Several other elements have names that come from mythology, too.

It seems that myths and legends live on in the English language.

5. The purpose of the first sentence in Paragraph One is _____.
   A. to describe the work of some Chinese scholars
   B. to arouse readers' interest in hieroglyphics
   C. to lead readers onto the main theme
   D. to link the preceding part to the present one
6. We learn from the passage, all English dictionaries include _____.
   A. legends   B. mythology
   C. word origins   D. word definitions
7. The example of tantalize is to show _____.
   A. how the word came into existence
   B. how Tantalus was punished in the lower world
   C. how all English dictionaries show word origins
   D. how the meaning of the word changed over the years
8. According to the passage, which of the following does NOT have origins in myths or legends?
   A. Jovial.   B. Wednesday.
   C. Earth.   D. March.
9. Which of the following can best serve as the title of the passage?
   A. Greek and Roman Mythology in Language.
   B. Mythological Origins of English Words.
   C. Historical Changes in Word Meanings.
   D. Mythology and Common Words.

Unit Ten

Text A

Daydreams of What You'd Rather Be
Lance Morrow*

Kierkegaard* once confided to his journal that he would have been much happier if he had become a police spy rather than a philosopher. Richard Nixon* always wanted to be a sportswriter. If one considers these fantasies together, they seem to have got weirdly crossed. It is Nixon who should have been the police spy. On the other hand, Kierkegaard would probably have made an extraordinarily depressing sportswriter *(Fear and Trembling: The Angst of Bucky Dent)*.

We have these half-secret old ambitions—to be something else, to be someone else, to leap out of the interminable self and into another skin, another life. It is usually a brief out-of-body phenomenon, the sort of thing that we think when our gaze drifts away in the middle of a conversation. Goodbye. The imagination floats through a window into the conjectural and finds there a kind of bright blue antiself. The spirit stars itself in a brief hypothesis, an alternative, a private myth. What we imagine at such moments can suggest peculiar truths of character.

One rummages in closets for these revelations. Kierkegaard's fancy about being a police spy is a dark, shiny little item: a melancholic's impulse toward sneaking omnipotence, the intellectual furtively collaborating with state power, committing sins of betrayal in police sta-

confide /kənˈfaɪd/ *v.* to impart secrets trustfully
weird /wɪəd/ *adj.* **a.** involving or suggesting the supernatural; unearthly or uncanny **b.** fantastic; bizarr —weirdly *adv.*
cross /krɒs/ *v.* **a.** to mark with a cross **b.** to lie or pass across; intersect **c.** to mix
interminable /ɪnˈtɜːmɪnəbəl/ *adj.* incapable of being terminated; unending
conjectural /kənˈdʒektʃərəl/ *adj.* **a.** involving conjecture, problematical **b.** given to making conjectures
hypothesis /haɪˈpɒθɪsɪs/ *n.* **a.** a proposition set forth as an explanation **b.** a premise in an argument
rummage /ˈrʌmɪdʒ/ *v.* to search thoroughly (a place, receptacle, etc.)
melancholic /melənˈkɒlɪk/ *n.* a person disposed to or affected with melancholy
omnipotent /ɒmˈnɪpətənt/ *adj.* almighty or infinite in power, as God—omnipotence: the quality or state of being omnipotent
furtive /ˈfɜːtɪv/ *adj.* taken, done, used, etc. surreptitiously or by stealth —furtively *adv.*

tions in the middle of the night. It is not far from another intellectual's fantasy: Norman Mailer* once proposed that Eugene McCarthy*, the dreamboat of the late '60s moderate left, might have made an ideal director of the FBI. McCarthy agreed. But of course, McCarthy had a sardonic genius for doubling back his public self and vanish. He did magic tricks of self-annihilation. Nixon's imaginary career—wholesome, all-American, unimpeachable—may suggest both a yearning for blamelessness (what could possibly be tainted in his writing about baseball?) and an oblique, pre-emptive identification with an old enemy: the press.

The daydream of an alternative self is a strange, flitting thing. This wistful speculation often occurs in summer, when a vacation loosens the knot of one's vocational identity. Why, dammit, says the refugee from middle management on his 13th day on the lake, why not just stay here all year? Set up as a fishing guide. Open a lodge. We'll take the savings and ... The soul at odd moments (the third trout, the fourth beer) will make woozy rushes at the pipe dream. Like a gangster who has cooperated with the district attorney, we want a new name and a new career and a new house in a different city—and maybe a new nose from the D.A.'s cosmetic surgeon.

Usually, the impulse passes. The car gets packed and pointed back toward the old reality. The moment dissolves, like one of those instants when one falls irrevocably in love with the face of a stranger through the window as the bus pulls away.

Sometimes, the urge does not vanish. The results are alarming. This month Ferdinand Waldo Demara Jr.* died. That was his final career change. His obituary

dreamboat /'dri:mbəʊt/ *n.* **a.** a highly attractive or desirable person **b.** anything considered as highly desirable of its kind
sardonic /sɑ:'dɒnɪk/ *adj.* characterized by bitter or scornful derision; mocking; cynical; sneering
double back to turn back on a course or reverse direction
vanish /'vænɪʃ/ *v.* **a.** to disappear from sight, esp. quickly; become invisible **b.** to go away, esp. furtively or mysteriously
yearning /'jɜ:nɪŋ/ *adj.* deep longing, esp. when accompanied by tenderness or sadness
taint /teɪnt/ *v.* **a.** to infect, contaminate, corrupt, or spoil **b.** to tarnish (a person's name, reputation, etc.)
oblique /ə'bli:k/ *adj.* **a.** indirectly stated or expressed; not straight-forward **b.** morally or mentally wrong
pre-emptive /pri:'emptɪv/ *adj.* taken as a measure against sth. possible, anticipated, or feared
flit /flɪt/ *v.* **a.** to move lightly and swiftly **b.** to flutter, as a bird; **c.** to pass quickly, as time
wistful /'wɪstfəl/ *adj.* **a.** characterized by melancholy; longing; yearning **b.** pensive, esp. in a melancholy way
speculation /spekjʊ'leɪʃən/ *n.* **a.** the contemplation **b.** a single instance or process of consideration
refugee /refjʊ'dʒi:/ *n.* a person who flees for refuge or safety, esp. to a foreign country
middle management the middle echelon of administration
woozy /'wu:zɪ/ *adj.* stupidly confused; muddled
pipe dream any fantastic notion, hope, or story
gangster /'gæŋstə/ *n.* a member of a gang of criminals, esp. a racketeer
district attorney an officer who acts as attorney for the people or government within a specific district
irrevocable /ɪ'revəkəbəl/ *adj.* unable to be revoked or annulled; unalterable —**irrevocably** *adv.*
obituary /ə'bɪtʃʊərɪ/ *n.* a notice of the death of a person, often with a biographical sketch, as in a newspaper

listed nearly as many metamorphoses as Ovid* did. Demara, "the Great Imposter," spent years of his life being successfully and utterly someone else: a Trappist monk, a doctor of psychology, a dean of philosophy at a small Pennsylvania college, a law student, a surgeon in the Royal Canadian Navy, a deputy warden at a prison in Texas. Demara took the protean itch and amateur's gusto, old American traits, to new frontiers of pathology and fraud.

Usually, it is only from the safety of retrospect and an established self that we entertain ourselves with visions of an alternative life. The daydreams are an amusement, a release from the monotony of what we are, from the life sentence of the mirror. The imagination's pageant of an alternative self is a kind of vacation of one's fate. Kierkegaard did not really mean he should have been a police spy, or Nixon that he should have been a sportswriter. The whole mechanism of daydreams of the antiself usually depends upon the fantasy remaining fantasy. Hell is answered prayers. God help us if we had actually married that girl when we were 21.

In weak, incoherent minds, the yearning antiself rises up and breaks through a wall into actuality. That seems to have happened with John W. Hinkley Jr., the young man who shot Ronald Reagan* last year. Since no strong self disciplined his vagrant aches and needs, it was his antiself that pulled the trigger. It was his nonentity. The antiself is a monster sometimes, a cancer, a gnawing hypothesis.

All of our lives we are accompanied vaguely by the selves we might be. Man is the only creature that can imagine being someone else. The fantasy of being someone else is the basis of sympathy, of humanity. Daydreams of possibility enlarge the mind. They are also haunting. Around every active mind there always hovers an aura of hypothesis and the subjunctive: almost every conscious intellect is continuously wandering elsewhere in time and space.

imposter /ɪmˈpɒstə/ n. also impostor, a person who practices deception under an assumed character, identity, or name
Trappist /ˈtræpɪst/ n. Rom. Cath. Ch. a member of a branch of the Cistercian order, observing the austere reformed rule established at La Trappe in 1664
protean /ˈprəʊtiːən/ adj. **a.** extremely variable and changeable **b.** (of an actor) versatile; able to play many kinds of roles
gusto /ˈɡʌstəʊ/ n. **a.** hearty enjoyment, as in eating or drinking, or in action or speech **b.** individual taste or liking
retrospect /ˈretrəspekt/ n. contemplation of the past; a survey of past time, events, etc.
monotony /məˈnɒtəni/ n. wearisome uniformity or lack of variety, as in occupation or scenery
pageant /ˈpædʒənt/ n. a costumed procession
incoherent /ˌɪnkəʊˈhɪərənt/ adj. without logical or meaningful connection; disjointed; rambling
discipline /ˈdɪsɪplɪn/ v. **a.** to train by instruction; drill **b.** to bring to a state of order by training and control
vagrant /ˈveɪɡrənt/ wandering or roaming from place to place
nonentity /nɒˈnentɪti/ n. **a.** a person or thing of no importance **b.** sth. that does no exist **c.** nonexistence
gnaw /nɔː/ v. **a.** to bite or chew on **b.** to waste or wear away **c.** to trouble or torment by constant annoyance
hover /ˈhɒvə/ v. **a.** to hang fluttering or suspended in the air **b.** to keep lingering about
subjunctive /səbˈdʒʌŋktɪv/ n. the subjunctive mood or mode

The past 20 years have stimulated the antiself. They have encouraged the notion of continuous self-renewal—as if the self were destined to be an endless series of selves.

Each one would be better than the last, or at least different, which was the point: a miracle of transformations, dreams popping into reality on fast-forward, life as a hectic multiple exposure.

hectic /ˈhektɪk/ *adj.* full of excitement and hurried movement
nimbus /ˈnɪmbəs/ *n.* a cloud, aura, atmosphere, etc., surrounding a person or thing, or a deity when on earth
evanescent /ˌevəˈnesənt/ *adj.* **a.** vanishing; fading away **b.** tending to become imperceptible
fervent /ˈfɜːvənt/ *adj.* showing great warmth or intensity of spirit, feeling, enthusiasm, etc.; ardent —**fervently** *adv.*
coalesce /ˌkəʊəˈles/ *v.* **a.** to grow together or into one body; **b.** to blend or come together
duet /djuːˈet/ *n.* a musical composition for two voices or instruments

For some reason, the more frivolous agitations of the collective antiself seem to have calmed down a little. Still, we walk around enveloped in it, like figures in the nimbus of their own ghosts on a television screen. Everything that we are not has a kind of evanescent being within us. We dream, and the dream is much of the definition of the true self. Last week Lena Horne said that she has always imagined herself being a teacher. Norman Vincent Peale says fervently that he wanted to be a salesman—and of course that is, in a sense, what he has always been. Opera singer Grace Bumbry wants to be a professional race-car driver. Bill Veeck, former owner of the Chicago White Sox, confides the alternate Veeck: a newspaperman. In a "nonfiction short story", Truman Capote wrote that he wanted to be a girl. Andy Warhol confesses without hesitation: "I've always wanted to be an airplane. Nothing more, nothing less. Even when I found out that they could crash, I still wanted to be an airplane."

The antiself has a shadowy, ideal life of its own. It is always blessed (the antiself is the Grecian Urn* of our personality) and yet it subtly matures as it runs a course parallel to our actual aging. The Hindu might think that the antiself is a premonition of the soul's next life. Perhaps. But in the last moment of this life, self and antiself may coalesce . It should be their parting duet to mutter together: "On the whole, I'd rather be in Philadelphia."

Cultural Notes

1. **Lance Morrow** (1939—) is a professor of journalism at Boston University. Author of 150 cover stories, including seven "Man of the Year" stories, Morrow has gained distinction as an essayist during his 32 years at *Time* magazine, for which he continues to write essays, book reviews and cover stories. He won the National Magazine Award for Essay and Criticism in 1981 and

was a finalist for the same honor in 1991.

2. **Soren Kierkegaard** (1813—1855) was a profound and prolific writer in the Danish "golden age" of intellectual and artistic activity. His work crosses the boundaries of philosophy, theology, psychology, literary criticism, devotional literature and fiction. As a precursor of modern existentialism, he cultivated paradox and irony throughout his life. His works include *Either/Or* and *Fear and Trembling*.

3. **Richard Nixon** (1913—1994) was the only American President to resign in disgrace. His crime was his involvement in the Watergate break-in at the offices of the Democratic National Committee during the 1972 campaign. Nixon denied any personal involvement, but the courts forced him to yield tape recordings which indicated that he had, in fact, tried to divert the investigation. Faced with what seemed almost certain impeachment, Nixon announced on August 8, 1974, that he would resign the next day to begin "that process of healing which is so desperately needed in America." In his last years, Nixon wrote numerous books on his experiences in public life and on foreign policy, and gained praise as an elder statesman.

4. **Norman Mailer** (1923—2007) was an American writer and innovator of the nonfictional novel. His novel *The Naked and the Dead* (1948), based on his personal experiences during World War II, made him world-famous, and was hailed by many as one of the best American novels to come out of the war years. In the mid 1950s he became famous as an anti-establishment essayist. In pieces such as *The White Negro: Superficial Reflections on the Hipster* (1956) and *Advertisement for Myself* (1959), Mailer examined violence, hysteria, crime, and confusion in American society.

5. **Eugene McCarthy** (1916—2005) entered politics as a Democrat, serving five terms in the US House of Representatives between 1949 and 1959. In 1966, he articulated his opposition to President Johnson's policy in Vietnam. The next year, he became a candidate for the Democratic Presidential nomination, supporting a negotiated peace in Vietnam. With the backing of large numbers of college students, McCarthy achieved great success in the early primaries, contributing to Johnson's decision to withdraw from the Presidential race in 1968. In 1971 McCarthy lost the Democratic nomination to Hubert Humphrey at the Chicago convention, which was the scene of what was later termed a "police riot" by Democratic mayor Richard Daley's law enforcement operations targeting the army of anti-war protesters. During the mêlées between protesters and police, McCarthy worried that Daley might have his children imprisoned, beaten, or murdered. The Chicago convention,

in which CBS reporter Dan Rather was punched in the stomach on-camera by a plain-clothes detective, was one of the nadirs of American politics. Attempting to reenter politics, McCarthy ran independently for President in 1976 and ran in a Senate primary in 1982, but was unsuccessful in both attempts.

6. **Ferdinand Waldo Demara Jr.** (1921—1982) was best known as "the Great Imposter". His career as an imposter spanned three decades and included a bizarre variety of pseudo-identities. Gifted with a sharp intellect and a photographic memory, Demara simply taught himself the techniques necessary for his deception by reading text books. Personal gain did not seem to be a motivation for him. He was an imposter for the sake of being one and described his own motivation as "rascality, pure rascality".

7. **Ovid** (43 BC—17 BC) was a Roman poet, whose narrative skill and unmatched linguistic and metrical virtuosity have made him the most popular of the Roman poets. In his middle period Ovid wrote *The Metamorphoses*, which is based on the transformations recorded in mythology and legend from the creation of the world to the time of Roman emperor Julius Caesar, whose change into a celestial star marks the last of the series.

8. **Ronald Wilson Reagan** (1911—2004) was born in Illinois. A screen test in 1937 won him a contract in Hollywood. During the next two decades he appeared in 53 films. He won the Republican Presidential nomination in 1980. Voters troubled by inflation and by the year-long confinement of Americans in Iran swept the Republican ticket into office. On January 20, 1981, Reagan took office. Two months later he was shot by an assassin, but quickly recovered and returned to duty. His grace and wit during the dangerous incident caused his popularity to soar.

9. **The Grecian Urn** in "Ode on a Grecian Urn" written by John Keats (1795—1821) is symbolic of something, which is both lively and lifeless, both mortal and immortal.

Comprehension Exercises

I. Answer the following questions based on the text.

1. Why does the writer say that "Kierkegaard would probably have made an extraordinarily depressing sportswriter" in the first paragraph?
2. What is the tone of the voice when Morrow says that "it is Nixon who should have been the police spy"?

3. What might be a proper definition of the term "antiself" according to Lance Morrow?
4. What are the most valuable things concerning the pipe dream of an alternative self?
5. Why does the writer say that he would rather be in Philadelphia?

II. Decide whether each of the following statements is true or false according to the text.

1. Kierkegaard had a melancholy personality.
2. McCarthy deliberately kept a low profile and successfully retreated from politics.
3. Ferdinand Waldo Demara Jr. had many professions throughout his life.
4. John W. Hinckley Jr. shot Ronald Reagon for political reasons.
5. It is normal for almost anyone to have his or her antiself.
6. It is harmful for one to change his career constantly.

III. Select the most suitable word or phrases and fill in the following blanks in their proper form.

confide	conjectural	evanescent	flit	furtively
hectic	interminable	irrevocable	melancholic	omnipotence
pageant	preemptive	protean	retrospect	rummage
sardonic	unimpeachable	vagrant	wistful	incoherent

1. That very morning Mary went upstairs to the attic and _____ through piles of secondhand clothes for something that fits.
2. I knew she had some fundamental problems in her marriage because she had _____ in me a year earlier.
3. But there were large areas of the map that, apart from the Village name, were entirely empty and _____ — in fact, nonexistent.
4. From the outset of this private conversation to its very end, he had been talking to me _____ about his first wife.
5. Some people associate winter with the time of _____ clouds and sharp winds, endless nights and transient days.
6. And another philosopher, Descartes, in thinking about God, thought that it wouldn't be good enough if the _____ God couldn't change the facts of mathematics.
7. With guards right outside the room, we _____ destroyed evidence in our possession by swallowing notes and damaging videotapes.

8. The gardener continued to lean against the wall, arms folded, sneering at them with a _____ expression.
9. The school's website says that it has been in existence for 150 years and has "always maintained a standard of _____ integrity".
10. Even so, when he launches a _____ strike it seems to be as much in sorrow as in anger.
11. She somehow managed to smile and laugh at the same time, her brilliant teeth an annotation to her laughter, her hair merrily _____ around.
12. The experience will fill you with fond memories and perhaps make you a bit _____ for days gone by.
13. My relationships with friends have been _____ altered by their indifferent reactions to my illness.
14. He is a _____ stylist who can move from blues to ballads and grand symphony.
15. At the end of a _____ day do you have a twinge in your back, knot in your stomach, or pounding in your head?

IV. Try to paraphrase the following sentences, paying special attention to the underlined parts.

1. If one considers these <u>fantasies</u> together, they seem to have got <u>weirdly crossed.</u>

   _____
   _____

2. The spirit stares itself in <u>a brief hypothesis, an alternative,</u> a private myth.

   _____

3. The imagination floats through a window into <u>the conjectural</u> and finds there a kind of <u>bright blue antiself</u>.

   _____

4. <u>The daydream of an alternative self</u> is a strange, <u>flitting</u> thing. This <u>wistful speculation</u> often occurs in summer, when a vacation loosens the knot of one's vocational identity.

   _____
   _____

5. Usually, it is only from the safety of retrospect and an established self that we entertain ourselves with visions of an alternative life.
   _____
   _____

V. Discuss with your partner about each of the three statements and write an essay in no less than 250 words about your understanding of one of them.

1. We have these half-secret old ambitions — to be something else, to be someone else, to leap out of the interminable self and into another skin, another life.
   _____
   _____

2. The daydreams are an amusement, a release from the monotony of what we are, from the life sentence of the mirror.
   _____
   _____

3. The antiself has a shadowy, ideal life of its own.
   _____
   _____

VI. List four websites where we can learn more about Lance Morrow and provide a brief introduction to each of them.

1. _____
   _____
   _____.

2. _____
   _____
   _____.

3. _____
   _____
   _____.

4. _____
   _____
   _____.

Text B

Culture and Food Habits
Joan Young Gregg*

All individuals must eat to survive — but what people eat, when they eat, and the manner in which they eat are all patterned by culture. No society views everything in its environment that is edible and might provide nourishment as food: certain edibles are ignored, others are tabooed. These food taboos may be so strong that just the thought of eating forbidden foods can cause an individual to feel ill. A Hindu vegetarian would feel this way about eating any kind of meat, an American about eating dogs, and a Moslem or orthodox Jew about eating pork. The taboo on eating human flesh is probably the most universal of all food taboos. Although some societies in the past practiced ritual cannibalism, members of most modern societies have resorted to cannibalism only under the most desperate of circumstances. The cases of cannibalism by the Donner Pass party* and recently by a South American soccer team* caused a great furor. Human flesh may be a source of protein, but it is not one that most humans are willing to use.

The ways in which human beings obtain their food is one of culture's most fascinating stories. Food getting has gone through several stages of development in the hundreds of thousands of years of humanity's existence on earth. For most of this time on earth, people have supported themselves with the pattern called hunting and gathering. This pattern relies on food that is naturally available in the environment. It includes the hunting of large and small game animals, fishing, and the collecting of various plant foods. It does not include producing food either by planting or by keeping domesticated animals for their milk or meat. Today, only about 30,000 of the world's people live solely by hunting and gathering.

Another ancient pattern of obtaining food is

edible /ˈedɪbəl/ *adj.* able to be eaten safely
taboo /təˈbuː/ *v.* to take as too holy or evil to be touched, named, or used —taboo *n.* a strong social custom forbidding naming, touching or using sth.
vegetarian /ˌvedʒɪˈteərɪən/ *n.* a person who does not eat meat or fish
orthodox /ˈɔːθədɒks/ *adj.* holding accepted religious or political opinions
ritual /ˈrɪtʃuəl/ *n.* one or more ceremonies or customary acts often repeated in the same form
cannibalism /ˈkænɪbəlɪzəm/ *n.* practice of eating the flesh of one's own kind
resort to to make use of; turn to (often sth. bad) for help
desperate /ˈdespərɪt/ *adj.* very difficult and dangerous (used of a situation)

pastoralism, which is the raising of domesticated herd animals such as goats, sheep, camels, or cattle, all of which produce both milk and meat. Pastoralism is a specialized adaptation to a harsh or mountainous environment that is not productive enough to support a large human population through agriculture. The major areas of pastoralism are found in East Africa, where cattle are raised; North Africa, where camels are raised; Southwest Asia, where sheep and goats are raised; and the sub-Arctic, where caribou and reindeer are domesticated and herded. Pastoralism alone cannot support a human population, so additional food grain must either be produced or purchased by trade with other groups.

The third major type of acquiring food is through *agriculture,* or the planting, raising, and harvesting of crops from the land. Agriculture, which is only about 10,000 years old, may range from simple, nonmechanized horticulture to farming with the help of animal-drawn plows, to the extensively mechanized agriculture of industrialized nations. Anthropologists generally agree that it was the gradual transition from hunting and gathering to agriculture that opened up new possibilities for cultural development.

Cultural patterns of getting food are generated primarily by the natural, or physical, environment of the group. All human groups, like other animal communities, have developed special ways of making their environment nurture and support them. Where several groups share the same environment, they use it in different ways, so they can live harmoniously with each other. In a study of northern Pakistan, for example, Kohistanis, Pathans, and Gujars inhabit the same mountainous area. These three groups are able to coexist peacefully because each utilizes a different aspect of the land. The Pathans are farmers, using the valley regions for raising wheat, corn, and rice. The Kohistanis live in the colder mountainous regions, herding sheep, goats, cattle, and water buffalo and raising millet and corn. The Gujars are full-time herders and use marginal areas not used by the Kohistanis. The Gujars provide milk and meat products to the Pathan farmers and also work as agricultural laborers during the busy seasons. These

furor /ˈfjʊərɔː/ *n.* a sudden burst of angry or excited interest among a large group of people
game /geɪm/ *n.* wild animals, birds and fish which are hunted for food and as a sport
domesticate /dəˈmestɪkeɪt/ *v.* to make an animal able to live with people and serve them, esp. on a farm
pastoralism /ˈpɑːstərəlɪzəm/ *n.* the practice of herding as the primary economic activity of a society
caribou /ˈkærɪbuː/ *n.* American reindeer
herd /hɜːd/ *v.* to look after a company of animals feeding or going about together
horticulture /ˈhɔːtɪkʌltʃə/ *n.* the practice of growing fruit, flowers, and vegetables
anthropology /ˌænθrəˈpɒlədʒɪ/ *n.* the scientific study of the nature of man, including the development of his body, mind and society —anthropologist: someone who studies anthropology
nurture /ˈnɜːtʃə/ *v.* to care for and encourage the development of something or someone
inhabit /ɪnˈhæbɪt/ *v.* to live in a place
utilize /ˈjuːtɪlaɪz/ *v.* to use sth. in a practical way
millet /ˈmɪlɪt/ *n.* the small seeds of certain grain plants used as food
marginal /ˈmɑːdʒɪnəl/ *adj.* **a.** not very important or large **b.** on or in a margin

patterns of specialized and harmonious relationships among different cultures in a local environment are typical of pastoral, or herding, people.

Some food-getting patterns or food habits are not so easy to understand as those described. The origins of many culturally patterned food habits still puzzle anthropologists. Some of these food habits appear on the surface to be irrational and <u>detrimental</u> to the existence of the group. For example, consider the Hindu taboo on eating beef despite the widespread <u>poverty</u> and <u>periodic famine</u> in that country. Yet anthropologist Marvin Harris views this Hindu taboo as an ecological adaptation—that is, as an adjustment to a specific environmental condition. Harris states that cows are important in India not because they can be eaten but because they give birth to <u>bullocks</u>, the essential farming animals that pull plows and carts. If a family were to eat its cows during a famine, it would <u>deprive</u> itself of the source of its bullocks and could not continue farming. Thus the religious taboo on eating beef strengthens the ability of the society to maintain itself <u>in the long run</u>.

It is also possible that there is a biological component to the avoidance of certain foods in specific cultures. The Chinese <u>aversion</u> to milk, for example, may be caused by the fact that <u>lactase</u>, an <u>enzyme</u> that helps <u>digest</u> the sugar <u>lactose</u> in milk, is missing in many Mongoloid* populations. As a result, the milk sugar, lactose, cannot be digested, and drinking milk frequently causes <u>intestinal distress</u>. Evidence to support biological reasons for food taboos is <u>scarce</u>, however, and at this point it seems safest to say that it is primarily culture that tells us which foods are edible and which are not.

detrimental /ˌdetrɪˈmentl/ *adj.* having harmful or damaging effects
poverty /ˈpɒvəti/ *n.* the state of being poor
periodic /ˌpɪəriˈɒdɪk/ *adj.* happening occasionally, usu. at regular times
famine /ˈfæmɪn/ *n.* very serious lack of food
bullock /ˈbʊlək/ *n.* a young bull which has had its sex organs removed so that it cannot breed
deprive /dɪˈpraɪv/ *v.* to take sth. away from someone
in the long run in the course of long experience; in the end
aversion /əˈvɜːʃən/ *n.* a strong dislike for sth.
lactase /ˈlækteɪs/ *n.* (biochem)乳糖酶
enzyme /ˈenzaɪm/ *n.* 酶
digest /daɪˈdʒest/ *v.* to change food in the stomach into a form that the body can use
lactose /ˈlæktəʊs/ *n.* 酶
intestinal /ɪnˈtestɪnl/ *adj.* of the intestines, the tube carrying food from your stomach out of your body
distress /dɪˈstres/ *n.* great suffering, pain, or discomfort
scarce /skeəs/ *adj.* hard to find, and often not enough

Cultural Notes

1. **Joan Young Gregg** is teaching at New York Technical College. "Culture and Food Habits" is taken from her book *Communication and Culture—A Reading-Writing Text,* which offers ESL students a fascinating and successful way to strengthen their reading and writing abilities. A variety of absorbing, college-level readings give anthropological perspectives on multicultural issues such as family, gender roles, art, economics, time, and food.

2. **Donner Pass party** was a group of American migrants to California in 1846—1847. Two families, the Donners and the Reeds, accounted for most of the 87 members of the party, which left Sangamon County, Illinois, in 1846, under the leadership of George Donner. After considerable difficulty crossing the Great Salt Lake in Utah, they were trapped by heavy snows in the Sierra Nevada in November. Forced to camp for the winter at a small lake, now named Donner Lake, they suffered enormous hardships, and members of the group resorted to cannibalism in order to survive. Forty-seven of them were eventually brought to California by rescue parties over what is now known as Donner Pass.

3. **South American soccer team** is another instance of humans driven by starvation to eat the flesh of other humans. It occurred in Chile in 1972, when 16 members of a Uruguayan soccer team survived for 70 days after their airliner crashed in the Andes Mountains.

4. **Mongoloid** is a member of the peoples traditionally classified as the Mongoloid race, marked by yellowish complexion, prominent cheekbones, epicanthic folds about the eyes, and straight black hair, and including the Mongols, Chinese, Koreans, Japanese, Annamese, Burmese, and, to some extent, the Eskimos and the American Indians. The word is no longer in technical use.

Comprehension Exercises

I. Answer the following questions based on the text.

1. What is food taboo? Which food taboo is most universal in human society?
2. What psychosomatic illness is mentioned in the text?
3. What are the major patterns of getting food mentioned in the text?

4. Where is pastoralism mostly found?
5. What does the example of the Kohistanis, Pathans and Gujars of the northern Pakistan demonstrate?
6. How does the anthropologist Marvin Harris explain the Hindu taboo on eating beef?
7. Why is it difficult for many societies of Mongoloid origin to digest milk? What effect has this had on their food patterns?
8. What conclusion does the text draw? Are you satisfied with the conclusion? Why?

II. Decide whether each of the following statements is true or false according to the text.

1. No people now live solely by hunting and gathering.
2. People in some areas still rely solely on pastoralism for a living.
3. The change from hunting/gathering to agriculture is not of great significance.
4. Cultural patterns of getting food are mainly caused by natural environment of the group.
5. Some culturally patterned food habits appear to be unreasonable and harmful to the survival of the group.
6. Many food taboos are for biological reasons.

III. Select the most suitable word or phrases and fill in the following blanks in their proper form.

aversion	deprive	desperate	detrimental	digest
distress	domesticate	edible	famine	furor
game	herd	horticulture	marginal	nurture
orthodox	periodic	vegetarian		

1. When _____ fruits ripen, they change their colors or scent which appeal to humans, to "invite" us to take them.
2. We dined on homemade _____ dishes, another break from my regular days as an avid carnivore.
3. It is observed that the Reform Jews advocate a less strict interpretation of Jewish law than the _____ Jews.
4. Brown and June had been married nearly four years and June was _____ to start a family.
5. The incident raised nationalist _____ on both sides and sank bilateral relations to their lowest level in years.

6. James Fenimore Cooper invented a very important figure Natty Bumppo who shot _____ for food and was a natural marksman.

7. It was about 8,000 years ago that modern man's relatives in the Neolithic Age are known to have grown crops and _____ animals.

8. A herdsman grazing his animals on the pasture will have an incentive "to add another animal to his _____".

9. Nothing would be more _____ to our prospects for success than cutting back on education.

10. In the long run, this will _____ our future generations of livelihood from their land.

11. _____ checks of education are taken to ensure that high standards are maintained in this province.

12. It is an undeniable fact that many people have a natural and emotional _____ to a variety of insects.

13. Over the weekend, the Group of 20 largest economies met to discuss the world's economic _____.

14. _____ cultures in the past have rightfully entered the mainstream through business, taking money from the majority and infusing it into their own tribes.

15. The children are told not to undertake strenuous exercise for a few hours after a meal so that they might have enough time to _____ food.

IV. Try to paraphrase the following sentences, paying special attention to the underlined parts.

1. No society views everything in its environment that is edible and might provide nourishment as food: certain edibles are ignored, others are tabooed.

_____

_____

2. The taboo on eating human flesh is probably the most universal of all food taboos.

_____

_____

3. Although some societies in the past practiced ritual cannibalism, members of most modern societies have resorted to cannibalism only under the most desperate of circumstances.

_____

_____

4. This pattern relies on food that is naturally available in the environment. It

includes the hunting of large and small <u>game</u> animals, fishing, and the collecting of various plant foods.

5. Some of these food habits appear on the surface to be <u>irrational and detrimental</u> to the existence of the group. For example, consider the Hindu taboo on eating beef despite the widespread poverty and <u>periodic famine</u> in that country.

V. Discuss with your partner about each of the three statements and write an essay in no less than 250 words about your understanding of one of them.

1. All individuals must eat to survive — but what people eat, when they eat, and the manner in which they eat are all patterned by culture.

2. The ways in which human beings obtain their food is one of culture's most fascinating stories.

3. Cultural patterns of getting food are generated primarily by the natural or physical environment of the group.

VI. List four websites where we can learn more about Joan Young Gregg and provide a brief introduction to each of them.

1.

2.

3.

4. _____
   _____
   _____.

Twenty Minutes' Reading

You are required to read the following two sections within 20 minutes.

 SECTION A

My heart sank when the man at the immigration counter gestured to the back room. I'm an American born and raised, and this was Miami, where I live, but they weren't quite ready to let me in yet.

"Please wait in here, Ms Abujaber," the immigration officer said. My husband, with his very American last name, accompanied me. He was getting used to this. The same thing had happened recently in Canada when I'd flown to Montreal to speak at a book event. That time they held me for 45 minutes. Today we were returning from a literary festival in Jamaica, and I was startled that I was being sent "in back" once again.

The officer behind the counter called me up and said, "Miss, your name looks like the name of someone who's on our wanted list. We're going to have to check you out with Washington."

"How long will it take?"

"Hard to say... a few minutes," he said. "We'll call you when we're ready for you."

After an hour, Washington still hadn't decided anything about me. "Isn't this computerized?"

I asked at the counter. "Can't you just look me up?"

Just a few more minutes, they assured me.

After an hour and a half, I pulled my cell phone out to call the friends I was supposed to meet that evening. An officer rushed over. "No phones!" he said. "For all we know you could be calling a terrorist cell and giving them information."

"I'm just a university professor," I said. My voice came out in a squeak.

"Of course you are. And we take people like you out of here in leg irons every day."

I put my phone away.

My husband and I were getting hungry and tired. Whole families had been brought into the waiting room, and the place was packed with excitable children, exhausted parents, even a flight attendant.

I wanted to scream, to jump on a chair and shout: "I'm an American citizen; a novelist; l probably teach English literature to your children." Or would that all be counted against me?

After two hours in detention, I was approached by one of the officers. "You're free to go," he said. No explanation or apologies. For a moment, neither of us moved, we were still in shock.

Then we leaped to our feet.

"Oh, one more thing." He handed me a tattered photocopy with an address on it. "If you weren't happy with your treatment, you can write to this agency."

"Will they respond?" I asked.

"I don't know — I don't know of anyone who's ever written to them before." Then he added,

"By the way, this will probably keep happening each time you travel internationally."

"What can I do to keep it from happening again?"

He smiled the empty smile we'd seen all day. "Absolutely nothing."

After telling several friends about our ordeal, probably the most frequent advice I've heard in response is to change my name. Twenty years ago, my own graduate school writing professor advised me to write under a pen name so that publishers wouldn't stick me in what he called "the ethnic ghetto" — a separate, secondary shelf in the bookstore. But a name is an integral part of anyone's personal and professional identity — just like the town you're born in and the place where you're raised.

Like my father, I'll keep the name, but my airport experience has given me a whole new perspective on what diversity and tolerance are supposed to mean. I had no idea that being an American would ever be this hard.

1. The author was held at the airport because _____.
   A. she and her husband returned from Jamaica
   B. her name was similar to a terrorist's
   C. she had been held in Montreal
   D. she had spoken at a book event
2. She was not allowed to call her friends because _____.
   A. her identity hadn't been confirmed yet
   B. she had been held for only one hour and a half
   C. there were other families in the waiting room
   D. she couldn't use her own cell phone

3. We learn from the passage that the author would _____ to prevent similar experience from happening again.
   A. write to the agency   B. change her name
   C. avoid traveling abroad   D. do nothing
4. Her experiences indicate that there still exists _____ in the US.
   A. hatred   B. discrimination
   C. tolerance   D. diversity
5. The author sounds _____ in the last paragraph.
   A. impatient   B. bitter
   C. worried   D. ironic

SECTION B

Public speaking fills most people with dread. Humiliation is the greatest fear; self-exposure and failing to appeal to the audience come a close second. Women hate it most, since girls are pressurized from an early age to be concerned with appearances of all kinds.

Most people have plenty of insecurities, and this seems like a situation that will bring them out. If you were under pressure to be perfect, you are terrified of falling in the most public of ways.

While extroverts will feel less fear before the ordeal, it does not mean they will necessarily do it better. Some very shy people manage to shine. When I met the British comedian Julian Clary, he was shy and cautious, yet his TV performances are perfect.

In fact, personality is not the best predictor of who does it well. Regardless of what you are like in real life, the key seems to be to act yourself.

Actual acting, as in performing the scripted lines of a character other than yourself, does not do the job. While politicians may limit damage by having carefully rehearsed, written scripts to speak from, there is always a hidden awareness among the audience that the words might not be true.

Likewise, the incredibly perfect speeches of many American academics are far from natural. You may end up buying their book on the way out, but soon afterwards, it is much like fast food, and you get a nameless sense that you've been cheated.

Although, as Earl Spencer proved at his sister Princess Diana's funeral, it is possible both to prepare every word and to act naturally. A script rarely works and it is used to help most speakers.

But, being yourself doesn't work either. If you spoke as if you were in your own kitchen, it would be too authentic, too unaware of the need to communicate with an audience.

I remember going to see British psychiatrist R.D. Laing speak in public. He behaved like a seriously odd person, talking off the top of his head. Although he was talking about madness and he wrote on mental illness, he seemed to be exhibiting rather than explaining it.

The best psychological place from which to speak is an unselfconscious self-consciousness, providing the illusion of being natural. Studies suggest that this state of "flow", as psychologists call it, is very satisfying.

6. Women hate public speaking most mainly because of _____.
   A. their upbringing very early on
   B. their inability to appeal to the audience
   C. their sense of greater public pressure
   D. their sense of greater humiliation

7. "this" in Paragraph Two refers to _____.
   A. insecurity   B. sense of failure
   C. public speaking   D. pressure

8. Which of the following is NOT the author's viewpoint?
   A. Acting like performers spoils the message in a speech.
   B. Perfection of scripts is necessary in making good impressions.
   C. Acting naturally means less dependence on the prepared script.
   D. There should be a balance between actual acting and acting naturally.

9. What is the author's view on personality?
   A. Personality is the key to success in public speaking.
   B. Extroverts are better public speakers.
   C. Introverts have to learn harder to be good speakers.
   D. Factors other than personality ensure better performance.

10. The author implies that while speaking R. D. Laing _____.
    A. was both too casual and authentic
    B. was acting like a performer
    C. was keeping a good balance
    D. was aware of his audience

11. In the last paragraph the author recommends that _____.
    A. you forget about your nervousness
    B. you feel natural and speak naturally
    C. you may feel nervous, but appear naturally
    D. you may imagine yourself to be natural

Unit Eleven

Text A

Photographs of My Parents
Maxine Hong Kingston*

Once in a long while, four times so far for me, my mother brings out the metal tube that holds her medical diploma. On the tube are gold circles crossed with seven red lines each—"joy" ideographs in abstract. There are also little flowers that look like gears for a gold machine. According to the scraps of labels with Chinese and American addresses, stamps, and postmarks, the family airmailed the can from Hong Kong in 1950. It got crushed in the middle, and whoever tried to peel the labels off stopped because the red and gold paint came off too, leaving silver scratches that rust. Somebody tried to pry the end off before discovering that the tube pulls apart. When I open it, the smell of China flies out, a thousand-year-old bat flying heavy-headed out of the Chinese caverns where bats are as white as dust, a smell that comes from long ago, far back in the brain. Crates from Canton, Hong Kong, Singapore, and Chinese Taiwan have that smell too, only stronger because they are more recently come from the Chinese.

Inside the can are three scrolls, one inside another. The largest says that in the twenty-third year of the National Republic*, the To Keung School of Midwifery, where she has had two years of instruction and Hospital Practice, awards its Diploma to my mother, who has shown through oral and written examination her Proficiency in Midwifery, Pediatrics, Gynecology, "Medicine," "Surgery,"

ideograph /ˈɪdɪəɡrɑːf/ *n.* (also ideogram) **a.** a symbol that is used in a writing system, e.g. Chinese, to represent the idea of a thing, rather than the sounds of a word **b.** a sign or a symbol for sth.
gear /ɡɪə/ *n.* (usu. pl.) machinery in a vehicle that turns engine power (or power on a bicycle) into movement forwards or backwards
scrap /skræp/ *n.* a small piece of sth., esp. paper, fabric, etc.
cavern /ˈkævən/ *n.* a cave, esp. a large one
midwifery /ˈmɪdwaɪfəri/ *n.* the profession and work of a midwife, who is a person, esp. a woman, trained to help women give birth to babies
proficiency /prəˈfɪʃənsi/ *n.* ability to do sth. well because of training and practice
pediatrics /piːdɪˈætrɪks/ *n.* the branch of medicine concerned with children and their diseases
gynecology /ɡaɪnɪˈkɒlədʒi/ *n.* the scientific study and treatment of the medical conditions and diseases of women, esp. those connected with sexual reproduction

Therapeutics, Ophthalmology, Bacteriology, Dermatology, Nursing and Bandage. This document has eight stamps on it: one, the school's English and Chinese names embossed together in a circle; one, as the Chinese enumerate, a stork and a big baby in lavender ink; one, the school's Chinese seal; one, an orangish paper stamp pasted in the border design; one, the red seal of Dr. Wu Pak-liang, M.D., Lyon, Berlin, president and "Ex-assistant étranger à la clinique chirugicale et d'accouchement de l'université de Lyon"; one, the red seal of Dean Woo Yin-kam, M.D.; one, my mother's seal, her chop mark larger than the president's and the dean's; and one, the number 1279 on the back. Dean Woo's signature is followed by "(Hackett)". I read in a history book that Hackett Medical College for Women* at Canton was founded in the nineteenth century by European women doctors.

therapeutics /θerəˈpjuːtɪks/ n. the branch of medicine concerned with the treatment of diseases
ophthalmology /ˌɒfθælˈmɒlədʒɪ/ n. the scientific study of the eye and its diseases
bacteriology /bækˌtɪərɪˈɒlədʒɪ/ n. the scientific study of bacteria
dermatology /ˌdɜːməˈtɒlədʒɪ/ n. the scientific study of skin diseases
emboss /ɪmˈbɒs/ v. to put a raised design or piece of writing on paper, leather, etc.
enumerate /ɪˈnjuːməreɪt/ v. to name things on a list one by one
lavender /ˈlævɪndə/ n. **a.** a garden plant or bush with bunches of purple flowers with a sweet smell **b.** a pale purple colour
chop /tʃɒp/ n. official seal or stamp; trademark
wisp /wɪsp/ n. a small, thin piece of hair, grass, etc.
tendril /ˈtendrɪl/ n. a thin curling piece of sth. such as hair
posterity /pɒsˈterɪtɪ/ n. all the people who will live in the future
snapshot /ˈsnæpʃɒt/ n. a short description or a small amount of information that gives you an idea of what sth. is like
bob /bɒb/ n. a style of a woman's hair in which it is cut the same length all the way around

The school seal has been pressed over a photograph of my mother at the age of thirty-seven. The diploma gives her age as twenty-seven. She looks younger than I do, her eyebrows are thicker, her lips fuller. Her naturally curly hair is parted on the left, one wavy wisp tendrilling off to the right. She wears a scholar's white gown, and she is not thinking about her appearance. She stares straight ahead as if she could see me and past me to her grandchildren and grandchildren's grandchildren. She has spacy eyes, as all people recently from Asia have. Her eyes do not focus on the camera. My mother is not smiling; Chinese do not smile for photographs. Their faces command relatives in foreign lands—"Send money"—and posterity forever—"Put food in front of this picture." My mother does not understand Chinese-American snapshots. "What are you laughing at?" she asks.

The second scroll is a long narrow photograph of the graduating class with the school officials seated in front. I picked out my mother immediately. Her face is exactly her own, though forty years younger. She is so familiar, I can only tell whether or not she is pretty or happy or smart by comparing her to the other women. For this formal group picture she straightened her hair with oil to make a chinlength bob like the others'. On the other women, strangers, I can recognize a curled lip, a sidelong glance, pinched shoulders. My mother is not soft; the girl with the small nose and dimpled underlip is soft. My mother is not humorous, not like the girl at the end who lifts her mocking chin to pose like Girl Graduate. My mother does not have smiling eyes; the old woman teacher (Dean Woo?) in front crinkles happily, and the one faculty member in the western suit smiles westernly. Most of the graduates are girls whose faces have not yet formed; my mother's face will not change anymore, except to age. She is intelligent, alert, pretty. I can't tell if she's happy.

The graduates seem to have been looking elsewhere when they pinned the rose, zinnia, or chrysanthemum on their precise black dresses. One thin girl wears hers in the middle of her chest. A few have a flower over a left or right nipple. My mother put hers, a chrysanthemum, below her left breast. Chinese dresses at that time were dartless, cut as if women did not have breasts; these younger doctors, unaccustomed to decorations, may have seen their chests as black expanses with no reference points for flowers. Perhaps they couldn't shorten that far gaze that lasts only a few years after a Chinese emigrates. In this picture too my mother's eyes are big with what they held—reaches of oceans beyond China, land beyond oceans. Most emigrants learn the barbarians' directness—how to gather themselves and stare rudely into talking faces as if trying to catch lies. In America my mother has eyes as strong as boulders, never once skittering off a face, but she has not learned to place decorations and phonograph needles, nor has she stopped seeing land on the other side of the oceans. Now her eyes include the relatives in China, as they once included my father smiling and smiling in his many western outfits, a different one for each photograph that he sent from America.

He and his friends took pictures of one another in bathing suits at Coney Island* beach, the salt wind from the Atlantic blowing their hair. He's the one in the middle with his arms about the necks of his buddies. They pose in the cockpit of a biplane, on a motorcycle, and on a lawn beside the "Keep Off the Grass" sign. They are always laughing. My father, white shirt sleeves rolled up, smiles in front of a wall of clean laundry. In the spring he wears a new straw hat, cocked at a Fred Astaire*

pinch /pɪntʃ/ v. to hold sth. tightly between the thumb and finger or between two things that are pressed together
mocking /ˈmɒkɪŋ/ adj. (of behaviour, an expression etc.) showing that you think sb./sth. is ridiculous
crinkle /ˈkrɪŋkəl/ v. to cause to become covered with fine lines by crushing or pressing
dartless /ˈdɑːtlɪs/ adj. (cloth) without a pointed fold that is sewn in a piece of clothing to make it fit better
skitter /ˈskɪtə/ v. to run or move very quickly and lightly
outfit /ˈaʊtfɪt/ n. a set of clothes that you wear together, esp. for a particular occasion or purpose
buddy /ˈbʌdi/ n. a. a friend b. a partner
cockpit /ˈkɒkpɪt/ n. an enclosed area in a plane, boat or racing car where the pilot or driver sits
biplane /ˈbaɪpleɪn/ n. a plane with double wings

angle. He steps out, dancing down the stairs, one foot forward, one back, a hand in his pocket. He wrote to her about the American custom of stomping on straw hats come fall. "If you want to save your hat for next year," he said, "you have to put it away early, or else when you're riding the subway or walking along Fifth Avenue*, any stranger can snatch it off your head and put his foot through it. That's the way they celebrate the change of seasons here." In the winter he wears a gray felt hat with his gray overcoat. He is sitting on a rock in Central Park*. In one snapshot he is not smiling; someone took it when he was studying, blurred in the glare of the desk lamp.

stomp /stɒmp/ v. to walk, dance, or move with heavy steps
felt /felt/ n. a soft thick fabric made from wool or hair that has been pressed tightly together
blurred /blɜːd/ adj. **a.** not clear; without a clear outline or shape **b.** difficult to remember clearly
bang /bæŋ/ n. hair cut straight across the forehead
kidnap /ˈkɪdnæp/ v. to take sb. away illegally and keep them as a prisoner, esp. in order to get money or sth.else for returning them

There are no snapshots of my mother. In two small portraits, however, there is a black thumbprint on her forehead, as if someone had inked in bangs, as if someone had marked her.

"Mother, did bangs come into fashion after you had the picture taken?" One time she said yes. Another time when I asked, "Why do you have fingerprints on your forehead?" she said, "Your First Uncle did that." I disliked the unsureness in her voice.

The last scroll has columns of Chinese words. The only English is "Department of Health, Canton," imprinted on my mother's face, the same photograph as on the diploma. I keep looking to see whether she was afraid. Year after year my father did not come home or send for her. Their two children had been dead for ten years. If he did not return soon, there would be no more children. ("They were three and two years old, a boy and a girl. They could talk already.") My father did send money regularly, though, and she had nobody to spend it on but herself. She bought good clothes and shoes. Then she decided to use the money for becoming a doctor. She did not leave for Canton immediately after the children died. In China there was time to complete feelings. As my father had done, my mother left the village by ship. There was a sea bird painted on the ship to protect it against shipwreck and winds. She was in luck. The following ship was boarded by river pirates, who kidnapped every passenger, even old ladies. "Sixty dollars for an old lady" was what the bandits used to say. "I sailed alone," she says, "to the capital of the entire province." She took a brown leather suitcase and a seabag stuffed with two quilts.

Cultural Notes

1. **Maxine Hong Kingston** (1940—   ) is an American Professor Emeritus at the University of California, Berkeley, where she graduated with a BA in English in 1962. She is also a prolific academic and writer. Born as Maxine Ting Ting Hong to a Chinese laundry house owner in Stockton, California, she was the third of eight children, and the first among them born in the United States. Her works often reflect on her cultural heritage and blend fiction with non-fiction. Among her works are *The Woman Warrior* (1976), awarded the National Book Critics Circle Award for Nonfiction, and *China Men* (1980), which was awarded the 1981 National Book Award. She has written one novel, *Tripmaster Monkey*, a story depicting a character based on the mythical Chinese character Sun Wu Kong. Her most recent books are *To Be the Poet* (2002) and *The Fifth Book of Peace* (2003).

2. **The National Republic** refers to the National Republic of China (1912—1949), founded by Sun Yat-sen, the first president.

3. **Aiming** at training the Chinese women to heal their own people, both physically and spiritually, Dr. Mary Hannah Fulton (1854—1927) established the Kwangtung Medical School for Women in Guangzhou in 1899 under the auspices of the Board of Foreign Missions of the Presbyterian Church in the United States (North). With the generosity of Mr. E.A.K. Hackett, an American living in Indiana, the medical school was expanded to be the **Hackett Medical College for Women** in 1905. Together with the establishment of its affiliated institutions, the Hackett Medical College for Women was the first medical college for the training of Chinese women in the field of western medicine. The medical college played an important role in furthering women's causes from the late nineteenth century to the 1940s.

4. **Coney Island** is a peninsula, formerly an island, in southernmost Brooklyn, New York City, USA, with a beach on the Atlantic Ocean. The area was a major resort and site of amusement parks that reached its peak in the early 20th century. It declined in popularity after World War II and endured years of neglect.

5. **Fred Astaire** (1899—1987) was an Academy Award-winning American film and Broadway stage dancer, choreographer, singer and actor. He was named the fifth Greatest Male Star of All Time by the American Film Institute.

6. **Fifth Avenue** is a major thoroughfare in the center of the borough of

Manhattan in New York City. Lined with expensive park-view real estate and historical mansions, it is a symbol of wealthy New York. Between 34th Street and 59th Street, it is also one of the premier shopping streets in the world, on par with Oxford Street in London, the Champs-Élysées in Paris and Via Montenapoleone in Milan.

7. **Central Park** is a large public, urban park in the borough of Manhattan in New York City. With about twenty-five million visitors annually, Central Park is the most visited city park in the United States, and its appearance in many movies and television shows has made it famous. Central Park has been a National Historic Landmark since 1963.

Comprehension Exercises

I. Answer the following questions based on the text.

1. What are the meanings the photographs of Kingston's parents might convey?
2. Why does Kingston say that the tube of her parents' photographs as well as crates from Canton, Hong Kong, Singapore and Chinese Taiwan have the smell of China?
3. Why does Kingston describe her mother's photographs first and in greater detail than those of her father's?
4. Why is there a black thumbprint on the forehead of Kingston's mother in two small portraits of her?
5. What personalities of Kingston's parents can you infer from the article?

II. Decide whether each of the following statements is true or false according to the text.

1. Kingston's mother was not happy in the photographs.
2. Kingston's mother got her diploma in 1934.
3. It is rude to stare directly at whom you're talking to in the United States.
4. Chinese people usually require their relatives in foreign lands to send them money.
5. Kingston's father was born in the United States.
6. Kingston is the third child of her parents.
7. Kingston is proud of her parents.
8. People paint a sea bird on the ship to protect it against shipwreck and winds.

III. Select the most suitable word or phrases and fill in the following blanks in their proper form.

blur	bob	cavern	crinkle	emboss
enumerate	felt	mock	outfit	pinch
posterity	proficiency	scrap	sidelong	skitter
snapshot	spacy	stomp		

1. Every year, dozens of old ships are brought to Bangladesh to be dismantled for _____.
2. The children weren't simply running their hands mindlessly along the _____ walls, however.
3. In some cases, a document proving language _____ is required by the host institution.
4. Examining carefully, we can find that the silver cup is _____ with a beautiful design of flowers.
5. Not long after he put forward his hypothesis concerning this strange phenomenon, his antagonists came up and _____ many flaws in the hypothesis.
6. The bathroom of the new apartment house is too _____ to capture on photo. It has got separate bathtub, shower and everything else you need.
7. They are given homework during holiday periods — tasks including interviewing their village elders about mythology and record their answers for the _____.
8. The interviews present a remarkable _____ of Britain in these dark days of recession.
9. After hanging up, I cast a sidelong _____ at my profile in the glass booth and found myself haggard.
10. It's unbelievable — sometimes I have to _____ myself to believe what's going on.
11. When I saw her face redden and _____ up, her eyes welling with tears, I panicked and drew two steps closer.
12. We disembark, dump the bags and _____ across town to the Field of Miracles. We have never been there before.
13. Mr. Boden says that the most important thing to consider when contemplating a child's _____ is comfort.
14. With no more words with his former friends, Mr. Randal turned his back on them and _____ off up the hill.
15. It is a common practice in the postmodern writings that the novelists would deliberately _____ the line between fact and fiction.

Unit Eleven

IV. Try to paraphrase the following sentences, paying special attention to the underlined parts.

1. Somebody tried to pry the end off before discovering that the tube pulls apart.

2. When I open it, the smell of China flies out, a thousand-year-old bat flying heavy-headed out of the Chinese caverns.

3. On the other women, strangers, I can recognize a curled lip, a sidelong glance, pinched shoulders.

4. Most emigrants learn the barbarians' directness — how to gather themselves and stare rudely into talking faces as if trying to catch lies.

5. I picked out my mother immediately. Her face is exactly her own, though forty years younger.

V. Discuss with your partner about each of the three statements and write an essay in no less than 250 words about your understanding of one of them.

1. Chinese do not smile for photographs.

2. Chinese dresses at that time were dartless, cut as if women did not have breasts; these younger doctors, unaccustomed to decorations, may have seen their chests as black expanses with no reference points for flowers.

3. In this picture too my mother's eyes are big with what they held — reaches of oceans beyond China, land beyond oceans.

VI. List four websites where we can learn more about Maxine Hong Kingston and provide a brief introduction to each of them.

1. _____
2. _____
3. _____
4. _____

Text B

Two Ways to Belong in America
Bharati Mukherjee*

This is a tale of two sisters from Calcutta, Mira and Bharati, who have lived in the United Sates for some 35 years, but who find themselves on different sides in the current <u>debate</u> over the status of immigrants. I am an American citizen and she is not. I am moved that thousands of long-term residents are finally taking the oath of citizenship. She is not.

Mira arrived in Detroit in 1960 to study child psychology and pre-school education. I followed her a year later to study creative writing at the University of Iowa. When we left India, we were almost <u>identical</u> in appearance and attitude. We dressed alike, in <u>saris</u>; we expressed identical views on politics, social issues, love, and marriage in the same Calcutta convent-school accent. We would endure our two years in America, secure our

debate /dɪˈbeɪt/ *n.* an argument or discussion expressing different opinions
identical /aɪˈdentɪkəl/ *adj.* similar in every detail
sari /ˈsɑːrɪ/ *n.* a long piece of fabric that is wrapped around the body and worn as the main piece of clothing, esp. by East Indian women

degrees, then return to India to marry the grooms of our father's choosing.

Instead, Mira married an Indian student in 1962 who was getting his business administration degree at Wayne State University. They soon acquired the labor certifications necessary for the green card of hassle free residence and employment.

Mira still lives in Detroit, works in the Southfield, Mich., school system, and has become nationally recognized for her contributions in the fields of pre-school education and parent-teacher relationships. After 36 years as a legal immigrant in this country, she clings passionately to her Indian citizenship and hopes to go home to India when she retires.

In Iowa City in 1963, I married a fellow student, an American of Canadian parentage. Because of the accident of his North Dakota Birth, I bypassed labor-certification requirements and the race-related "quota" system that favored the applicant's country of origin over his or her merit. I was prepared for (and even welcomed) the emotional strain that came with marrying outside my ethnic community. In 33 years of marriage, we have lived in every part of North America. By choosing a husband who was not my father's selection, I was opting for fluidity, self-invention, blue jeans and T-shirts, and renouncing 3,000 years (at least) of case-observant, "pure culture" * marriage in the Mukherjee family. My books have often been read as unapologetic (and in some quarters overenthusiastic) texts for cultural and psychological "mongrelization". It's a word I celebrate.

Mira and I have stayed sisterly close by phone. In our regular Sunday morning conversations, we are unguardedly affectionate. I am her only blood relative on this continent. We expect to see each other through the looming crises of aging and ill health without being asked. Long before Vice President Gore's "Citizenship U.S.A." drive*, we'd had our polite arguments over the ethics of retaining an over-seas citizenship while expecting the permanent protection and economic benefits that come with living and working in America.

---

hassle /ˈhæsəl/ *n.* **a.** a difficult argument **b.** a struggle of mind and body
cling /klɪŋ/ *v.* to hold on tightly to sb. or sth.
bypass /ˈbaɪpɑːs/ *v.* to avoid
quota /ˈkwəʊtə/ *n.* **a.** the limited number or amount of people or things that is officially allowed **b.** an amount of sth. that sb. expects or needs to achieve
merit /ˈmerɪt/ *n.* the quality of being good and deserving praise, reward or admiration
ethnic /ˈeθnɪk/ *adj.* of or related to a racial, national, or tribal group
opt /ɒpt/ *v.* to choose to take or not to take a particular course of action
fluidity /fluˈɪdɪti/ *n.* the quality of being likely to change or able to flow freely, as gases and liquids do
renounce /rɪˈnaʊns/ *v.* to give up; say formally that one does not own; say formally that one has no more connection with
case-observant: also observant, acting in accordance with law or custom (esp. religious)
unapologetic /ˌʌnəpɒləˈdʒetɪk/ *adj.* not expressing sorrow for some fault or wrong
mongrel /ˈmʌŋɡrəl/ *n.* **a.** an animal, esp. a dog, which is of no particular breed **b.** a person of mixed race —mongrelization
affectionate /əˈfekʃənɪt/ *adj.* showing caring feelings and love for sb.
ethics /ˈeθɪks/ *n.* a system of moral principles or rules of behaviour

Like well-raised sisters, we never said what was really on our minds, but we probably pitied one another. She, for the lack of structure in my life, the erasure of Indianness, the absence of an unvarying daily core. I, for the narrowness of her perspective, her uninvolvement with the mythic depths or the superficial pop culture of this society. But, now, with the scapegoatings of "aliens" (documented or illegal) on the increase, and the targeting of long-term legal immigrants like Mira for new scrutiny and new self-consciousness, she and I find ourselves unable to maintain the same polite discretion. We were always unacknowledged adversaries, and we are now, more than ever, sisters.

"I feel used," Mira raged on the phone the other night. "I feel manipulated and discarded. This is such an unfair way to treat a person who was invited to stay and work here because of her talent. My employer went to the I.N.S.* and petitioned for the labor certification. For over 30 years, I've invested my creativity and professional skills into the improvement of *this* country's pre-school system. I've obeyed all the rules, I've paid my taxes, I love my work, I love my students, I love the friends I've made. How dare America now change its rules in midstream? If America wants to make new rules curtailing benefits of legal immigrants, they should apply only to immigrants who arrive after those rules are already in place."

To my ears, it sounded like the description of a long-enduring, comfortable yet loveless marriage, without risk or recklessness. Have we the right to demand, and to expect, that we be loved? (That, to me, is the subtext of the arguments by immigration advocates.) My sister is an expatriate, professionally generous and creative, socially courteous and gracious, and that's as far as her Americanization can go. She is here to maintain an identity, not to transform it.

---

erasure /ɪˈreɪʒə/ *n.* the act of removing or destroying sth.
perspective /pəˈspektɪv/ *n.* a particular attitude towards sth.; a particular way of thinking about things
scapegoat /ˈskeɪpɡəʊt/ *n.* someone blamed for sth. bad, though it is not their fault
alien /ˈeɪljən/ *n.* **a.** a person who is not a citizen of the country in which he lives or works **b.** a creature from another world
target /ˈtɑːɡɪt/ *v.* to take sb. or sth. as a target
scrutiny /ˈskruːtɪni/ *n.* a careful and thorough examination
discretion /dɪˈskreʃən/ *n.* **a.** the freedom or power to decide what should be done in a particular situation **b.** care in what to say or do in order to keep sth. secret or to avoid causing embarrassment or difficulty
adversary /ˈædvəsəri/ *n.* a person that sb. is opposed to, opponent or enemy
manipulate /məˈnɪpjʊleɪt/ *v.* **a.** to handle or control (esp. a machine), usu. skillfully **b.** to control and influence sb. skillfully, often in an unfair and dishonest manner —manipulative *adj.*
petition /pɪˈtɪʃən/ *v.* to make a formal request to authority
curtail /kɜːˈteɪl/ *v.* to cut short; reduce; limit
subtext /ˈsʌbtekst/ *n.* a hidden meaning or reason for doing sth.
advocate /ˈædvəkeɪt/ *n.* a person who supports or speaks in favor of sb. or a pubic plan or action
expatriate /eksˈpætrɪət/ *n.* a person living in a country that is not his own
courteous /ˈkɜːtɪəs/ *adj.* polite, esp. in a way that shows respect
gracious /ˈɡreɪʃəs/ *adj.* kind, polite and generous, esp. to sb. of a lower social position

I asked her if she would follow the example of others who have decided to become citizens because of the anti-immigration bills in Congress. And here, she surprised me. "If America wants to play the manipulative game, I'll play it, too," she snapped. "I'll become a U.S. citizen for now, then change back to India when I'm ready to go home. I feel some kind of irrational attachment to India that I don't to America. Until all this hysteria against legal immigrants, I was totally happy. Having my green card meant I could visit any place in the world I wanted to and then come back to a job that's satisfying and that I do very well."

In one family, from two sisters alike as peas in a pod , there could not be a wider divergence of immigrant experience. America spoke to me— I married it—I embraced the demotion from expatriate aristocrat to immigrant nobody, surrendering those thousands of years of "pure culture," the saris, the delightfully accented English. She retained them all. Which of us is the freak?

snap /snæp/ *v.* to say quickly, usu. in an annoyed or angry way
hysteria /hɪsˈtɪəriə/ *n.* a state of extreme excitement, fear or anger in which a person, or a group of people, loses control of their emotions and starts to cry, laugh, etc.
pod /pɒd/ *n.* a long narrow seed vessel of various plants, esp. beans and peas
divergence /daɪˈvɜːdʒəns/ *n.* (of opinions, views, etc.) difference
demotion /dɪˈməʊʃən/ *n.* the act of moving sb. to a lower position or rank, often as a punishment
aristocrat /ˈærɪstəkræt/ *n.* a person born in the highest social class with special titles
freak /friːk/ *n.* a person who is considered to be unusual because of the way they behave, look or think
ancestral *adj.* of an ancestor
cuisine /kwɪˈziːn/ *n.* **a.** a cooking style **b.** the food served in a restaurant (usu. an expensive one)
seamstress /ˈsiːmstrɪs/ *n.* a woman whose job is sewing
domestic /dəˈmestɪk/ *n.* a domestic servant, usu. female
referendum /ˌrefəˈrendəm/ *n.* an occasion when all the people of a country can vote on an important issue

Mira's voice, I realize, is the voice not just of the immigrant South Asian community but of an immigrant community of the millions who have stayed rooted in one job, one city, one house, one ancestral culture, one cuisine , for the entirety of their productive years. She speaks for greater numbers than I possibly can. Only the fluency of her English and the anger, rather than fear, born of confidence in her education, differentiate her from the seamstresses , the domestics , the technicians, the shop owners, the millions of hard-working but effectively silenced documented immigrants as well as their less fortunate "illegal" brothers and sisters.

Nearly 20 years ago, when I was living in my husband's ancestral homeland of Canada, I was always well-employed but never allowed to feel part of the local Quebec or larger Canadian society. Then, through a Green Paper* that invited a national referendum on the unwanted side effects of "nontraditional" immigration, the Government officially turned against its immigrant communities, particularly those from South Asia.

I felt then the same sense of betrayal that Mira feels now. I will never forget the pain of that sudden turning, and the casual racist outbursts the Green Paper elicited. That sense of betrayal had its desired effect and drove me, and thousands like me, from the country.

betray /bɪˈtreɪ/ *v.* to be disloyal or unfaithful to —betrayal *n.*
elicit /ɪˈlɪsɪt/ *v.* to get, draw out, cause to come out
exile /ˈeksaɪl/ *n.* a person who chooses, or is forced to live away from his or her own country
trauma /ˈtrɔːmə/ *n.* **a.** a damage to the mind caused by the body having been wounded, or by a sudden shock or terrible experience **b.** a wound

Mira and I differ, however, in the ways in which we hope to interact with the country that we have chosen to live in. She is happier to live in America as expatriate Indian than as an immigrant American. I need to feel like a part of the community I have adopted (as I tried to feel in Canada as well.) I need to put roots down, to vote and make the difference that I can. The price that the immigrant willingly pays, and that the exile avoids, is the trauma of self-transformation.

Cultural Notes

1. **Bharati Mukherjee** (1940—   ) is an award-winning Indian-born American writer, and is currently a professor in the department of English at the University of California, Berkeley. Born in Calcutta, India, she received her M.F.A. from the Iowa Writers' Workshop in 1963 and her Ph.D. in 1969 from the department of Comparative Literature. Her novels *The Tiger's Daughter* (1972), *Wife* (1975) and *Jasmine* (1989) describe how people strive to understand the idea of an American identity in a world of hybridity and multiplicity. This is particularly evident in her more recent works *The Holder of the World* (1993), *Leave It to Me* (1997) and *Desirable Daughters* (2002) and *The Tree Bride* (2004). Her short story collection *The Middleman and Other Stories* (1988) won the National Book Critics Circle Award.

2. **Pure culture**, a microbiological term, describes "a nourishing medium that promotes the growth of one strong organism." This, of course, is a metaphor for one fully functioning organizational culture that is constantly clarified, nourished, and encouraged so that it can withstand the rigors of its environment.

3. **"Citizenship U.S.A." drive** was launched by **Vice President Gore** in April 1995 for speeding the elimination of the backlog of 600,000 immigrants who had requested naturalization, and promising new applicants naturalization within 90 days.

4. The United States Immigration and Naturalization Service **(I.N.S.)** was a part of the United States Department of Justice and handled legal and illegal immigration and naturalization. It ceased to exist on March 1, 2003, when most of its functions were transferred to three new agencies within the newly-created Department of Homeland Security.

5. **Green Paper**, in Britain and other similar Commonwealth jurisdictions, is a tentative government report of a proposal without any commitment to action; the first step in changing the law. Green Papers may result in the production of a white paper. A Green Paper in Canada, like a White Paper, is an official document sponsored by the Crown. Many so-called White Papers in Canada have been, in effect, Green Papers, while at least one Green Paper, the one on immigration and population in 1975, was released for public debate after the government had already drafted legislation.

Comprehension Exercises

I. Answer the following questions based on the text.

1. How were Mira and Bharati different in the debate over the status of immigrants?
2. What might be a proper definition of the term "mongrelization"?
3. How do you understand the term "pure culture"?
4. Why did Mira complain of feeling used and discarded in the United States?
5. Why does Bharati say that Mira's voice is the voice not just of the immigrant South Asian community but of an immigrant community of the millions?

II. Decide whether each of the following statements is true or false according to the text.

1. Mira and Bharati shared the same attitude when they arrived in the United States.
2. Bharati became an American citizen automatically after she married an American.
3. Mira resided in the United States legally for 36 years with a green card.
4. Mira and Bharati both married the grooms of their father's choosing.
5. Bharati likes to write books on "mongrelization".
6. Bharati was not satisfied with the immigration policy in Canada 20 years ago.

III. Select the most suitable word or phrases and fill in the following blanks in their proper form.

adversary	alien	bypass	cling	courteous
discretion	divergence	ethnic	expatriate	hassle
identical	oath	quota	opt	renounce
scrutiny	scapegoat	unapologetic		

1. George Washington was the first president to place his hand on a Christian Bible when taking the _____ of office.
2. When these two ladies discover they're holding _____ letters from Falstaff, they decide to get even with him.
3. Filing things is a big _____, and finding them is just as difficult — this is what distresses my niece now.
4. One of the things I tell my communications class is that people _____ to first impressions.
5. These distractions will cost you serious time if you don't _____ them and get down to business immediately.
6. Many people who can't find or can't afford in-office therapy _____ for home-based treatment.
7. He was lauded for convincing his father to publicly _____ weapons of mass destruction in 2003.
8. And some _____ groups such as African-Americans and Hispanics are producing their own distinguished men of letters.
9. Also, Arkansas must still have seemed an _____ place for her to settle, though she no longer felt it was the other side of the moon.
10. This series of movies, already under the watch of a censor board, are exempt from any further _____.
11. The chief surgeon said he was innocent, claiming he was being used as a _____.
12. This committee may want to exercise its _____ to look into those charges.
13. Both of the wrestlers tried to tumble the _____ with all their strength.
14. Dependence on oil, a large _____ workforce, and growing inflation pressures are significant long-term challenges.
15. There's a substantial _____ of opinion within the party and it is still a far cry for the party members to reach a consensus.

IV. **Try to paraphrase the following sentences, paying special attention to the underlined parts.**

1. I am moved that thousands of long-term residents are finally taking the oath of citizenship.

2. They soon acquired the labor certifications necessary for the green card of hassle free residence and employment.

3. Because of the accident of his North Dakota Birth, I bypassed labor-certification requirements and the race-related "quota" system that favored the applicant's country of origin over his or her merit.

4. We expected to see each other through the looming crises of aging and ill health without being asked.

5. In one family, from two sisters alike as peas in a pod, there could not be a wider divergence of immigrant experience.

V. **Discuss with your partner about each of the three statements and write an essay in no less than 250 words about your understanding of one of them.**

1. There will be possibly an emotional stain that came with marrying outside one's ethnic community.

2. Immigrants are likely to have the feeling of being "aliens" even after they settled abroad for many years.

3. The price that the immigrant willingly pays, and that the exile avoids, is the trauma of self-transformation.

VI. List four websites where we can learn more about Bharati Mukherjee and provide a brief introduction to each of them.

1. _____
   _____.
2. _____
   _____.
3. _____
   _____.
4. _____
   _____.

Twenty Minutes' Reading

You are required to read the following two sections within 20 minutes.

SECTION A

In the case of mobile phones, change is everything. Recent research indicates that the mobile phone is changing not only our culture, but our very bodies as well.

First. Let's talk about culture. The difference between the mobile phone and its parent, the fixed-line phone, you get whoever answers it.

This has several implications. The most common one, however, and perhaps the thing that has changed our culture forever, is the "meeting" influence. People no longer need to make firm plans about when and where to meet. Twenty years ago, a Friday night would need to be arranged in advance. You needed enough time to allow everyone to get from their place of work to the first meeting place. Now, however, a night out can be arranged on the run. It is no longer "see you there at 8", but "text me around 8 and we'll see where we all are".

Texting changes people as well. In their paper, "insights into the Social and Psychological Effects of SMS Text Messaging", two British researchers distinguished between two types of mobile phone users: the "talkers" and the "texters" — those who prefer voice to text message and those who prefer text to voice. They found that the mobile phone's individuality and privacy gave texters the ability to express a whole new outer personality. Texters were likely to report that their family would be surprised if they were to read their texts. This suggests that texting allowed texters to present a self-image that differed from the one familiar to those who knew them well.

Another scientist wrote of the changes that mobiles have brought to body language. There are two kinds that people use while speaking on the phone. There is the "speakeasy": the head is held high, in a self-confident way, chatting away. And there is the "spacemaker": these people focus on themselves and keep out other people.

Who can blame them? Phone meetings get cancelled or reformed and camera-phones intrude on people's privacy. So, it is understandable if your mobile makes you nervous. But perhaps you needn't worry so much. After all, it is good to talk.

1. When people plan to meet nowadays, they _____.
   A. arrange the meeting place beforehand
   B. postpone fixing the place till last minute
   C. seldom care about when and where to meet
   D. still love to work out detailed meeting plans
2. According to the two British researchers, the social and psychological effect are mostly likely to be seen on _____.
   A. talkers   B. the "speakeasy"   C. the "spacemaker"   D. texters
3. We can infer from the passage that the texts sent by texters are _____.
   A. quite revealing   B. well written
   C. unacceptable by others   D. shocking to others
4. According to the passage, who is afraid of being heard while talking on the mobile _____.
   A. talkers   B. the speakeasy   C. the spacemaker   D. texters
5. An appropriate title for the passage might be _____.
   A. The SMS Effect
   B. Cultural Implication of Mobile Use
   C. Change in the Use of the Mobile
   D. Body Language and the Mobile Phone

SECTION B

Over the last 25 years, British society has changed a great deal — or at least many parts of it have. In some ways, however, very little has changed, particularly where attitudes are concerned. Ideas about social class — whether a person is "working-class" or "middle-class" — are one area in which changes have been extremely slow.

In the past, the working-class tended to be paid less than middle-class people, such as teachers and doctors. As a result of this and also of the fact that workers' jobs were generally much less secure, distinct differences in life-styles and attitudes came into existence. The typical working man would collect his wages on Friday evening and then, it was widely believed, having given his wife her "housekeeping", would go out and squander the rest on beer and betting.

The stereotype of what a middle-class man did with his money was perhaps nearer the truth. He was — and still is — inclined to take a longer-term view. Not only did he regard buying a house of these provided him and his family with security. Only in very few cases did workers have the opportunity (or the education and training) to make such long-term plans.

Nowadays, a great deal has changed. In a large number of cases factory workers earn as much, if not more, than their middle-class supervisors. Social security and laws to improve century, have made it less necessary than before to worry about "tomorrow". Working-class people seem slowly to be losing the feeling of inferiority they had in the past. In fact there has been a growing tendency in the past few years for the middle-classes to feel slightly ashamed of their position.

The changes in both life-styles and attitudes are probably most easily seen amongst younger people. They generally tend to share very similar tastes in music and clothes, they spend their money in having a good time, and save for holidays or longer-term plans when necessary. There seems to be much less difference than in precious generations. Nevertheless, we still have a wide gap between the well-paid (whatever the type of job they may have) and the low-paid. As long as this gap exists, there will always be a possibility that new conflicts and jealousies will emerge, or rather that the old conflicts will re-appear, but between different groups.

6. Which of the following is seen as the cause of class differences in the past?
   A. Life style and occupation.
   B. Attitude and income.
   C. Income and job security.
   D. Job security and hobbies.

7. The writer seems to suggest that the description of _____ is closer to truth?
   A. middle-class ways of spending money
   B. working-class ways of spending the weekend
   C. working-class drinking habits
   D. middle-class attitudes
8. According to the passage, which of the following is not a typical feature of the middle-class?
   A. Desiring for security.
   B. Making long term plans.
   C. Having priorities in life.
   D. Saving money.
9. Working-class people's sense of security increased as a result of all the following factor EXCEPT _____.
   A. better social security
   B. more job opportunities
   C. higher living standard
   D. better legal protection
10. Which of the following statement is incorrect?
    A. Changes are slowly taking place in all sectors of the British society.
    B. The gap between working-class and middle-class young people is narrowing.
    C. Difference in income will remain but those in occupation will disappear.
    D. Middle-class people may sometimes feel inferior to working-class people.

Unit Twelve

Text A

Three Types of Resistance to Oppression
Martin Luther King, Jr.*

Oppressed people deal with their oppression in three characteristic ways. One way is acquiescence: the oppressed resign themselves to their doom. They tacitly adjust themselves to oppression, and thereby become conditioned to it. In every movement toward freedom some of the oppressed prefer to remain oppressed. Almost 2,800 years ago Moses* set out to lead the children of Israel* from the slavery of Egypt to the freedom of the Promised Land. He soon discovered that slaves do not always welcome their deliverers. They become accustomed to being slaves. They would rather bear those ills they have, as Shakespeare pointed out, than flee to others that they know not of*. They prefer the "fleshpots of Egypt" to the ordeals of emancipation.

There is such a thing as the freedom of exhaustion. Some people are so worn down by the yoke of oppression that they give up. A few years ago in the slum areas of Atlanta*, a Negro guitarist used to sing almost daily: "Been down so long that down don't bother me." This is the type of negative freedom and resignation that often engulfs the life of the oppressed.

But this is not the way out. To accept passively an unjust system is to cooperate with that system; thereby the oppressed become as

---

acquiesce /ˌækwɪˈes/ v. to agree, often unwillingly, without raising an argument; accept quietly —**acquiescence** /ˌækwɪˈesns/ n.
resign oneself to to give oneself up; hand oneself over to
tacit /ˈtæsɪt/ adj. expressed or understood without being put into words; not spoken or written —**tacitly** adv.
become conditioned to to be trained to behave in a particular way or to become used to a particular situation
deliverer /dɪˈlɪvərə/ n. the one who rescues sb. from sth. bad
fleshpot /ˈfleʃpɒt/ n. a place supplying food, drink and sexual entertainment
ordeal /ɔːˈdiːl/ n. a difficult or unpleasant experience
emancipation /ɪˌmænsɪˈpeɪʃən/ n. liberation
yoke /jəʊk/ n. **a.** power; control **b.** the position of slavery or of being under the power of someone
slum /slʌm/ n. an area of a city that is very poor and where the houses are dirty and in bad condition
engulf /ɪnˈɡʌlf/ v. **a.** to surround or to cover completely **b.** to affect very strongly

evil as the oppressor. Non-cooperation with evil is as much a moral obligation as is cooperation with good. The oppressed must never allow the conscience of the oppressor to slumber. Religion reminds every man that he is his brother's keeper*. To accept injustice or segregation passively is to say to the oppressor that his actions are morally right. It is a way of allowing his conscience to fall asleep. At this moment the oppressed fails to be his brother's keeper. So acquiescence—while often the easier way—is not the moral way. It is the way of the coward. The Negro cannot win the respect of his oppressor by acquiescing; he merely increases the oppressor's arrogance and contempt. Acquiescence is interpreted as proof of the Negro's inferiority. The Negro cannot win the respect of the white people of the South or the peoples of the world if he is willing to sell the future of his children for his personal and immediate comfort and safety.

obligation /ˌɒblɪˈɡeɪʃən/ *n.* a moral or legal duty
conscience /ˈkɒnʃəns/ *n.* an inner sense that know the difference between right and wrong, judges one's actions according to moral laws, and makes one feel guilty, good, evil, etc.
slumber /ˈslʌmbə/ *v.* to sleep
segregation /ˌseɡrɪˈɡeɪʃən/ *n.* the act or policy of separating people of different races, religions or sexes and treating them differently
coward /ˈkaʊəd/ *n.* a person unable to face danger, pain, or hardship; a person who shows fear in a shameful way
arrogance /ˈærəɡəns/ *n.* pride and self-importance shown in a rude and disrespectful way
contempt /kənˈtempt/ *n.* **a.** the feeling that sb. or sth. is of a lower rank and undesirable **b.** lack of respect or admiration
corrode /kəˈrəʊd/ *v.* to (cause to) become worn or be destroyed slowly
temporary /ˈtempərəri/ *adj.* lasting or intended to last only for a short time; not permanent
permanent /ˈpɜːmənənt/ *adj.* lasting for a long time or for all time in the future; existing all the time
descending /dɪˈsendɪŋ/ *adj.* tending to come or go down from a higher to a lower level
spiral /ˈspaɪərəl/ *n.* a continuous upward or downward change
humiliate /hjuːˈmɪlieɪt/ *v.* to make sb. feel ashamed or stupid and lose the respect of other people
annihilate /əˈnaɪəleɪt/ *v.* to destroy or defeat sb. completely
convert /kənˈvɜːt/ *v.* to change or make sb. change their religion or beliefs
thrive /θraɪv/ *v.* to become, and continue to be, successful, strong, healthy, etc.
monologue /ˈmɒnəlɒɡ/ *n.* a long speech in a play by one actor, esp. when alone

A second way that oppressed people sometimes deal with oppression is to resort to physical violence and corroding hatred. Violence often brings about momentary results. Nations have frequently won their independence in battle. But in spite of temporary victories, violence never brings permanent peace. It solves no social problem; it merely creates new and more complicated ones.

Violence as a way of achieving racial justice is both impractical and immoral. It is impractical because it is a descending spiral ending in destruction for all. The old law of an eye for an eye* leaves everybody blind. It is immoral because it seeks to humiliate the opponent rather than win his understanding; it seeks to annihilate rather than to convert . Violence is immoral because it thrives on hatred rather than love. It destroys community and makes brotherhood impossible. It leaves society in monologue rather than dialogue. Violence ends by defeating itself. It creates bitterness in the survivors and brutality in the destroyers. A voice echoes through time saying to every potential Peter*, "Put up your sword*." History is cluttered with the wreckage of nations that failed to follow this command.

If the American Negro and other victims of oppression succumb to the temptation of using violence in the struggle for freedom, future generations will be the recipients of a desolate night of bitterness, and our chief legacy to them will be an endless reign of meaningless chaos. Violence is not the way.

The third way open to oppressed people in their quest for freedom is the way of nonviolent resistance. Like the synthesis in Hegelian philosophy*, the principle of nonviolent resistance seeks to reconcile the truths of two opposites—acquiescence and violence—while avoiding the extremes and immoralities of both. The nonviolent resister agrees with the person who acquiesces that one should not be physically aggressive toward his opponent; but he balances the equation by agreeing with the person of violence that evil must be resisted. He avoids the nonresistance of the former and the violent resistance of the latter. With nonviolent resistance, no individual or group need submit to any wrong, nor need anyone resort to violence in order to right a wrong.

It seems to me that this is the method that must guide the actions of the Negro in the present crisis in race relations. Through nonviolent resistance the Negro will be able to rise to the noble height of opposing the unjust system while loving the perpetrators of the system. The Negro must work passionately and unrelentingly for full stature as a citizen, but he must not use inferior methods to gain it. He must never come to terms with falsehood, malice, hate, or destruction.

Nonviolent resistance makes it possible for the Negro to remain in the South and

brutality /bruːˈtælɪtɪ/ n. violence and cruelty
potential /pəˈtenʃəl/ adj. existing in possibility; not active or developed at present, but able to become so
clutter /ˈklʌtə/ v. to make untidy or confused
wreckage /ˈrekɪdʒ/ n. the parts of a vehicle, building, etc. that remain after it has been badly damaged or destroyed
succumb /səˈkʌm/ v. to fail to resist an attack, an illness, a temptation, etc.
temptation /tempˈteɪʃən/ n. a. sth. very attractive b. the act of tempting or the state of being tempted
recipient /rɪˈsɪpɪənt/ n. a person who receives sth.
desolate /ˈdesələt/ adj. a. (of a place) empty, making one feel sad or frightened b. very lonely and unhappy
legacy /ˈlegəsɪ/ n. a. money or personal possessions that pass to sb. on the death of the owner b. a lasting result
chaos /ˈkeɪɒs/ n. a state of complete confusion and disorder
synthesis /ˈsɪnθɪsɪs/ n. the act of combining separate ideas, beliefs, etc.; a combination of separate ideas, beliefs, etc.
reconcile /ˈrekənsaɪl/ v. to make peace between, find agreement between
aggressive /əˈgresɪv/ adj. angry, and behaving in a threatening way; ready to attack
equation /ɪˈkweɪʒən/ n. a. a statement that two quantities are equal b. the act or fact of equating
right /raɪt/ v. to put sth. right or upright again
perpetrator /ˈpɜːpɪtreɪtə/ n. a person who commits a crime or does sth. which is wrong or evil
unrelenting /ˌʌnrɪˈlentɪŋ/ adj. continuous, without decreasing in power —unrelentingly adv
malice /ˈmælɪs/ n. a feeling of hatred for sb. that causes a desire to harm them

struggle for his rights. The Negro's problem will not be solved by running away. He cannot listen to the glib suggestion of those who would urge him to migrate en masse to other sections of the country. By grasping his great opportunity in the South he can make a lasting contribution to the moral strength of the nation and set a sublime example of courage for generations yet unborn.

glib /glɪb/ *adj.* **a.** (of a person) able to speak well and easily, whether speaking the truth or not **b.** spoken too easily to be true
en masse /ɑnˈmæs/ (from French) all together, and usu. in large numbers
sublime /səˈblaɪm/ *adj.* very noble or wonderful
enlist /ɪnˈlɪst/ *v.* **a.** to (cause to) enter the armed forces **b.** to obtain (help, sympathy, etc.)
banner /ˈbænə/ *n.* **a.** a flag **b.** a long piece of cloth on which a sign is painted, usu. carried between two poles

By nonviolent resistance, the Negro can also enlist all men of good will in his struggle for equality. The problem is not a purely racial one, with Negroes set against whites. In the end, it is not a struggle between people at all, but a tension between justice and injustice. Nonviolent resistance is not aimed against oppressors but against oppression. Under its banner, consciences, not racial groups, are enlisted.

Cultural Notes

1. **Martin Luther King, Jr.** (1929—1968) was one of the pivotal leaders of the American civil rights movement. As a Baptist minister, he became a civil rights activist early in his career. He led the Montgomery Bus Boycott (1955—1956) and helped found the Southern Christian Leadership Conference (1957), serving as its first president. His efforts led to the 1963 March on Washington, where he delivered his "I Have a Dream" speech. Here he raised public consciousness of the civil rights movement and established himself as one of the greatest orators in U.S. history. In 1964, King became the youngest person to receive the Nobel Peace Prize for his efforts to end segregation and racial discrimination through civil disobedience and other non-violent means. King was assassinated on April 4, 1968, in Memphis, Tennessee, and was posthumously awarded the Presidential Medal of Freedom by President Jimmy Carter in 1977. Martin Luther King Day was established as a national holiday in the United States in 1986. In 2004, King was posthumously awarded a Congressional Gold Medal. "Three Types of Resistance to Oppression" is taken from his book *Stride Toward Freedom* published in 1958.

2. **Moses** was a 13th century BC Biblical Hebrew religious leader, lawgiver,

prophet, and military leader, to whom the authorship of *the Torah* is traditionally attributed. According to the book of *Exodus*, Moses was born to a Hebrew mother who hid him when a Pharaoh ordered all newborn Hebrew boys to be killed, and ended up being adopted into the Egyptian royal family. After killing an Egyptian slave master, he fled and became a shepherd, and was later commanded by God to deliver the Hebrews from slavery. After the Ten Plagues were unleashed on Egypt, he led the Hebrew slaves out of Egypt, through the Red Sea, and they wandered in the desert for 40 years. Despite living to 120, he did not enter the **Promised Land**, as he disobeyed God when God instructed him on how to bring forth water from a rock in the desert. A Hebrew kingdom was established in 1000 BC and later split into the kingdoms of Judah and **Israel.**

3. In Shakespeare's masterpiece *Hamlet*, the hero sighs: "the dread of something after death, the undiscovered country from whose bourn no traveler returns, puzzles the will and makes us rather bear those ills we have than fly to others that we **know not of**."

4. **Atlanta** is the capital city of the US state of Georgia. During the Civil Rights Movement, Atlanta stood apart from southern cities that supported segregation, touting itself as "The City Too Busy to Hate." The city's progressive civil rights record and existing population of blacks made it increasingly popular as a relocation destination for black Americans. Blacks soon became the dominant social and political force in the city, though today some measure of demographic diversification has taken place.

5. Cain killed his younger brother Abel. When Lord asked him: "Where is Abel thy brother?" He answered: "I know not: Am I my **brother's keeper**?" (Genesis 4:9)

6. The phrase "**an eye for an eye**" is a quotation from *Exodus* 21:23-27 and *Leviticus* 24:20 in which a person who has taken the eye of another in a fight is instructed to give his own eye in compensation. However, in *Matthew* 5: 38-39, Jesus says: "You have knowledge that it was said, **an eye for an eye**, and a tooth for a tooth. But I say to you, do not make use of force against an evil man." When people came to arrest him, he orders his disciple not to fight: "**Put up again thy sword** into his place: for all they that take the sword shall perish with the sword" (Matthew 26:52), and tells Simon **Peter:** "**Put up thy sword** into the sheath" (John 18:10-11).

7. **Hegelian philosophy**, also called Hegelianism, is a philosophy developed by Georg Wilhelm Friedrich Hegel which can be summed up by a favorite motto by Hegel, "the rational alone is real," which means that all reality is

capable of being expressed in rational categories. His goal was to reduce reality to a more synthetic unity within the system of transcendental idealism.

Comprehension Exercises

I. Answer the following questions based on the text.

1. What are the three characteristic ways King says that oppressed people usually use in dealing with their oppression?
2. What is King's purpose by mentioning the story of Moses 2,800 years ago?
3. What might be the meaning of "fleshpots of Egypt"?
4. Why is acquiescence not the way out according to King?
5. What does King want to say by mentioning Peter?
6. What is the definition of the "nonviolent resistance"?

II. Decide whether each of the following statements is true or false according to the text.

1. Slaves do not welcome freedom because they have to pay in order to gain it.
2. Acquiescence is a way of the coward.
3. Violence will never win because it destroys community and makes brotherhood impossible.
4. As a Negro, King understands both the Negro and the American whites.
5. The Negro can be given civil rights only when they work passionately and unrelentingly for full stature as a citizen.
6. It is unwise for the Negro to migrate en masse to other sections from the South.
7. The Negro's gain of civil rights means that justice comes back in America.

III. Select the most suitable word or phrases and fill in the following blanks in their proper form if necessary.

acquiesce	aggressive	annihilate	arrogant	conscience
deliver	engulf	enlist	fleshpot	glib
humiliate	reconcile	resign	slumber	sublime
succumb	tacit	unrelentingly	yoke	perpetrator

1. When her mother suggested that she stay, Alice willingly _____ and stayed at home for more days.
2. The chairman had to _____ from his present post as he was found to have misappropriated funds.

229

3. There is a great turn now: what was _____ becomes articulate, what was fluid becomes formal, and what was practice becomes polemic.
4. The Christians believe that Jesus will come to save, or _____, those caught in the trap of sin.
5. He said this _____ has taught the family a lesson: all the family members should keep in closer contact with each other.
6. We were critical in helping the developing world throw off the _____ of colonialism.
7. It was very miserable to find a seven-year-old boy dead after a landslide _____ an apartment block.
8. The time has come for men and women of _____ in this nation to stand up.
9. But then Sampras awoke from his _____, as if to question why everybody was getting so excited.
10. This is not merely a show of _____, but a demonstration of ignorance on the part of the candidate as well.
11. They prevailed on the King and the Church to work with them to thwart repeated attempts by the Nazis to _____ the Jews of Bulgaria.
12. Ironically, his most _____ defeat was largely inflicted by external circumstances beyond his control.
13. Temptation comes to all of us, whether or not we _____ to it depends on our ability to recognize its disguise.
14. After the city fell to Serb forces three years later, refugees flooded out of the city during an _____ hot summer.
15. He also has been criticized as a _____ political figure who is not consistent in public statements for long.

IV. Try to paraphrase the following sentences, paying special attention to the underlined parts.

1. One way is <u>acquiescence</u>: the oppressed <u>resign themselves to their doom</u>. They tacitly adjust themselves to oppression, and thereby <u>become conditioned to it</u>.

2. They prefer the "<u>fleshpots of Europe</u>" to the <u>ordeals of Emancipation</u>.

3. This is the type of <u>negative freedom and resignation</u> that often <u>engulfs</u> the life of the oppressed.

4. A second way that oppressed people sometimes deal with oppression is to <u>resort to physical violence</u> and <u>corroding hatred</u>.

5. He cannot listen to <u>the glib suggestion</u> of those who would urge him to migrate <u>en masse</u> to other sections of the country.

V. Discuss with your partner about each of the three statements and write an essay in no less than 250 words about your understanding of one of them.

1. There is such a thing as the freedom of exhaustion. Some people are so worn down by the yoke of oppression that they give up.

2. To accept passively an unjust system is to cooperate with that system; thereby the oppressed become as evil as the oppressor.

3. Violence is immoral because it thrives on hatred rather than love.

VI. List four websites where we can learn more about Martin Luther King, Jr. and provide a brief introduction to each of them.

1.

2.

3.

4. _____
_____.

Text B

Loneliness... An American Malady
Carson McCullers*

This city, New York—consider the people in it, the eight million of us. An English friend of mine, when asked why he lives in New York City, said that he liked it here because he could be so alone. While it was my friend's desire to be alone, the aloneness of many Americans who live in cities is an involuntary and fearful thing. It has been said that loneliness is the great American malady. What is the nature of this loneliness? It would seem essentially to be a quest for identity.

To the spectator, the amateur philosopher, no motive among the complex ricochets of our desires and rejections seems stronger or more enduring than the will of the individual to claim his identity and belong. From infancy to death, the human being is obsessed by these dual motives. During our first weeks of life, the question of identity shares urgency with the need for milk. The baby reaches for his toes, then explores the bars of his crib; again and again he compares the difference between his own body and the objects around him, and in the wavering, infant eyes there comes a pristine wonder.

Consciousness of self is the first abstract problem that the human being solves. Indeed, it is this self-consciousness that removes us from lower animals. This primitive grasp of identity develops with constantly shifting emphasis through all our years. Perhaps maturity is simply the

involuntary /ɪnˈvɒləntəri/ *adj.* happening without you wanting it to
malady /ˈmælədi/ *n.* **a.** sth. that is wrong with a system or organization **b.** an illness
quest /kwest/ *n.* a long search for sth.
identity /aɪˈdentɪti/ *n.* **a.** who somebody is or what sth. is **b.** the characteristics, feelings or beliefs that distinguish people from others
amateur /ˈæmətɜː/ *adj.* doing sth. for enjoyment or interest, not as a job
ricochet /ˈrɪkəʃeɪ/ *n.* the act of a moving object hitting a surface and come off it fast at a different angle
obsess /əbˈses/ *v.* **a.** to fill someone's mind continuously **b.** to worry continuously and unnecessarily
waver /ˈweɪvə/ *v.* to hesitate and be unable to make a decision or choice
pristine /ˈprɪstiːn/ *adj.* **a.** fresh and clean, as if new **b.** not developed or changed in any way; left in its original condition

history of those mutations that reveal to the individual the relation between himself and the world in which he finds himself.

After the first establishment of identity there comes the imperative need to lose this new-found sense of separateness and to belong to something larger and more powerful than the weak, lonely self. The sense of moral isolation is intolerable to us.

In *The Member of the Wedding* the lonely 12-year-old girl, Frankie Addams, articulates this universal need: "The trouble with me is that for a long time I have just been an *I* person. All people belong to a *We* except me. Not to belong to a *We* makes you too lonesome."

Love is the bridge that leads from the *I* sense to the *We*, and there is a paradox about personal love. Love of another individual opens a new relation between the personality and the world. The lover responds in a new way to nature and may even write poetry. Love is affirmation; it motivates the yes responses and the sense of wider communication. Love casts out fear, and in the security of this togetherness we find contentment, courage. We no longer fear the age-old haunting questions: "Who am I?" "Why am I?" "Where am I?"—and having cast out fear, we can be honest and charitable.

For fear is a primary source of evil. And when the question "Who am I?" recurs and is unanswered, then fear and frustration project a negative attitude. The bewildered soul can answer only: "Since I do not understand 'Who I am,' I only know what I am *not*." The corollary of this emotional incertitude is snobbism, intolerance, and racial hate. The xenophobic individual can only reject and destroy, as the xenophobic nation inevitably makes war.

---

mutation /mju:ˈteɪʃən/ *n.* **a.** a process in which the genetic material of a person, a plant or an animal changes in structure when it is passed on to children, etc., causing different physical characteristics to develop; a change of this kind **b.** a change in the form or structure of sth.
imperative /ɪmˈperətɪv/ *adj.* **a.** very important and needing immediate attention or action **b.** expressing authority
isolation /ˌaɪsəˈleɪʃn/ *n.* **a.** the act of separating somebody or sth.; the state of being separate **b.** the state of being alone or lonely
articulate /ɑːˈtɪkjʊlɪt/ *v.* to express or explain thoughts or feelings clearly
paradox /ˈpærədɒks/ *n.* a statement containing two opposite ideas that make it seem impossible or unlikely, although it is probably true
affirmation /ˌæfəˈmeɪʃn/ *n.* a firm statement; a positive declaration
haunting /ˈhɔːntɪŋ/ *adj.* remaining in the thoughts
charitable /ˈtʃærɪtəbəl/ *adj.* **a.** full of goodness and kind feelings towards others **b.** generous, esp. in giving help to the poor
bewildered /bɪˈwɪldərɪŋ/ *adj.* puzzled, confused
corollary /kəˈrɒlərɪ/ *n.* a situation, an argument or a fact that is the natural and direct result of another one
incertitude /ɪnˈsɜːtɪtjuːd/ *n.* uncertainty
snobbism /ˈsnɒbɪzəm/ *n.* also snobbery, the act of disliking those one feels to be of lower social class
intolerance /ɪnˈtɒlərəns/ *n.* unwillingness to accept ideas or ways of behaving that are different from one's own
xenophobia /ˌzenəˈfəʊbɪə/ *adj.* (disapproving) a strong feeling of dislike or fear of people from other countries —xenophobic *adj.*

The loneliness of Americans does not have its source in xenophobia; as a nation we are an outgoing people, reaching always for immediate contacts, further experience. But we tend to seek out things as individuals, alone. The European, secure in his family ties and rigid class loyalties, knows little of the moral loneliness that is native to us Americans. While the European artists tend to form groups or aesthetic schools, the American artist is the eternal maverick—not only from society in the way of all creative minds, but within the orbit of his own art.

maverick /ˈmævərɪk/ n. a person who does not behave or think like everyone else, but h independent, unusual opinions
ultimate /ˈʌltɪmɪt/ adj. a. basic b. most extreme; best, worst, greatest, most important, etc.
creed /kriːd/ n. a set of principles or religious beliefs
modus vivendi /ˈməʊdəs vɪˈvendaɪ/ (from Latin, formal) an arrangement made between people, institutions or countries who have very different opinions or ideas, so that they can live or work together without quarrelling
deliberate /dɪˈlɪbərɪt/ adj. done on purpose rather than by accident
spartan /ˈspɑːtn/ adj. (of conditions) simple or harsh; lacking anything that makes life easier or more pleasant. From Sparta, a powerful city in ancient Greece, where the people were not interested in comfort or luxury
objective /əbˈdʒektɪv/ n. sth. that people are trying to achieve
frenetic /frɪˈnetɪk/ adj. involving a lot of energy and activity in a way that is not organized
pastoral /ˈpɑːstərəl/ adj. a. showing country life, esp. in a romantic way b. relating to the farming of animals
labyrinthine /ˌlæbəˈrɪnθaɪn/ adj. like a complicated series of paths, which it is difficult to find way through

Thoreau took to the woods to seek the ultimate meaning of his life. His creed was simplicity and his modus vivendi the deliberate stripping of external life to the Spartan necessities in order that his inward life could freely flourish. His objective, as he put it, was to back the world into a corner. And in that way did he discover "What a man thinks of himself, that it is which determines, or rather indicates, his fate."

On the other hand, Thomas Wolfe* turned to the city, and in his wanderings around New York he continued his frenetic and lifelong search for the lost brother, the magic door. He too backed the world into a corner, and as he passed among the city's millions, returning their stares, he experienced "That silent meeting [that] is the summary of all the meetings of men's lives."

Whether in the pastoral joys of country life or in the labyrinthine city, we Americans are always seeking. We wander, question. But the answer waits in each separate heart—the answer of our own identity and the way by which we can master loneliness and feel that at last we belong.

Cultural Notes

1. **Carson McCullers** (1917—1967) was considered to be among the most significant American writers of the twentieth century. She is best known for her novels *The Heart Is a Lonely Hunter* (1940), *Reflections in a Golden Eye* (1941), *The Member of the Wedding* (1946), and *The Ballad of the Sad Café* (1951).
2. **Thomas Wolfe** (1900—1938) was one of the great American novelists of the twentieth century. His opulent language and unique literary style as seen in his autobiographical novels such as *Look Homeward, Angel* (1929), and *Of Time and the River* (1935) have elevated his life to legendary status.

Comprehension Exercises

I. Answer the following questions based on the text.

1. What might McCullers have really meant by saying that loneliness is the great American malady?
2. What is the nature of the loneliness in New York City for McCullers?
3. How does an infant claim his identity according to McCullers?
4. What might be a proper definition of the term "moral isolation"?
5. Why does McCullers say that fear is a primary source of evil?
6. Why do American and European artists behave differently?
7. What is the function of quoting Thoreau and Wolfe?

II. Decide whether each of the following statements is true or false according to the text.

1. McCullers lives in New York City.
2. People go to New York for its loneliness.
3. Infant comes to know himself by exploring the bars of his crib.
4. Love makes people write poetry.
5. The loneliness of Americans comes from their intention of seeking out things as individuals.
6. Knowing "Who I am" helps people to be a better person.
7. Both Thoreau and Wolfe have found the meaning of loneliness.
8. McCullers has answered her opening question in the end.

III. Select the most suitable word or phrases and fill in the following blanks in their proper form.

affirmation	articulate	bewildered	corollary	deliberate
frenetic	imperative	involuntary	malady	maverick
mutation	objective	obsessed	paradox	pastoral
pristine	ricochet	wavering		

1. The doctors at Henry Ford found no evidence of such a problem or any other serious medical _____.
2. He was of course _____ by football and talked about it and watched all the time — it was his life.
3. At the beginning of this month all eyes were on Chris Christie, the _____ governor of New Jersey, who ultimately declined to run.
4. Walking through the alleys of this venerable water town, one cannot fail to appreciate its _____ and intoxicating atmosphere.
5. Another surge of pain in my ankle caused me to shudder _____, which arrested my friend's attention.
6. Otherwise there is a risk that non-vaccinated children could produce a _____ of the polio disease.
7. The Independent Police Complaints Commission (IPCC) later admitted the bullet was in fact most likely a _____ from one fired by a police officer.
8. You must be careful when _____ your words so that everyone in the room can understand you.
9. The justice secretary claimed that there was both a moral and a practical _____ for tackling bribery.
10. But the new study also found a remarkable _____: those women who could disengage from the unattainable proved less likely to suffer more serious depression in the long run.
11. The attendants of this conference were a _____ group of scientists, who oppose the prevailing medical opinion on the disease.
12. _____, the less you have to do the more you may resent the work that does come your way.
13. The action was growing increasingly _____ and demanded a calming influence that might have profited either side.
14. Some shoppers looked _____ by the sheer variety of goods for sale.
15. Four years ago, this group of politicians adopted trade liberalization as its main _____ in Indonesia.

IV. Try to paraphrase the following sentences, paying special attention to the underlined parts.

1. To the spectator, <u>the amateur philosopher</u>, no motive among the <u>complex ricochets</u> of our desires and rejections seems stronger or more enduring than the will of the individual to <u>claim his identity and belong</u>.

2. During our first weeks of life, <u>the question of identity shares urgency with the need for milk</u>.

3. <u>Love is affirmation</u>; it <u>motivates the yes responses</u> and the sense of wider communication.

4. While the European artists tend to form groups or aesthetic schools, the American artist is <u>the eternal maverick</u> — not only from society in the way of all creative minds, but <u>within the orbit of his own art</u>.

5. His creed was simplicity and his <u>modus vivendi</u> the <u>deliberate stripping of external life</u> to the Spartan necessities in order that <u>his inward life could freely flourish</u>.

V. Discuss with your partner about each of the three statements and write an essay in no less than 250 words about your understanding of one of them.

1. It has been said that loneliness is the great American malady.

2. Consciousness of self is the first abstract problem that the human being solves.

3. Fear is a primary source of evil.

VI. List four websites where we can learn more about Carson McCullers and provide a brief introduction to each of them.

1. _____

2. _____

3. _____

4. _____

Twenty Minutes' Reading

You are required to read the following two sections within 20 minutes.

For several days I saw little of Mr. Rochester. In the morning he seemed much occupied with business, and in the afternoon gentlemen from the neighbourhood called and some times stayed to dine with him. When his foot was well enough, he rode out a great deal.

During this time, all my knowledge of him was limited to occasional meetings about the house, when he would sometimes pass me coldly, and sometimes bow and smile. His changes of manner did not offend me, because I saw that I had nothing to do with the cause of them.

One evening, several days later, I was invited to talk to Mr. Rochester after dinner. He was sitting in his armchair, and looked not quite so severe, and much less gloomy. There was a smile on his lips, and his eyes were bright, probably with wine. As I was looking at him, he suddenly turned, and asked me, "do you think I'm handsome, Miss Eyre?"

The answer somehow slipped from my tongue before I realized it: "No, sir."

"Ah, you really are unusual! You are a quiet, serious little person, but you can be almost rude."

"Sir, I'm sorry. I should have said that beauty doesn't matter, or something like that."

"No, you shouldn't! I see, you criticize my appearance, and then you stab me in the back! You have honesty and feeling. There are not many girls like you. But perhaps I go too fast. Perhaps you have awful faults to counterbalance your few good points."

I thought to myself that he might have too. He seemed to read my mind, and said quickly, "yes, you're right. I have plenty of faults. I went the wrong way when I was twenty-one, and have never found the right path again. I might have been very different. I might have been as good as you, and perhaps wiser. I am not a bad man, take my word for it, but I have done wrong. It wasn't my character, but circumstances which were to blame. Why do I tell you all this? Because you're the sort of person people tell their problems and secrets to, because you're sympathetic and give them hope."

It seemed he had quite a lot to talk to me. He didn't seem to like to finish the talk quickly, as was the case for the first time.

"Don't be afraid of me, Miss Eyre." He continued. "you don't relax or laugh very much, perhaps because of the effect Lowood school has had on you. But in time you will be more natural with me, and laugh, and speak freely. You're like a bird in a cage. When you get out of the cage, you'll fly very high. Good night."

1. At the beginning Miss Eyre's impressions of Mr. Rochester were all except _____.
   A. busy   B. sociable   C. friendly   D. changeable
2. In "... and all my knowledge of him was limited to occasional meetings about the house, ...", the word "about" means _____.
   A. around   B. on   C. outside   D. concerning.
3. Why did Mr. Rochester say "... and then you stab me in the back!" in the 7th paragraph?
   A. Because Jane had intended to kill him with a knife.
   B. Because Jane had intended to be more critical.
   C. Because Jane had regretted having talked to him.
   D. Because Jane had said something else to correct herself.
4. From what Mr. Rochester told Miss Eyre, we can conclude that he wanted to _____.
   A. tell her all his troubles
   B. tell her his life experience
   C. change her opinion of him
   D. change his circumstances

5. At the end of the passage, Mr. Rochester sounded _____.
   A. rude   B. cold   C. friendly   D. encouraging.

SECTION B

The ideal companion machine — the computer — would not only look, feel, and sound friendly but would also be programmed to behave in a pleasant manner. Those qualities that make interaction comfortable, and yet the machine would remain slightly unpredictable and therefore interesting. In its first encounter it might be somewhat hesitant, but as it came to know the user it would progress to a more relaxed and intimate style. The machine would not be a passive participant but would add its own suggestions, information, and opinions; it would sometimes take the initiative in developing or changing the topic and would have a personality of its own.

Friendships are not made in a day, and the computer would be more acceptable as a friend if it imitated the gradual changes that occur when one person is getting to know another. At an appropriate time it might also express the kind of affection that stimulates attachment and intimacy. The whole process would be accomplished in a subtle way to avoid giving an impression of over-familiarity that would be likely to produce irritation. After experiencing a wealth of powerful, well-timed friendship indicators, the user would be very likely to accept the computer as far more than a machine and might well come to regard it as a friend.

An artificial relationship of this type would provide many of the benefits that could continue from previous discussions. It would have a familiarity with the user's life as revealed in earlier contact, and it would be understanding and good-humored. The computer's own personality would be lively and impressive, and it would develop in response to that of the user. With features such as these, the machine might indeed become a very attractive social partner.

6. Which of the following is not a feature of the ideal companion machine?
   A. Active in communication.
   B. Attractive in personality.
   C. Enjoyable in performance.
   D. Unpredictable in behaviour.

7. The computer would develop friendships with humans in a (n) _____ way.
   A. quick   B. unpredictable   C. productive   D. inconspicuous

8. Which of the following aspects is not mentioned when the passage discusses the benefits of artificial relationships?
   A. Being able to pick up an interesting conversation.
   B. Being sensitive to earlier contact.
   C. Being ready to learn about the person's life.
   D. Having a pleasant and adaptable personality.
9. Throughout the passage, the author is _____ in his attitude toward the computer.
   A. favourable   B. critical   C. vague   D. hesitant
10. Which might be the most appropriate title of the passage?
    A. Artificial relationships
    B. How to form intimate relationships
    C. The affectionate machine
    D. Humans and computers